"If it has long been a mystery why so many writers have argued that baseball explains life, Keith Law's *The Inside Game* addresses its corollary: why life explains baseball. Inside these pages the senior baseball writer for the Athletic website examines the assumptions that animate baseball—both on the field and in the opinionated realms of fandom."

—*Wall Street Journal*

"Law's take is as entertaining as it is informative. This intelligent and accessible work is a grand slam."

—*Publishers Weekly* (starred review)

"In a market saturated with baseball books, Law's stands out by exploring key decisions in the game. Highly recommended for serious followers of baseball and readers interested in how statistical analysis and trends can be applied in any sport."

—*Library Journal*

"*Moneyball* changed the baseball world forever, but the reasons why those inefficiencies existed in the first place were never explained. Keith Law finally does, as he takes you on a wild ride—with Kahneman seemingly riding shotgun—through baseball's decision-making and the fascinating ways our minds lead us astray."

—Sig Mejdal, Assistant General Manager, Baltimore Orioles

"This is a terrific book about the many ways in which we make irrational choices—inside and outside of baseball. We are misled by sunk costs, anchoring, hot streaks, hindsight bias, and much, much more. *The Inside Game* is chock-full of clear explanations and compelling stories that can help us all make better decisions."

—Professor Gary Smith, author of *Standard Deviations: Flawed Assumptions, Tortured Data, and Other Ways to Lie with Statistics*

"Some of my favorite days at the ballpark are just sitting next to Keith Law and listening to him explain what he sees. He has a brilliant sense of players and the game. *The Inside Game* is double the fun because here he also delves into the sociology and psychology of baseball, opening up all new worlds on topics as diverse as robot umpires, Pete Rose, and pitch counts. You'll see the game in a whole different way."

—Joe Posnanski, *New York Times* bestselling author

"You might spend a lot of time thinking about baseball, but do you ever think about . . . thinking? The joy of Keith's book is that each chapter is a meditation on a way that the brains we keep tucked away under our favorite team's ballcap can fool us. At the end of this book, you'll understand baseball a little better, and hopefully yourself as well."

—Russell A. Carleton, PhD, author of *The Shift: The Next Evolution in Baseball Thinking*, contributor to Baseball Prospectus

# The Inside Game

ALSO BY KEITH LAW

*Smart Baseball*

# THE
# Inside
# Game

**BAD CALLS, STRANGE MOVES, AND WHAT BASEBALL
BEHAVIOR TEACHES US ABOUT OURSELVES**

# Keith Law

WM

WILLIAM MORROW
*An Imprint of* HarperCollins*Publishers*

To Meredith,
*my person*

HarperCollins books may be purchased for educational, business, or
sales promotional use. For information, please email the Special Markets
Department at SPsales@harpercollins.com.

A hardcover edition of this book was published in 2020 by William Morrow,
an imprint of HarperCollins Publishers.

FIRST WILLIAM MORROW PAPERBACK EDITION PUBLISHED 2021.

Library of Congress Cataloging-in-Publication Data has been applied for.

ISBN 978-0-06-294273-9

21 22 23 24 25   LSC   10 9 8 7 6 5 4 3 2 1

# Contents

# Introduction

This is a baseball book. It's also, I hope, not really a baseball book.

When the idea for *The Inside Game* first came to me, I had a hard time figuring out whether I wanted to use baseball to explain some key ideas about how we think and make decisions, or whether I wanted to use those same ideas, drawn from cognitive psychology and behavioral economics, to explain a bunch of otherwise disconnected events from baseball history. I just liked the idea of putting the two things together and telling a bunch of stories, while also providing readers with enough of the basics of the philosophy to walk away feeling like they've learned something.

Since the genesis of this book, though, I've decided to embrace its duality: it's a baseball book that uses concepts from economics to make you think more about irrational decisions people have made over the last century in baseball; it's also, I hope, a book for the lay audience that explains cognitive biases and illusions, using examples from the baseball world, enough to make you think about them at home or at work, and maybe to decide you want to go read more about the topic.

The idea wasn't some instance of spontaneous generation, of course. As much as I'd love to tell you, like a proud toddler, that "I do it myself," the reality is that front office personnel around Major League Baseball have been reading about these topics for almost a decade now, spurred by the influx of analysts who have nontraditional academic backgrounds like decision sciences or machine learning. The sabermetric revolution was televised; the revolution in front office thinking was not. Just as some general managers embraced data to try to gain an advantage over other clubs, and then tried to find new advantages in the data before other clubs did, some general managers looked at how they think to try to avoid falling into the kind of cognitive traps that all humans face whenever we make decisions.

My first exposure to this came in the spring of 2014, when, on the recommendation of Sig Mejdal, then the director of decision sciences for the Houston Astros, I read Daniel Kahneman's book *Thinking, Fast and Slow*. Kahneman won the Nobel Memorial Prize in Economics Sciences in 2002 "for having integrated insights from psychological research into economic science, especially concerning human judgment and decision-making under uncertainty."[1] His work with longtime colleague Amos Tversky (who died in 1996) pioneered the field of behavioral economics, showing that much of what economics long believed and taught about humans being strictly rational when making economic decisions was not supported by evidence. We're not that rational—or we are rational subject to the constraints imposed on us by our thinking, which is subject to all kinds of cognitive biases and illusions that Kahneman, Tversky, Richard Thaler (who won the same Nobel in 2017), and others have elucidated over decades of research and numerous publications.

*Thinking, Fast and Slow* went from unknown to must-read within baseball front offices in a fairly short period of time, a shocking development in a sport that generally moves at the pace of a sloth that is still hungover after a weekend bender. When Jeff Luhnow became General Manager of the Astros before the 2012 season, he and his lieutenant Sig Mejdal, now assistant GM of the Orioles, made it required reading for all new front office hires. The A's, Cubs, and Red Sox all followed suit, and by the time I started working on this book in earnest in 2019, every front office source I contacted had either read the book or at least started to do so.

Kahneman's book isn't a sports-ball book at all, although it has a few sports examples because it's such a universal interest; it's not even an analytics book, although I think in the false dichotomy of the sports world it would be characterized as one. It is a book that asks you to think about thinking so that you will make better, more reasoned decisions. So many choices made in the baseball world are done quickly, using only what Kahneman calls the brain's "system 1," using intuitive reasoning, including heuristics and shortcuts, which is good if you're in a burning building and need to get out as fast as you can, but less good if you're a major-league general manager trying to decide how many years to give a free-agent reliever. These decisions happen all over baseball, on the field and off, during the season and across the winter. Free agents go to the highest bidder, and draft-eligible players go to the first team to select them, both of which are choices that can easily go astray because of system 1, "fast" thinking that is prone to errors and biases—if you're the one team that doesn't stop and think about whether your projections are too optimistic or you haven't considered all possible scenarios, you're going to make an expensive mistake.

*Thinking, Fast and Slow* is a wonderful book that changed my thinking, making me hyperaware of these deficits in my own thinking (like, I could stand to talk about this stuff a little less), but it's also not for everybody. It's a dense read, and assumes a fair bit of foreknowledge on the part of the reader; if you come in cold, it might be tough sledding. There are other books in the genre that are a bit easier for the lay reader, which I'll cite over the course of this book, and many of them helped inspire passages or even whole chapters here. I'll give a list of such books at the end if you'd like to delve further into this area and learn more from the folks who've done the research themselves.

I use a lot of baseball terminology and notation in *The Inside Game,* although I've tried to be very consistent in that usage and to stick to the same handful of stats and terms as much as I can. The most common of these include:

- The "triple-slash" line for a hitter, which looks like .300/.400/.550. That's batting average, on-base percentage, and slugging percentage. Benchmarks for the three vary from year to year, but the numbers I just used would all be above average in any season. When you hear elsewhere that a player led the league "in hitting," they mean batting average. On-base percentage, also called OBP, and slugging percentage, both include batting average as a partial component but include more important information. OBP is a measure of how often a hitter reaches base safely by any means—hits, walks, hit by pitch. Slugging percentage is a crude measure of power, where a single is worth one base, a double two, a triple three, and a home run four, all added up and divided by the hitter's at bats.
- WAR, or Wins Above Replacement. This construct adds together values that represent everything a player does on the field to give us a single number that approximates how many extra wins the player was worth to his team in that year. For a

hitter, that's his bat, his defense (glove, range, arm), his base-running, and the value of playing his particular position, since some are harder than others. For a pitcher, that's how good he was at preventing runs, and how much he pitched. There are different ways to calculate these components; the two most popular public calculations come from Baseball-Reference and Fangraphs. I use both in this book. More is better, obviously; a negative number means the player's performance actively hurt his team, and they would have been better off grabbing the best "free" talent available to take that playing time.

- Replacement level. A replacement-level player is worth zero wins under WAR, and represents the hypothetical value you'd get from just calling up a random minor leaguer from triple-A at that position, or claiming such a player who had been waived by another team. To put it another way, a replacement-level player is neither helping nor hurting his team with his performance.

I have, however, tried to assume that readers have no background in any sort of economics or psychology when I am writing about the various cognitive biases and illusions I cover in the text. I do have some economics background from college and grad school, but it was twenty-plus years ago, and all of my coursework was in the realm of classical economics, which works from the assumption that humans are rational beings who will always make economically sound choices. This is all kinds of wrong, and we've actually known that for a good forty years now, but even in the early 1990s you couldn't find much if any behavioral economics instruction even at my alma mater, Fancy Pants University. I had to learn this stuff myself, on the fly, and of course I'm still learning as I go along. I've enjoyed the journey, and wanted to share it with readers who share my curiosity. I hope this book piques your interest in this subject as Kahneman's and Tversky's work did mine.

I've organized this book in a couple of different ways to allow you to read it straight through or pick and choose the parts you'd like to read. Each chapter adheres to the same general format: I'll start with a baseball story, then explain what cognitive bias or illusion I think underlies the error I'm describing, and will return to baseball with another salient example. I've footnoted this book to allow interested readers to go read some of the key research papers or texts that helped prove these biases exist, especially if you'd like to see more concrete proof that people really do act in this "predictably irrational"[2] way.

The key phrase there is that I think I'm matching the right bias to each story. You can't prove what people were thinking, especially since many of these biases occur at the subconscious level—nobody sits down and plans to fall into the availability bias trap; it's hard even to identify this looking back at your own decisions. In some cases, I could at least rely on contemporary quotes from the decision-makers from which we might infer a specific cognitive error, but that's it. You might read some of these chapters and think, "Keith's wrong about this story resulting from that cognitive bias," and I'm fine with that. I don't present these links as definitive proof; I present them to explain the cognitive errors, and to tell good baseball stories, some of which you'll know and, I hope, some you won't. Psychology professor James Shanteau pointed out this difficulty in a 1989 paper: "The problem is that when a bias (error) exists, it is difficult to establish a logical connection to any particular heuristic."[3] We can make educated guesses, and that's what I've tried to do throughout this book.

Like Brian Cohen and friends, though, I always look on the bright side of life, so I end the book with a chapter on some good decisions, ones that appeared counterintuitive at the time the executives made those choices but that have turned out in time to be correct. I spoke to the decision-makers in each case about their processes in making those calls, to tease out what the rest of us might learn from their preparations, and to see how those decision-makers overcame these potential traps, like the GM who chose to give a player a lucrative five-year contract extension off what appeared to be a single outlier season. Good outcomes don't always result from good processes, but when the world thinks a decision is bad and it turns out good, it's instructive to try to understand why.

My hope here is that you'll find yourself a more informed base-ball fan as a result, even though there are no new analytical tools or concepts within this book. Outsiders, whether writers like myself, game broadcasters, or fans at home screaming at their televisions (don't worry, I do that, too), have the luxury of time to rethink those initial, system 1 thoughts. If you're considering whether a manager or GM or player made a good decision—including, often, the decision not to do something—considering all possible scenarios and whether they fell prey to the biases I discuss in this book will lead you to more reasoned conclusions, and maybe you'll yell smarter things at your TV in the end.

# 1

# The Case for Robot Umpires

## How Anchoring Bias Influences Strike Zones and Everything Else

If you've spent any time on Twitter during baseball season, especially the postseason the last few years, you've probably stumbled on fans arguing for #RobotUmpsNow against those who argue for "the human element," two sides of the ongoing debate over whether baseball should move to automated calling of balls and strikes. It came up yet again in the 2019 World Series, when umpire Lance Barksdale missed two obvious calls in Game 5, one of which he openly blamed on Washington catcher Yan Gomes, which led Nationals manager Davey Martinez to yell at Barksdale to "wake up"; and another so egregious that the victim, Victor Robles, jumped in anger and tossed his batting gloves after Barksdale called him out on a pitch that never even saw the strike zone.[1] Both calls were bad, and in both cases, there was at least the appearance that Barksdale was punishing the Nationals—punishing Gomes for assuming the strike call before it happened, then punishing the whole team later for questioning him in the first place. They may have simply been "human errors," but the perception was worse.

I'm unabashedly in the former camp; calling balls and strikes is a difficult task, virtually impossible for a human to do well (especially when there's another human, the catcher, sitting in his way), and just a few errant calls can sway the outcome of a game or series. There are some practical arguments against this, notably that the existing pitch-tracking technology isn't definitively more accurate than good umpires, but the latter argument, that we're okay with nonplayers affecting the outcomes of games because of this "human element," is codswallop. Humans shouldn't be making these calls because humans, as you know by now from this book, are subject to so many biases.

We have proof that umpires are biased, too, in at least two ways. I'm not talking about the sort of player-specific bias where Davey Strikethrower always gets the benefit of the doubt on a pitch that's an inch or two off the plate, or Joey Bagodonuts gets squeezed a lot as a hitter because umpires don't like how much he complains. Those biases may exist, and, yes, they'd go away with an automated system, but the evidence for those biases isn't very strong and their effects aren't universal.

I am talking about two very specific ways in which umpires consistently make mistakes because of cognitive biases, and these are far more pervasive because they're not player- or even umpire-specific. If you're human, you have these cognitive issues, and since umpires are asked to make ball/strike calls immediately after each pitch and have almost zero latitude to change a call even if they think better of it, there is no corrective procedure available to them when they do miss a call. This is not a bug of using human umpires, but a feature.

The first known issue with human umpires is that the way they call a pitch is biased by their calls on the previous pitches, especially the pitch that came right before. There is no reason why the ball/strike status of one pitch should be affected by previous pitches; pitches are independent events, and if you can predict, even with a little success, whether a pitcher is going to throw a ball or strike on his next pitch, then that pitcher is too predictable and hitters will catch onto him.

In a paper published in 2016, Daniel Chen, Tobias Moskowitz, and Kelly Shue report their findings in a study of all pitches tracked by Major League Baseball's Pitch f/x system from 2008 to 2012. They looked at consecutive pitches that were "called" by the umpire—that is, not hit into play, hit foul, swung at and missed, or otherwise not adjudicated by the umpire—and found 900,000 such pairs. They also categorized all called pitches as obvious, meaning that the pitch's status as a ball or strike was clear, or ambiguous, referring to pitches on or near the edges of the strike zone. They report that 99 percent of "obvious" pitches were called correctly, while only 60 percent of "ambiguous" pitches were.

They began with the specific question of whether an umpire was more likely to call pitch 2 a ball if they had called pitch 1 a strike—that is, whether the call on the previous pitch biased their call on the next one. They found a small but significant effect on all pitches, where umpires were 0.9 percent more likely to call pitch 2 a ball if they'd called the previous pitch a strike, and the effect rose to 1.3 percent if the previous two pitches were called strikes. The effect was more blatant when the next pitch was "ambiguous," with biasing effects 10 to 15 times larger than those on "obvious" pitches.

The authors categorize this as a manifestation of the "gambler's

fallacy," the errant belief that random or even semi-random outcomes will always even out in a finite sample. For example, gamblers may claim that a roulette wheel that has come up black five
times in a row is more likely to come up red on the next spin
because the wheel is "due"—which, by the way, you'll hear quite
often about hitters who are having a "cold" streak at the plate,
and which is equally absurd. They also cite the possibility of self-
imposed quotas, where umpires might feel that they have to call a
certain number or percentage of strikes in each game.

Anchoring effect, a different cognitive bias, provides us with
a simpler explanation. Some previous piece of information independent of the next decision still affects that next decision by
changing the mind's estimate of the probabilities of certain outcomes. The umpire's call on the previous pitch should have no
impact on their call on the next pitch, or on their probability of
getting the call right on the next pitch, but it does because the umpire's mind does not treat these two events as independent, even
though the umpire may not be aware of this biasing. It could be a
matter of an internal quota: "I called that last pitch a strike, so I
should try to even things out." It could be a subconscious expectation: "The last pitch was a strike, and the pitcher isn't that likely
to throw two strikes in a row, so this pitch is more likely to be a
ball." Whatever the cause is, the simplest explanation is that the
umpire's mind is anchored on that last called pitch, and therefore
the umpire's internal calibration is thrown off for the next pitch.
That means they're less likely to get the next call right—and that's
another point in favor of giving the job of calling balls and strikes
to machines, not humans.

The anchoring effect was first proposed by Tversky and
Kahneman back in 1974, in a landmark paper modestly titled "Judg-

ment Under Uncertainty."[2] The section title "Adjustment and Anchoring" begins with a statement that sounds obvious but contains multitudes: "In many situations, people make estimates by starting from an initial value that is adjusted to yield the final answer."

When you are asked to estimate something, or find yourself in a situation where you need to make an estimate for yourself, you don't just start the thought process from a blank slate. You begin with some piece of information that your mind deems relevant, and then you make adjustments up or down from there based on other factors or how the spirits move you. It's a mental game reminiscent of *The Price Is Right*, the popular game show where contestants are often given some price for an item and asked to say whether the actual price is higher or lower. (Some games ask contestants to adjust specific digits of the price, which feels like an anchoring-and-adjustment game within an anchoring-and-adjustment game.) Your mind sets that initial anchor, grasping at whatever number is handy, and then you adjust it from there.

The most shocking result in their paper showed that research subjects' minds would use totally irrelevant numbers as anchors for estimates. They spun a wheel that showed a random number from 0 to 100 in front of the test subjects and then asked the subjects what percentage of countries in the United Nations were African. They write: "For example, the median estimates of the percentage of African countries in the United Nations were 25 and 45 for groups that received 10 and 65, respectively, as starting points. Payoffs for accuracy did not reduce the anchoring effect."[3] (The correct answer would have been 32 percent, assuming they did the study in 1973.)

They characterized this as "insufficient adjustment," although it looks more like "incompetent anchoring." Their term applies more to their second experiment, where they asked two groups of high school students to calculate an eight-figure product, giving them five seconds and asking them to estimate the answer at that time. One group received the question as 8 x 7 x 6 x 5 x 4 x 3 x 2 x 1, while the other received it as 1 x 2 x 3 x 4 x 5 x 6 x 7 x 8. The first group's median guess was 2,250; the latter's was 512.[4]

Dan Ariely, author of *Predictably Irrational*,[5] describes a similar experiment he conducted at the Massachusetts Institute of Technology with his colleague Drazen Prelec where they would ask students to bid on some item, but first asked the students to write down the last two digits of their Social Security numbers as if that were the list price of the item. Those students with numbers above 50 bid more than three times as much as those students with numbers below 50. The anchor was meaningless. Its total irrelevance to the question at hand had no effect whatsoever on the students' brains; the number was in front of them, and therefore it became an anchor from which the students adjusted up or down.

Anchoring and adjustment is one of many cognitive heuristics, or mental shortcuts, we use every day to cope with the sheer volume of information coming into our brains and the number of decisions we are expected to make. You can't spend six hours at the grocery store trying to figure out whether each item meets or beats your optimal price, nor can you spend an hour each at six grocery stores to comparison shop. You make snap decisions on whether a price is good, and sometimes those decisions will be skewed by misinformation (for example, an item that is on sale may not be a bargain compared to other stores, or even that much of a discount from the regular price).

Umpires are asked to make most of their calls in, at most, about two seconds; when they take longer than that, there will be chirping from one dugout and probably some announcers about a "delayed call." They make those ball/strike decisions a little faster by the use of heuristics, even ones they're not quite aware they're using. My hypothesis, at least, is that they are anchoring and adjusting from the previous pitch, or the previous few pitches, and thus the evidence of bias we see in their calls is the result of a persistent human cognitive error.

Before I continue with how the anchoring bias shows up in baseball, there's another cognitive error that affects how home plate umpires call pitches, one you may have seen already if you've read the wonderful book *Scorecasting: The Hidden Influences Behind How Sports Are Played and Games Are Won*, by Tobias Moskowitz and L. Jon Wertheim. The book takes a *Freakonomics*-style look at issues across multiple sports, from home-field advantage to NFL draft pick values to whether "defense wins championships" to why the Chicago Cubs are cursed. (Well, they weren't, but it's still a good book.)

Moskowitz was a coauthor of the 2016 paper I cited earlier that looked at umpire accuracy and bias. A second effect that he and his coauthors found (also reported in *Scorecasting*) was that umpires were much less likely to call a pitch a ball if it would result in a batter drawing a walk, or to call a strike if it would result in a strikeout. Moskowitz and his coauthors refer to this as *impact aversion,* which you might think of as a bias toward doing nothing. (In fact, that's first cousin to another bias, *omission bias,* which says that we view doing nothing as less harmful than doing something, even if the outcomes are the same.)

In *Scorecasting,* the authors looked at Pitch f/x data on pitch calls and locations over the 2007–2009 seasons, with 1.15 million called pitches in their sample. In overall situations, they found that umpires made the correct ball/strike call 85.6 percent of the time. However, when the count on the batter went to two strikes, meaning a third would result in a strikeout, and the pitch was within the strike zone, the umpires only correctly called the pitch a strike 61 percent of the time. (They excluded full counts, where either a called strike or ball would end the at bat, and thus impact aversion was not in play.) Umpires' error rate more than doubled in those situations, likely because they shied away at least a little bit from making a decision that had a higher impact than other called pitches.

The converse situation, where there's a three-ball count on the batter and the pitch is out of the strike zone, also showed evidence of this impact aversion. Umpires correctly called pitches out of the strike zone as balls 87.8 percent of the time, but in three-ball counts (excluding full counts) they made the correct call just 80 percent of the time. In baseball jargon, the umpire squeezes pitchers with two strikes, and expands the zone with three balls.

They further demonstrated that the evidence of impact aversion was highest at the two ends of the spectrum of ball-strike counts. Umpires are way more likely to errantly call a ball a strike in 3–0 counts, and way more likely to call a pitch in the strike zone a ball on 0–2 counts.[6] This is hardly a surprise if you've watched much baseball; there's no greater chance of a gift strike call than with a 3–0 count. Writing for the *Hardball Times* back in 2010, Pitch f/x expert John Walsh found that the strike zone was 50 percent larger in a 3–0 count than it was in an 0–2 count, saying "these umpires are a bunch of softies."[7] Walsh goes on to point out that the run values of each count, meaning the expected value to the hitter of any specific ball-strike count, reach their two extremes at 3–0 (+.22 runs to the hitter, in his research) and 0–2 (-.11 runs to the hitter), so by altering the size of the strike zone more in those counts, umpires are flattening the expected values of these at bats—pulling both run values back toward zero. A previous article by Dave Allen, which Walsh references, found that an additional strike in the count had as much effect on the probability that an umpire would call a pitch a strike as would an additional inch of distance away from the center of the strike zone.[8] Allen found that once you controlled for the ball-strike count and the amount of break on a pitch, the changes in the size of the strike zone across pitches became insignificant.

There's an alternative explanation for this beyond "umpires are dumb." (I'm not saying that, by the way; I happen to think the job of calling balls and strikes accurately enough in an MLB environment is beyond the capabilities of any human.) Etan Green and David Daniels argue in a 2018 paper[9] that umpires employ statistical discrimination, using disallowed information like the count or batter handedness to improve their decision-making on balls and strikes, and a loose form of Bayesian updating (just nod and keep reading) to make more accurate and more rational calls over the course of a game. Doing so does not require knowing or using Bayes's theorem, which allows you to calculate the probability of one event based on your prior knowledge of a condition related to the event.[10] Green and Daniels write that this kind of intuitive correction is a heuristic honed over years of practice and constant feedback. A scout or baseball executive might call it "feel." I see it as further argument that we should turn this job over to machines: if umpires feel the need to use information, like the game state, to get to the desired level of accuracy in ball/strike calls, that is in and of itself a problem with the system.

Labels about players can be their own form of anchoring, and baseball does love its labels. This guy's an ace, but this other guy's just a number two starter. Joey Bagodonuts? He's a bust. Twerpy McSlapperson's a grinder, a gamer, a professional hitter (duh), or, my absolute favorite, a baseball player. (Which distinguishes him how, exactly?)

Most of these labels do more to confuse fans or readers than elu-
cidate, but I think one in particular really skews decision-making
in baseball even years after the label was applied. I refer to the tag
of "first-rounder," which becomes an anchoring point for executives, scouts, and coaches when they're evaluating a player.

In 2019, Danny Hultzen, the number two overall pick in 2011
whose career appeared to be over after a substantial shoulder injury, made his major-league debut for the Chicago Cubs at age
twenty-nine. It was an incredible turn of events after he missed
all of 2014, threw just 10 innings total in 2015–16, and then was
out of baseball for all of 2017 and most of 2018, throwing 8.2
innings in August for the Cubs' rookie-league and triple-A teams.
Most pitchers who miss as much time as he did due to shoulder
woes don't come back the way he did, and it's to his credit that he
worked his way to the majors when he could have walked away
forever.

His ascension to the majors also gave the loaded 2011 draft an
unofficial record: the first 29 players selected have now all played
in the majors. The first round of that draft, which looked historically great at the time and has fulfilled that promise, has produced
at least six players I'd comfortably call stars: Gerrit Cole, Anthony
Rendon, Francisco Lindor, George Springer, Javier Báez, and the
late José Fernández. It's produced a half-dozen other guys who've
had some time as regulars in the majors. But, like all first rounds,
it's produced some players who just didn't pan out. Chris Reed,
the 16th overall pick, appeared in just two games and threw four
innings in 2015, and he's now out of baseball. Alex Meyer, the
23rd overall pick, appeared in 22 career games, posted a 4.63
ERA, and is probably finished after major shoulder surgery.
Bubba Starling, a two-sport star who turned down a scholarship
to be the University of Nebraska's quarterback when he signed
with his hometown Kansas City Royals, also debuted in 2019,

but currently has the lowest WAR of any first-rounder from 2011 at −0.8.

Once a first-rounder, however, always a first-rounder. A player drafted in the first round has that tag attached to him forever, even once it's clear that he probably shouldn't have gone in the first round, either because the team that drafted him goofed or because the industry incorrectly evaluated him in the first place. Yet if you're a first-rounder, you're perceived as a more valuable prospect in trade talks. Does that also mean that you will get more chances to prove yourself than players taken later in the draft?

The answer is yes, somewhat. The evidence says that first-rounders do get more opportunity to appear in the majors, although the effect is weaker than I expected it to be (based strictly on my own intuition, which was that teams are overly generous with former first-round picks) and could be explained by other factors. For example, Jacob Turner, the 9th overall pick in 2009, spent parts of seven seasons in the majors, pitched for five organizations (two of them twice), and as of this writing is at −2.5 WAR for his career and appears to be out of baseball.

I looked at all first- and second-round picks, including "supplemental" picks,[11] from 1992 to our glorious draft year of 2011, twenty years in total, and only considered players who signed out of those drafts. That leaves us with 859 first-rounders in the period and 580 second-rounders, with the difference the result of the greater number of supplemental picks attached to round one.

Only 33.8 percent of first-rounders in the study period never played in the majors, compared to 52.9 percent of second-rounders, an enormous drop-off in probability—especially if, say, you're a scouting director in charge of the draft and you know that you're being evaluated at least in part by the sheer quantity of big leaguers your drafts have produced. This could indicate that former first-rounders get more opportunities to reach the majors, either as a direct result of their status—let's give that guy a chance, he was a first-rounder—or an indirect result, such as preferential treatment in playing time, off-season assignments, or training with coaches or other staff members. A team, having already invested heavily in a player they drafted in the first round, may invest more time and money in that player to try to ensure his success. (This is called an "escalation of commitment," and I'll discuss it more in chapter 11, where I cover the fallacy of the sunk cost.)

However, the more likely explanation here is that first-rounders are in aggregate simply better players than second rounders—that's why they're drafted in the first round. While the draft is hardly perfect, it is not "a crapshoot," as you will often hear from fans or even from writers who cover baseball as a whole but don't cover the draft. The best players typically come from the first round; Mike Trout was a first-rounder, as was 2018 NL MVP Christian Yelich and 2018 AL Cy Young Award winner Blake Snell. Five of the top six pitchers by vote totals for the 2018 AL Cy were first-rounders, as were the first two runners-up in the NL. Twenty-four of the 75 All-Stars in 2019 were first-round picks, representing 35 percent of the players in the game who entered pro baseball via the draft. Six of the top ten MLB players by WAR in 2019, per Baseball-Reference, were first-rounders; via Fangraphs, it's five of the top ten, eleven of the top 17 (and also top 20). Not all first-rounders turn out to be stars, or good players, but more stars come from the first round than anywhere else.

So what if we look at the margins of the first and second rounds, where we would expect the differences between players to be smaller? The draft may unfold rationally at the round level, but not even draftnik Jim Callis would say teams draft players in the perfect order. The gap between the players taken at picks 35 and

36, or the expected return of those two selections, is negligible. If there's a difference between the opportunities given to players based on the rounds in which they were selected, we might expect to see it at the margins between rounds.

We do . . . sort of. Comparing the last ten picks of the first rounds to the first ten picks of the second rounds in those same twenty drafts shows a small preference for first-round players. Of those selected first-rounders, 55.4 percent reached the majors, while 52.9 percent of the second-rounders did—the predicted direction, but a smaller gap than I expected. The gap widens if we look at players who did make it, but weren't very good: 84 percent of those late first-rounders who did reach the majors produced 5 career WAR or less, while 73 percent of those early second-rounders did the same.

There are other factors to consider here that might also explain the gaps I highlighted above. One is that teams may have just drafted exceptionally well in those years. Most drafts have first-rounders who never make it and players drafted in the second round and beyond who should have been drafted in the first round, although we usually only know that with the benefit of hindsight. However, perhaps they did well in the study period within the picks I examined, and that's why the higher-drafted players made the majors at a higher rate.

Another factor to consider is that the twenty picks I examined, comprising the last ten of the first round and the first ten of the second round, do not always fall in the same spot in the draft. The number of picks in the first round varies from year to year, as the rules around picks have changed with each new labor agreement, and teams have gained or lost picks due to free-agent signings, so the twenty picks that counted for this study aren't the same absolute picks from year to year.

The first round plus supplemental picks have included as many as 64 picks (2005) and as few as 30 picks (1995). So I think there's an effect here where teams cut first-rounders a little more slack, or give them more opportunities, but it's weaker than I believed, at least when it comes to player development.

There's still one belief about first-rounders to which I can cling for a little longer, until someone figures out a way to test this hypothesis: GMs overvalue former first-rounders in trade due to the anchoring effect. This might be a direct result of the anchoring effect altering evaluations of the players (he must be good, he was a first-round pick!) or because the GMs believe that their stakeholders are subject to that same anchor, thus improving the "optics" of acquiring a first-rounder (wow, we got a first-rounder in return, that's good!). They're certainly traded often; at the 2019 trade deadline on July 31, twelve former first-round picks were included in deals, ten of whom were either still prospects or were major leaguers who had not yet established themselves. The Detroit Tigers made two trades where they dealt veterans Nick Castellanos and Shane Green for a total of four prospects, three of whom were first-round picks, with the fourth a second-rounder. All three former first-rounders have underperformed relative to expectations, at least. The Diamondbacks and Astros made the largest deal of the deadline, with Arizona sending Zack Greinke to Houston for a four-player deal that included the Astros' last two first-round picks, both of whom had seen some loss in value in 2019, plus a second-rounder who was injured. Again, this is purely my own speculation, but it does make me reevaluate any trade where the prospects changing hands were all drafted high, because I know I too can be subject to this same anchoring bias.

Anchoring bias is pervasive inside or outside of baseball because it is such a fundamental shortcut for our brains. You can see how widespread its effects might be just in the world of base-ball. If umpires are subject to anchoring bias in their calling of balls and strikes, then hitters and pitchers would have to try to adjust, consciously or subconsciously, to those variable strike zones from game to game and even within games or within in-nings. If umpires are especially averse to calling ball four or strike three, that will almost certainly alter how hitters and pitchers approach pitches in those counts. If a manager anchors on the first thing they learn about a player, such as the first live look they have at the player in spring training or in his first few games in the majors, it would likely impact how often the manager uses the player (or doesn't use him) or how he deploys the player in the lineup or on the field. If general managers use a player's draft status or signing bonus as an anchor, that's a potentially large inefficiency for other executives to exploit in trades, or a trap to avoid for yourself in those same situations. Even the armchair fan can fall prey to this—perhaps you slightly overvalue players who were drafted high, or whom writers like me have pushed up our prospect rankings.

How do you overcome anchoring bias? Like many cognitive biases, anchoring is a heuristic—a shortcut your mind uses to re-place what might be a complex evaluation process, one you can't do in your head or in a short period of time, with a quick one. It's a gut reaction, and those often aren't useful or accurate. If you can buy the time to engage in your normal process for making decisions, you always want to do so. Listing the actual variables that should go into a decision, and then basing your evaluation or calculations just on those variables, can give you evidence that is free of the anchoring bias. For example, a major-league general manager may receive a trade offer shortly before the deadline that sounds great because it includes two former first-round picks. They may feel the time pressure to respond quickly, and their

unconscious mind may say that it's a good offer because those
two players are former first-rounders (or just because they're familiar names, which would invoke availability bias as well). It
may be a fair offer, but the GM can't know that without a proper
evaluation—speaking to the team's analysts and scouts about the
players involved, gathering essential data, and then using that to
drive the decision.

Sometimes the optimal solution will involve removing people from the decision-making process entirely. If Major League
Baseball chose to automate calling of balls and strikes, investing
further in the existing technology to improve its accuracy at the
margins of the zone, even without any immediate improvement
in the frequency of inaccurate ball/strike calls, the missed calls
would at least be more predictable, because they'd all come at the
edges of the strike zone where the calls are ambiguous. Machines
are not subject to anchoring bias, while people are. A computer
might mistake a pitch an inch outside of the zone for a strike,
but it won't miss on a pitch right down the middle because prior
pitches informed its expectations. Some decisions are just hard
for humans to make without bias because they lack the time to
work around it. Recognizing which type of decision you're facing
is the first step in figuring out how to avoid this trap.

# 2

## Never Judge an Iceberg by Its Tip

### How Availability Bias Shapes the Way Commentators Talk About Sports

Ted Williams's 1941 season was truly one for the ages. He hit .406/.553/.735, leading the majors in all three of those categories (batting average/on-base percentage/slugging percentage), and to this day remains the last player to post a .400 batting average in a full season. He also led the majors with 37 homers and 147 walks, and reached base more times than any other hitter in the majors. According to Baseball-Reference, his 10.6 Wins Above Replacement made it the 29th most valuable season of all time,[1] and put him a win and a half—about 15 runs of production—ahead of the second most valuable player, Joe DiMaggio.

Astute readers may see where I'm going with this. DiMaggio and 1941 go together, along with a third number, 56, in baseball lore. That was the season when Joe DiMaggio, not just a star on the field but a bona fide celebrity off it, recorded at least one base hit in 56 consecutive games, a streak that is still the major-league record through the 2019 season; no one has come within ten games of his mark before or since. The streak itself became national news, beyond the sports pages, giving baseball publicity they couldn't buy even if they wanted to do so.

When the season ended—with a Yankees world championship, as most seasons of that era ended—the writers of the Baseball Writers' Association of America, entirely white and male (which has scarcely changed in seventy-eight years), chose to give the American League MVP award to DiMaggio rather than to Williams. It remains one of the most absurd miscarriages of trivial justice in baseball history; DiMaggio's season was great, but Williams's was unequivocally better, and we shouldn't even be having this conversation.

The *New York Times*' John Drebinger, in a piece reporting on the voting results while simultaneously cheering them on, was certain of the reason for the choice. Writing for the Grey Lady on November 12, 1941, he said:

Thus the writers made it clear that they considered DiMaggio's spectacular 56-game hitting streak, together with Joe's vastly superior defensive skill and base running ability, had more than offset Williams's impressive .406 average and 37 homers, though both these figures topped all others in the majors. The Yankee star, who had won the batting crown in 1939 and 1940, last Summer [*sic*] hit .357. It was the fifty-six-game hitting streak, all-time high for the major leagues, which doubtless clinched the verdict.[2]

If you need a moment to grab your toothbrush and get that treacle off your teeth, take your time.

Ben Bradlee Jr., writing in his book *The Kid: The Immortal Life of Ted Williams,* has a less saccharine take on the situation, even if it's not quite the rational view:

> Thanks in part to his good press and strong relationships with the baseball writers, Joe won three MVPs to Ted's two. Despite Ted's .406, the 1941 vote in favor of DiMaggio was defensible because of Joe's streak and because the Yankees won the pennant, but the narrow 1947 tally for DiMaggio, in the face of Williams' overwhelmingly superior numbers that year, was not.[3]

I'm looking at this contest with modern eyes, though; although DiMaggio won by a modest margin, he was also expected to win. Mark Armour said in an article on Baseball Prospectus's site in 2003 that "in 1941 it would have been somewhat astonishing if Williams had won the award," noting both the streak and the fact that DiMaggio's team went to the playoffs while Williams's finished 17 games out of first place.

Coverage at the time assumed that the streak was the deciding factor for voters. The Associated Press's article on the results noted that "Di Maggio batted .357 in 139 games in 1941, but he was more outstanding because of his record-breaking feat of hitting safely in 56 consecutive games," before even mentioning his 30 homers or league-leading 125 RBI.[4] George Kirksey, then a writer for the United Press who would later become part of the first ownership group of the Houston Astros, had an even stronger take that the streak was the coup de grâce for the Yankee Clipper:

> Although the writers do not amplify their figures with explanations, it is apparent that DiMaggio was selected on the

basis of his value to the team. . . . There is plenty of evidence to back up the committee's selection. DiMaggio's spectacular hitting streak, which broke all major league records, ignited the winning spark which sent the Yanks on to the pennant and subsequently the world's title. When Joe started his streak on May 15, the New York club was in fourth place, 5½ games behind Cleveland. When he was stopped, the Yanks were first.[5]

As Kirksey said, voters at the time did not reveal their votes—that only became compulsory within the last five years, and many voters still decline to explain their ballots—so we don't know exactly why DiMaggio beat out Williams despite the latter's superior performance. Contemporary coverage, at least, seemed to focus more on DiMaggio's hitting streak than any other single factor, and writers writing about that MVP vote in the ensuing decades have assumed that the streak was the primary reason he won. To borrow a line from Bob Wallace and Phil Davis, it's not good, but it's a reason.

From today's perspective, it looks like the streak trumped the entirety of Williams's performance, and the obvious question is why the voters allowed it to do so. The streak was great, but that's hardly the purpose of the MVP award, even if we allow some latitude in what "valuable" really means. Here's my hypothesis, based primarily on that media coverage and subsequent historical coverage of the season and the vote: the streak was so unavoidable that season that it became the first thing voters thought about when they thought about DiMaggio and Williams.

In a year where the news was mostly bad, and would only get worse that December, DiMaggio's streak was a major, positive story that newspapers across North America would update daily, taking stories from the Associated Press, leading with his streak rather than with the results of the games in which he played. You couldn't get away from it, and I can only imagine that, by the end of that season, if you heard DiMaggio's name the streak would pop right into your head before you could say "Joltin' Joe."

When a specific fact or example comes to mind more readily, we tend to overemphasize that fact or example—maybe we ascribe too much importance to it, or perhaps we extrapolate and assume that that example is representative of the whole. This phenomenon is called *availability bias,* and I think it's one of the easiest cognitive biases to understand but one of the hardest to catch in yourself, because it's not just natural but easy. Your brain is just doing what you asked, right? You thought about some question, and your brain went right to the hard drive and pulled out something relevant. Your brain didn't go to the archives, though, and it probably just gave you one thing when you actually needed the whole set.

Kahneman and Tversky—I don't know how to tell you this, but they're kind of a big deal—describe availability bias as a "phenomenon of illusory correlation," painting it as a cognitive illusion where you misjudge the frequency of some event or characteristic because of how much you can remember seeing it. It's a sampling error: you may think that your memory provides an adequate sample of the whole, and sometimes it might, but often it won't and you can't bank on it doing so.

For example, one may assess the divorce rate in a given community by recalling divorces among one's acquaintances; or one may evaluate the probability that a politician will lose an election by considering various ways in which he may lose support. In both of these cases, the estimation of the frequency of a class or the probability of an event is mediated by an assessment of availability. A person is said to employ the availability heuristic whenever he estimates frequency or probability by the ease with which instances or associations could be brought to mind.[6]

I ran into an example of availability bias with my own daughter, aged thirteen, when I took her to a high school baseball showcase event called the Under Armour All-American Game at Wrigley Field in 2019. (She isn't a baseball fan at all; the bribe was that she got to eat her way around Chicago with me the day before, although she told me she enjoyed the game and the home run derby that came before it.) We got a program that listed all of the players, mostly rising high school seniors, in the game, along with their schools, hometowns, heights, and weights.

She noticed rather quickly that all but two of the 41 players in the program—just under 5 percent—were listed at 6'0" or taller, and asked if a player had to be at least that tall to play professional baseball. That's not an unreasonable question, since the sport has a long-standing bias toward taller players, and the six-foot mark is a common threshold used in scouting reports despite its arbitrary nature. (Six feet is about 183 centimeters, which doesn't roll off the tongue so easily; if baseball were primarily played in any other country, would the threshold suddenly drop to 180 cm?)

As of this writing, early September 2019, there have been 1,368 players who've appeared in at least one major-league game this season. Of those, 199 are listed with heights of 5'11" or shorter, or 14.5 percent, three times the frequency of sub-six-footers in the Under Armour game. If you had used that one (admittedly inapt) proxy to estimate how many MLB players were shorter than six feet tall, you'd have underestimated the actual rate by two-thirds.

(I'm ignoring one of the elephants in the room, which is that the listed heights of baseball players are about as accurate as airline schedules. There are 48 percent more players listed at 5'11" than at 5'10", 89 percent more players listed at 6'0" than at 5'11" . . .

and just 1 percent more players listed at 6'1" than at 6'0". That seems a bit suspicious, at least.)

My daughter wasn't entirely wrong; there is a clear preference for players who are or at least claim to be six feet or taller. For the game we attended, the third-party company Baseball Factory selects the best prospects in the class, who, of course, will tend to be taller; the last time a player under 6'1" went first overall in the draft was in 2004. But that's availability bias in a nutshell: the only sample of baseball players she saw was not representative of the body of baseball players as a whole. This group had been skimmed off the top, and represented the preferences of MLB teams and their scouts—taller players, faster players, pitchers who throw hard, hitters with big power, and so on. There are a lot of major leaguers, some of whom are very good, who don't fit into those categories, but teams continue to gravitate to certain arche- types and that's what this sample showed.

In *Thinking, Fast and Slow*, Kahneman illustrates how avail- ability bias can manifest itself in both directions with a pair of hypothetical statements. The first: "Because of the coincidence of two planes crashing last month, she now prefers to take the train. That's silly. The risk hasn't really changed; it is an availability bias."

Everyone has experienced that same trepidation when a plane crash occurs; I will never forget the hush that fell over the entire office of the consulting firm where I worked in the fall of 1994 after the news of USAir flight 427's crash near Pittsburgh broke. The risk of flying, which was an intrinsic part of the job of consul- tants, had not changed, but the reality of that small risk—all 132 people on board the flight were killed—was suddenly in front of, and thus more available, to everyone.

The next passage Kahneman provides goes the other way to show a sort of unavailability bias: "He underestimates the risks of indoor pollution because there are few media stories on them. That's an availability effect. He should look at the statistics."

The last sentence there always applies: You should always look at the overall statistics even if an individual instance or two seems to tell you what you need to know.

A small cluster in time of murders in New York City in 2016, including the murder of a young woman who was jogging alone in Queens, led to increased fears of such seemingly random homicides. The *New York Times'* Michael Wilson pointed out that such murders remained extremely rare, noting that in 2014, "homicides involving strangers represented 11 percent of the nationwide total" in FBI statistics, not including cases where the relationship between the killer and victim was marked as "unknown."[7]

Perhaps the classic example of this involves the statistics on missing children. All parents worry about their children being assaulted or kidnapped by someone they don't know; we talk to our kids about "stranger danger" as a matter of course, and have been doing so since the phrase first appeared in the 1960s. Yet the overwhelming majority of child abductions are by family members, friends, or other close acquaintances; David Finkelhor, the director of the Crimes Against Children Research Center at the University of New Hampshire, wrote in 2013 that "children taken by strangers or slight acquaintances represent only one-hundredth of 1 percent of all missing children."[8] That's one in about 10,000 missing children cases, which includes not just kidnappings but runaways, children who get lost, or any other instance that is reported to authorities (not necessarily abductions). The National Center for Missing & Exploited Children says that abductions by strangers are actually the rarest cases of missing children.[9]

But doesn't it feel like these cases are getting more common— that more kids are abducted and hurt by strangers? Finkelhor, writing in the wake of a high-profile child abduction case in

Cleveland, also puts the lie to that myth, stating that "many state missing-children agencies show declining numbers of cases" and that "FBI statistics [show] fewer missing persons of all ages— down 31 percent between 1997 and 2011."[10]

Why do we feel like our children are in so much more danger from strangers than they actually are? It's availability bias in our thinking, cutting both ways. When a child is abducted, especially in the extremely rare cases where the outcome is bad, it becomes a major news story—often a national one. But our minds don't get any news on the positive end. "Jimmy wasn't abducted on the way to school today or on the way home" doesn't make the news. There are no non-kidnapping stories—nor should there be, mind you. There's just no balance in the flow of information coming toward us on this subject. It's all bad, and our brains are not capable of calibrating these loud examples by comparing them to the overall population to realize that, while undeniably awful, these incidents are extremely rare and unlikely to occur. Most children never experience this trauma, and those who do are much more likely to be the victims of friends, family members, teachers, members of the clergy, and so on. "Stranger danger" is availability bias run amok.

Andre Dawson's 1987 season has also entered the lore of bad awards voting, in large part because of the specific narrative of how he ended up with the Cubs for that season. Voters went against their own established pattern of not voting for players whose teams finished well out of the playoffs—in Dawson's case, the Cubs finished dead last in the six-team National League East—and gave Dawson an MVP that was as irrational as it was improbable.

The history of Major League Baseball from the mid-1970s

through 1995 was dominated as much by what happened off the field as on it, as the owners and the nascent players' union engaged in a two-decade war that resulted in one long midseason strike (1981), several shorter strikes, and eventually the 1994 strike—the union's response to the owners' attempt to enact a hard salary cap—that led to the cancellation of that year's World Series. The owners spent much of this time trying to claw back the gains the players had made with the advent of free agency in December 1975, after arbitrator Peter Seitz ruled in favor of two players, Andy Messersmith and Dave McNally, who argued that they should have the right to become free agents after playing one year under the automatic contract renewals enabled by baseball's "reserve clause," which owners had used for decades to keep players in a form of indentured servitude to their employers. Owners' unwillingness to give up their control—or pay players anything approaching a fair wage—led to extensive collusion among owners agreeing not to bid on free agents, driving down player salaries and eventually leading to the owners paying players $280 million in penalties for violating the terms of their collective bargaining agreement (CBA).

Dawson was one of the most notable victims of what is now called Collusion II, as it was the second year of owner collusion on free agency. Dawson had hit .284/.338/.478 in 1986, with 20 homers and 78 RBI, and had won six consecutive Gold Glove Awards, indicative at least of the belief that he was a good defender. He received no offers from teams that winter, and during spring training, his agent, Dick Moss, presented the Cubs' general manager at the time, Dallas Green, with a one-year contract that had the dollar amount left blank, essentially saying Dawson would sign for whatever the Cubs would pay him. Green gave Dawson a base salary of $500,000, half of what the three-time

All-Star had earned the previous year for Montreal, and told the *Chicago Tribune*'s Fred Mitchell in 2010 that "it wasn't a very nice contract ($500,000) for Andre at the time, particularly after what he had done,"[11] but that it was the most the Cubs' ownership, the Tribune Company (owners of the same *Tribune*), would allow him to spend.

Dawson, who eventually received an additional $200,000 in bonuses[12] for 1987 and $1 million as part of the collusion settlement, responded with career highs in home runs and RBI. Aided by the "rabbit ball" of 1987, where MLB averaged more than one home run per game for the first time in history,[13] Dawson led the majors with 49 homers and 137 RBI. It is true that, for much of the history of postseason awards voting, the player who led his league in RBI would win the MVP award or at least be near the top of the results. The previous year, Mike Schmidt led the NL in RBI and won its MVP award, while in 1985, Don Mattingly had the same exacta in the American League.

What made Dawson's MVP win so improbable was that he did it for the Cubs, who finished last in the National League East. No player in history had won the MVP in either league while playing for a last-place team. The idea, still pervasive today if less universally believed, was that a player could not be the "most valuable" if his team didn't reach the playoffs or at least contend for a spot. I know it's crazy, but it's true: people charged with writing about baseball for a living thought you should be judged based on how well your teammates played.

How did Dawson overcome this impediment? It looks like voters were just more cognizant of his performance, particularly in the two statistical categories that at the time weighed most heavily in voters' minds, because he was in the news so much more that very spring. You could not miss what Dawson did because he was a story before he took his first at bat for the Cubs, and continued coverage of him throughout the season would mention his preseason situation. The *New York Times'* own article on his MVP win started by mentioning the contract: "Andre Dawson, who had neither a contract nor a team to play for last spring before he finally signed with the Chicago Cubs . . ."[14] The *Chicago Tribune*'s coverage of his award had a similar tone, mentioning in the first sentence that Dawson "is going to cost the Cubs some hard cash" after his win, and then explaining in the second sentence how he "came to the Cubs hat in hand last spring as a spurned free-agent slugger," telling the entire story of his almost futile search for a new employer later in the article.[15]

This isn't just my hypothesis, of course. Writing for ESPN's Sweet Spot in 2011, Chip Buck said the same thing. "There were two primary factors in Dawson winning the 1987 NL MVP Award: (1) his impressive, but deceiving raw statistics; and (2) the story of him overcoming collusion to sign a blank contract with the Cubs in March of that year. What other reasons could there be?"[16] Buck may have meant that voters were directly crediting Dawson with extra points for his contract, but I think he was getting at the same point I am—that his name was already in boldface in the voters' minds because the story of his contract and subsequent season received so much more coverage.

Dawson wasn't the best or most valuable—there isn't any difference, by the way—player in the National League that year. By Baseball-Reference's Wins Above Replacement, he ranked 19th just among position players. Leading the league was eventual Hall of Famer Tony Gwynn, widely acknowledged even at the time as one of the great hitters for batting average in that era, whose San Diego Padres finished in last place with a worse record than the Cubs; second was Eric Davis, who went 30/30 (at least 30 homers and 30 steals) with 37 homers and 50 stolen bases while playing for a Cincinnati Reds team that did contend for the playoffs and finished in second.

The best example of availability bias in awards voting has to be the 1999 American League Gold Glove voting, when Rafael Palmeiro won the award for first basemen despite spending almost the entire year as a designated hitter. The voting results were immediately and widely criticized, and did enough to delegitimize the Gold Gloves themselves that Rawlings, the company that created the award in 1958, eventually added an analytical component to the awards in 2013.

Palmeiro had won the AL Gold Glove award at first base in 1997 and 1998, playing almost every game at first base in both of those seasons, so he had the benefit of incumbency—the best way to win a Gold Glove is to already have won one—and of a positive reputation as a fielder. Herbert A. Simon referred to this as the "Matthew Effect" in his memoir, *Models of My Life,* writing that "one wins awards mainly for winning awards. . . . Once one becomes sufficiently well known, one's name surfaces automatically as soon as an award committee assembles."[17] The term "Matthew Effect" came from sociologist Robert K. Merton, who coined it in a 1968 paper,[18] alluding to Matthew 25:29 from the New Testament: "For unto every one that hath shall be given, and he shall have abundance: but from him that hath not shall be taken away even that which he hath."

It probably did not hurt that Palmeiro was also, even at age thirty-four, still a great hitter; even though the award is ostensibly just for defense, there is a long history of players appearing to win it because they're just good all-around players. Derek Jeter, by any metric a well-below-average defensive shortstop, won five Gold

Gloves, the last at age thirty-six, because he was then–future Hall of Famer Derek Jeter.

In 1999, however, Palmeiro played just 28 games at first base for the Texas Rangers; Lee Stevens, whom Palmeiro himself pushed for the award, was the Rangers' primary first baseman. It's the fewest games played for any nonpitcher who won a Gold Glove Award, of course, and the result showed, in the words of the unnamed AP writer who wrote about the results, "Seems like some managers and coaches weren't paying much attention this year."[19] Palmeiro himself was bemused by the outcome, but I think he nailed one of the reasons for the vote when he humbly said "the only way I can look at it is that people have respect for what I've done at the position in the past and they recognize me as one of the best in the game."

Gold Glove voting at the time was done entirely by coaches from that specific league; coaches would get ballots showing all players at each position and would pick one per spot. While it is entirely possible that these coaches would take their ballots home, examine all of the relevant statistics, maybe review some video, call advance scouts, and so on . . . I'm guessing that's probably not how it happened. The far more likely scenario is that coaches just checked off the names that "sounded" right to them—and, at first base in the American League, they would look at the names, and Palmeiro's name would be especially available to their memories. He'd won the last two awards, he had a reputation as an above-average defender, and he was a good hitter. His name would, figuratively speaking, appear to be in a larger font than the other names. The same likely landed Jeter those five Gold Gloves, of which he deserved exactly zero. Jeter's name is going to jump off the page in any group of names, because he was so good and so famous (and played for the Yankees, who are on national television what seems like every other night).

There's no way to avoid availability bias; it's a feature of how our memories work, not a bug you can fix with new code. Any solution should thus aim to reduce the effects of availability bias on our decision-making—that is, to accept that availability bias will show up early in the process and then engage in additional steps to overcome it. The simplest approach is to incorporate a step into your decision-making processes to ensure that you have gathered all of the relevant data, not just what came to mind or was easy to get, and that your sample sizes are sufficient for you to draw some sort of conclusions. In *Standard Deviations,* Gary Smith counsels readers to actively consider the data that *doesn't* easily come to mind, a strategy to reduce survivorship bias and availability bias:

> We naturally draw conclusions from what we see—workers' wages, damaged aircraft, successful companies. We should also think about what we do not see—the employees who left, the planes that did not return, the companies that failed. The unseen data may be just as important, or even more important, than the seen data.[20]

Ensuring that your sample size is large enough to let you draw some conclusions is another powerful heuristic in fighting availability bias, because it forces you to think about and look for additional data beyond what you could easily obtain or remember.

As a writer, I've had to retrain myself to get out of the habit of relying on my memory, which is more fallible than I'd like it to be, whether I'm just citing facts or trying to provide evidence for a hypothesis or opinion I've included in my writing. I've discarded many ideas over the thirteen years I've been a professional baseball writer, including many that would have appeared in *Smart*

*Baseball,* because the data didn't support an initial impression, whether it was about a specific player, a class of players, or the league as a whole. One of the most common manifestations of this problem for me is when I go to scout a player in person and see something glaring—for example, a right-handed hitter who seems to have particular trouble with breaking balls (curveballs and sliders), or a shortstop whose arm appears too weak to make the throw from the hole (toward the shortstop's right, almost behind the third baseman, in short left field). After some mistakes early in my career, I developed the habit of writing down what I saw, but always trying to verify, whether with data for that hypothetical right-handed hitter, or by talking to other evaluators who might have seen the player more often or simply on different nights. I still glean a lot from in-person evaluations, but my process starts by assuming that those evaluations, which will always be more available to my mind because I saw them myself, are inherently limited.

As a fan, understanding availability bias helps you filter out sports coverage and commentary that falls for it—the color commentator who talks about a player's great defense because he's made a few highlight plays, even though the player is a poor defender; or the columnist who goes out of his way to denigrate the team's best player while praising another player who just had a few "big hits." It's especially true in radio and TV, which I've experienced myself: when you're live, there's such pressure to talk that you want to go with whatever examples pop into your mind as you're speaking. That's not a great approach to any medium, and you risk misinforming the audience if you rely too much on your automatic memory rather than preparing talking points with evidence in advance. (The more I do my job, the more I've learned to just say "I don't know the answer to that, but I can tell you . . ." or "I don't think I have enough information." It may feel evasive or unhelpful, but it's better to do that than say something inaccurate or misleading.)

You, as a fan, don't have that limitation; when you hear someone talking up or down a player, ask if all the evidence really supports that conclusion—or if that person is just relying on the information that was readily at hand. Baseball commentary is often a victim of the tropes that have long defined it—and availability bias is behind much of it, if for no other reason than it's convenient and often obvious.

# 3

## Winning Despite Your Best Efforts

### Outcome Bias and Why Winning Can Be the Most Misleading Stat of All

Baseball is a game of outcomes: the best-laid schemes of (Johnny) Mize and (Ramiro) Mendoza often go askew, and history records the results, not the processes, even if the two don't align.

The 2001 World Series has long stood out as one where the efforts of a few players overwhelmed a huge mismatch between the managers, as the Yankees' Joe Torre was playing chess while Diamondbacks manager Bob Brenly was playing Candyland, with the Yankees coming a few outs away from taking the series because of Brenly's blunders. The Diamondbacks won, thanks to the herculean efforts of their top two pitchers and the rare blown save by Mariano Rivera, and Brenly, then a rookie manager, will forever be known as a World Series–winning manager despite a series of tactical errors that cost his team runs and likely stretched the series longer than it needed to run. Even with clear evidence he was a poor on-field manager, the Diamondbacks retained him through the end of his contract and picked up his fourth-year option before finally releasing him halfway through the 2004 season, at which point the club was 29–50 and en route to the worst record in the majors that year.

Brenly's blunders started before the first pitch of the first game of the World Series, as he seemed to be operating from a nineteenth-century playbook. The Diamondbacks' offense that year was driven by a career year from Luis Gonzalez, who, at age thirty-three, nearly doubled his previous career high with 57 home runs and was the third-best hitter in the National League behind Barry Bonds and Sammy Sosa. Gonzalez wasn't just a power hitter, but also finished sixth in the NL in on-base percentage at .429, which means that he reached first base safely via hit, walk, or being hit by a pitch in 43 percent of his plate appearances that year. That made him a double threat—pitchers had a hard time getting him out by any means, and when he put the ball in play, he frequently put it right back out of play by hitting it into the seats.

Brenly batted Gonzalez third in his lineup, which was standard at the time and for many years afterward—batting your best hitter third, with the idea that the two hitters ahead of him would get on base and you could hope for a three-run homer or other positive outcome, had been conventional wisdom in baseball since at least the early 1900s. It was suboptimal, as we know today; you should bat your best hitter second, because that allows you to optimize his results across two different variables—his chance to come up with men on base, and his total number of chances to bat at all and perhaps get on base himself. The further down in the lineup a batter hits, the fewer times he'll get to the plate over the course of a season. This was a mistake by Brenly, but I tend to give him something of a pass on this because every manager at the time would have done the same thing.

Brenly's lineup error wasn't in batting Gonzalez third, but in who he put ahead of him. Brenly installed shortstop Tony Womack as his leadoff hitter for Game 1, which demonstrated very old-school thinking: conventional wisdom said to bat your fastest guys at the top of the lineup. That's all well and good except that you can't steal first base, and Womack wasn't very good at getting to first base the legal way. Womack posted a .307 OBP in 2001, identical to the OBP he posted in 2000, so that was probably a good indication of his true talent level at the time—and that is not a good figure at all. Out of 77 National League hitters who played enough to qualify for the batting average leadership in 2001 (usually 502 plate appearances), Womack ranked 71st in OBP. Of the Diamondbacks' nine players who had at least 400 trips to the plate in 2001, Womack had the *worst* on-base percentage; only thirty-five-year-old Matt Williams, then at the very tail end of his career, was even below .330. So Brenly chose the hitter least likely to get on base out of all of his options and put him in the lineup spot that will come to the plate most often in a game, series, or even season.

Brenly batted Womack leadoff in 73 games over the course of 2001, so this wasn't a new choice for the rookie manager, but it was still the worst option. The player he used in the leadoff spot most often besides Womack was utility infielder Craig Counsell, who led off in 63 games in 2001, and posted a .359 OBP over the course of the season, which was the third-best mark on the team after Gonzalez and Mark Grace. To Brenly's credit, he batted Counsell second in the first game, so he did get one thing right, although he was to misuse Counsell several times in the series.

This was a process error—Brenly either ignored the relevant information (the on-base percentages of their hitters) or didn't understand what it meant in practical terms, but regardless of the reason, he screwed up royally—yet it proved immaterial, as the Diamondbacks won the game 9–1 and the lineup construction probably wouldn't have made one iota of difference in the outcome. The diminutive Counsell, who had four home runs in all of the regular season, hit his second home run of the month of October, tying the game in the first inning.

Brenly repeated the same lineup the next day, when the mistake was even more glaring because of who started for the opposing Yankees. New York started right-handed pitcher Mike Mussina in Game 1, and then came back with left-hander Andy Pettitte in Game 2. In baseball, hitters typically fare better against pitchers who throw with the opposite hand—so a left-handed hitter does better against right-handed pitchers than left-handed ones. You may have a guess where this story is going.

Tony Womack was a left-handed batter, so as bad as he was overall, he was utterly useless as a hitter when the opposing pitcher was left-handed. His on-base percentage against lefties in 2001 was .235, the worst performance of his career against southpaws to that date, while Pettitte had limited left-handed batters to a .284 OBP that year. This was a terrible matchup for Arizona from the start, made worse by the individual players involved, especially Pettitte, who was good against all hitters but always tougher on lefties. Brenly reacted to this matchup by . . . batting Womack leadoff again. Womack went 0 for 4, as did Counsell batting second, so Luis Gonzalez came to the plate three times and didn't bat once with a man on base, and was left in the on-deck circle after Counsell made the final out for Arizona in the bottom of the eighth.

Once again, it didn't matter. Randy Johnson threw a shutout, allowing just four Yankees to reach base at all, and the Diamond-backs won again, 4–0. Brenly's process did hurt the Diamond-backs a little bit, but not enough to sway the outcome of the game.

The Yankees won Game 3 of the series, 2–1, with Womack batting ninth and Steve Finley now batting ahead of Gonzalez—a much better lineup than the ones Brenly used in Games 1 and 2, at least, although Roger Clemens and Mariano Rivera limited the Diamondbacks to just seven baserunners. But in Game 4, Brenly once again made a brutal error, this time costing the Diamond-backs the game.

Arizona's designated closer that year was twenty-two-year-old Korean right-hander Byung-Hyun Kim, who threw with an underhand delivery that is often called a "submarine" delivery, since his hand was so low to the ground and, to a hitter, the ball appears to surface from below, while most pitchers use an over-hand delivery so that the ball comes down at the hitter. Kim was effective all year, but like just about every pitcher who has a low arm slot (sidearm or submarine), he had a platoon split, meaning that left-handed batters did much better against him than right-handed batters. This happens to low-slot pitchers because hitters on the other side of the plate have a better view of the ball out of the pitchers' hands, removing the deception that makes the deliv-ery so effective.

Kim wasn't awful against lefties in 2001, but he was definitely worse. He gave up 10 homers on the year, and 8 of them were hit by left-handed batters. The previous year, he gave up more hom-ers to right-handers, but allowed a .385 OBP to lefties. Using Kim against right-handed batters was an obvious choice, but against left-handed batters in a critical situation should at least have given Brenly some pause.

Brenly brought Kim into the game in relief of starter Curt Schil-ling for the eighth inning, which might qualify as progressive for a time when managers typically preferred to save their designated closer for the ninth inning, and only if their team was leading, and only if they were leading by a small enough amount that the closer would be eligible for a statistic called a "save." It's absurd—you're managing to a stat, not to the actual game state itself—but, to Brenly's credit, he at least brought Kim into the game an inning earlier than the conventional wisdom argued.

With the Diamondbacks ahead 3–1, Kim faced three right-handed hitters in the eighth inning and retired them all, then retired Derek Jeter, also right-handed, to lead off the ninth. Paul O'Neill, the first left-handed hitter Kim faced, then singled, which meant that the batter became the potential tying run. The next two batters were Bernie Williams, a switch hitter, and Tino Martinez, a left-handed hitter, the top two home run hitters on the Yankees in 2001. Brenly had two left-handed pitchers on the postseason roster, and could have gone to either of them in this situation either for both hitters or just for Martinez, since Williams would always have the upper hand as a switch hitter.

Instead, Brenly stuck with Kim, who struck out Williams, then gave up a game-tying homer to Martinez. Brenly left Kim in the game into the tenth inning, when Derek Jeter homered to give the Yankees a 4–3 victory.

That wasn't Brenly's only error in Game 4, however; it's just the one everybody remembers. Womack, back in the leadoff spot, reached base three times ahead of Counsell and Gonzalez, and every time, Brenly had Counsell lay down a sacrifice bunt, giving up an out to advance Womack a base (twice from first to second, once from second to third). Sacrifice bunts are, in most cases, terrible strategy, as they reduce your chances of scoring multiple runs while doing little or nothing to improve your chance of scoring one run. In this case, however, Brenly's error was egregiously, monstrously inane.

Luis Gonzalez hit more home runs than any National League player in 2001 other than Barry Bonds, who was still in the midst of an offensive peak that is unmatched in major-league history, and Sammy Sosa. The cool thing about a home run is that everyone on base when you hit one scores, no matter what. It's in the rules. Whatever base you were on when the ball left the stadium, you score. And you score one run. You don't score an extra run for being on second or third rather than first. Everybody scores. It's a party at home plate and everyone's invited.

Brenly's decision to have Counsell give up an out to advance Womack, rather than to try to reach base himself—Counsell's best skill as a hitter was getting on base—made no sense whatsoever. Gonzalez singled, walked, and was hit by a pitch (again), but Womack did not score at all in the game. The ninth inning meltdown may never have occurred had Brenly let Counsell swing away in those three plate appearances with Womack on base, which could have created a situation where there were two men on for Gonzalez to drive in. The best way to avoid blowing a small lead in the late innings is to have a large lead going into the late innings. Brenly's strategy reduced the Diamondbacks' odds of getting a larger lead, and helped create the situation where Arizona would lose the lead and eventually the game.

There was plenty of contemporary criticism of Brenly's mishandling of Kim and the ninth inning, at least, and some criticism of his other blunders. Joe Sheehan, a colleague of mine at the time at Baseball Prospectus, led off his column the next morning[1] with the line "He deserved to lose," and then called the sac bunting "idiotic, reflexive, counterproductive, [and] self-immolative," which seems kind, really. Sheehan also pointed out that Brenly might have used Kim in the eighth inning to preserve Schilling to start in a potential Game 7, and had other options to get through the Williams/Martinez gauntlet without Kim. Brenly confirmed the first part, telling the *New York Times'* Murray Chass that saving Schilling for a hypothetical seventh game "certainly that entered into it somewhat." Andrew Marchand of the *New York Post* wrote of similar sentiments from Brenly, while saying the move defied the manager's stated belief in winning tonight's game and worrying about future games later. (Marchand also quoted Brenly saying that second-guessing from the media was "the lowest form of journalism." Would that that were still true.)

Brenly did the same thing the next night, bringing Kim into the ninth inning because it was a "save situation," which means you have to use your closer no matter what.[2] In Game 4, Kim threw 61 pitches, the most he'd thrown in any game all year and the second-most he'd ever thrown in any MLB appearance, which today at least would probably lead to a day off for any pitcher given what we know about how fatigue affects both performance and injury risk. Arizona had a 2–0 lead entering the ninth inning; Kim gave up a double to switch hitter Jorge Posada and, three batters later, a game-tying home run to right-handed hitter Scott Brosius. The Yankees eventually won the game 3–2 in twelve innings, giving them a series lead as the teams headed back to Arizona for Game 6 and, if necessary, Game 7.

The Diamondbacks won Game 6 in a blowout, and then won Game 7 with a ninth-inning comeback of their own, scoring the game-winning run on a bloop single off Hall of Famer Mariano Rivera after Randy Johnson, their Game 6 starter, came in and threw just over an inning in relief to keep the Diamondbacks' deficit to just one run. Even in that situation, Brenly couldn't help himself, bunting twice in the ninth inning, but this time he benefited from Rivera making an errant throw on the first bunt as he tried to retire the lead runner, resulting in two men on base with nobody out. Brenly bunted *again*, this time with pinch-hitter Jay Bell (.349 OBP in 2001); the next three batters singled, reached on a hit by pitch, and singled to give Arizona its first and, as of right now, only World Series championship.

The narrative of Bob Brenly's career was determined largely by that ninth inning. If the Diamondbacks don't score, the Yankees win the Series, and there would have been volumes written on how Brenly managed the team out of at least one victory. That's not what happened, consigning that sort of analysis to the realm of the academic. The Diamondbacks did win the series, which made Bob Brenly a World Series–winning manager, a tag that sticks to a manager forever. The fact that the players won the series, and did so in spite of Brenly managing like he'd never so much as seen a baseball game before, is immaterial; media coverage of him in 2018–19 still often includes reference to the 2001 World Series, such as when Brenly went on a possibly racist tirade against Padres players Manny Machado and Fernando Tatis Jr. in April 2019.[3]

Brenly didn't win that World Series, of course. His players did, first of all, but his on-field decisions hurt his team's chances of winning. Giving him credit for the win, as is standard in baseball writing—the manager won the World Series, the players were just the hired hands—disconnects the process from the outcome.

There's a name for the mental mistake that leads to this fallacy, of course: outcome bias. We would all like to believe that good process yields good results and bad process yields bad results, so that we can tell from the results whether a process was good or bad. That would be true if life were deterministic, but it's not. Sometimes you do all the right things and are stymied by bad luck. Other times you do everything wrong and are subsequently rewarded for it. That's outcome bias.

In *Thinking, Fast and Slow*, Kahneman lists outcome bias in his section on biases or illusions of overconfidence, even slipping in a baseball reference of his own by listing third-base coaches among decision-makers often judged most harshly by outcome or hindsight bias (along with physicians, CEOs, financial advisers, social workers, and others):

> We are prone to blame decision makers for good decisions that worked out badly and to give them too little credit for successful moves that appear obvious only after the fact. There is a clear *outcome bias*. . . . Actions that seemed prudent in foresight can look irresponsibly negligent in hindsight.

Kahneman cites the revelation after the attacks on the United States on September 11, 2001, that the CIA had received information two months earlier that al-Qaeda might be planning an attack of this magnitude, but that George Tenet, then the CIA's director, chose to bring it to National Security Adviser Condoleezza Rice rather than to President George W. Bush. Much post-9/11 analysis of intelligence "failures" focused on the information that the CIA and other agencies had collected that indicated an attack was brewing, but ignored the quantity of additional conflicting or irrelevant information around it.

Nassim Nicholas Taleb, author of *The Black Swan* and *Fooled by Randomness*, wrote in a 2004 editorial for the *New York Times* called "Learning to Expect the Unexpected"[4] that the 9/11 Commission risked squandering an opportunity to reconsider how to prepare for future terror attacks due to "hindsight distortion": "To paraphrase Kierkegaard, history runs forward but is seen backward." It was easy for the commission to look into the past and see negligence in the intelligence process as the members appeared "to be looking for precise and narrowly defined

accountability." The commission's mandate was to find someone
or something to blame, rather than starting with the premise, as
Taleb argues, that the extent and sophistication of the 9/11 attacks made it an extremely unlikely event such that it was almost
inconceivable, and our inability to conceive of it is what made the
attacks possible. In hindsight, we say, of course, we should have
seen that coming. In real time, however, we almost never foresee
these extremely rare yet historically significant events—if we did,
we would stop or alter them, but their very nature makes them
possible.

In their 1988 paper "Outcome Bias in Decision Evaluation,"[5]
Jonathan Baron and John C. Hershey write, "A fault condemned
but seldom avoided is the evaluation of the intention of an act in
terms of the act's outcome." They further cite a 1974 book, *Decision Analysis for the Manager,* in saying that "[d]ecision makers
cannot infallibly be graded by their results." You can make all
the right moves and still lose. You can choose the right players
in the draft, or make a trade that appears to be a huge win for
your side, and yet come out behind because of bad luck, player
injuries, or the simple fact that any decision that involves human
beings brings in some unpredictable factors. This is the fundamental problem with second-guessing or Monday morning quar-
terbacking (a now-dated expression)—we are driven, naturally, to
judge decisions by their outcomes, instead of asking whether the
process that led to that decision was sound, and therefore likely to
lead to a good outcome even if, in reality, it did not.

Baron and Hershey's paper includes the results of five studies
where they presented undergraduate subjects with the descriptions of decisions and the outcomes, and then asked the subjects
to rate the decision-makers' competence or the quality of their
decisions. The authors found consistent evidence of outcome bias
in all five experiments, and explain its existence and consistent

appearance by several suppositions: that people believe luck or clairvoyance is a personal trait of some people, the general heuristic most people use that a bad outcome proves a bad process, and, worst of all from the subjects' perspective, a tendency to disbelieve information about what the decision-maker knew if the outcome appears to contradict it. They conclude that "[o]ur results suggest that people may confuse their evaluations of decisions with the evaluations of the consequences themselves."

Outcome bias also skews the way we think about and discuss leaders in worlds beyond that of sport. Kahneman points out that "the CEO of a successful company is likely to be called flexible, methodical, and decisive. Imagine that a year has passed and things have gone sour. The same executive is now described as confused, rigid, and authoritarian."

We can see this effect at work with baseball managers, who are the first people credited when a team exceeds expectations and the first people blamed when a team falls short. After each regular season, members of the Baseball Writers' Association (BBWAA) vote for postseason awards, including each league's Most Valuable Player, Rookie of the Year, and Manager of the Year, with thirty writers voting for each of those honors. The Manager of the Year award has long been the squishiest of all, as we have little to no idea of how to properly value the manager's job, other than the general sense among analysts that the effect of a manager, positive or negative, on a team's record in one season is smaller than the conventional wisdom indicates.

Given the award's nebulous nature and the apparent default voting strategy of "pick the guy whose team won more games than they were supposed to win," we see all kinds of hindsight distortion and outcome bias in the voting results and in how quickly sentiment turns against those same managers. There have been 69 winners of this nice award since its inception in 1983 (due to a tie one year), and 35 of those managers were eventually fired or "resigned" under pressure. What's more amazing is how fast the wind changed direction:

- One manager was fired between his last game and the announcement that he'd won the award (Joe Girardi, Florida, 2006).
- Six were fired during or after the following season.
- Twelve were fired/resigned during the second season after they won the award, or after two seasons.
- Eight were fired during season three or after three more seasons.

Nineteen men won the Manager of the Year award and were bounced within two years of the honor. If we extend it one more year, that's 27 such winners, or 39 percent of every manager to win the award—nearly two in five. With odds like that, maybe some manager will go all George C. Scott and refuse the honor.

There are two explanations at work here, and I think they both apply. (I've cast a ballot for the award once, and would be fine to never do that again.) The first is that the writers are not good at choosing the winners: because we don't really know how much effect managers have, and struggle to measure the effects we can identify, voters tend to employ outcome bias and pick the guy whose team did the best relative to preseason expectations. That might have had nothing to do with the manager—it could be that a couple of players had unexpected breakout seasons, and maybe the preseason expectations themselves were wrong—but the manager is just standing there, looking respectable and such, so let's hand him the credit.

The second explanation is that teams themselves don't really know when a manager is good, and so decisions to hire and especially fire managers are rather arbitrary. There's hindsight distortion here, too—we thought we would win so many games, but we won fewer games than we thought, so let's blame the manager. (As the old sports saying goes, you can't fire the players.) It's outcome bias in the other direction. We ascribe wins and losses to managers, saying that a manager had such-and-such a record, even though it was the players who played those games, and the manager, while bearing some small responsibility for the results, didn't play enough of a role to be handed credit for all of the wins and all of the losses.

We've seen plenty of managers post poor records when handed mediocre rosters and then find success when handed better players, perhaps none more significant than Joe Torre, who was fired by the St. Louis Cardinals early in the 1995 season, giving him a career "record" of 894 wins and 1003 losses, with just one playoff appearance and zero postseason wins. His hiring by the Yankees after they fired Buck Showalter (less than twelve months after Showalter won the Manager of the Year award in the American League) earned this description by Joe Sheehan (a lifelong Yankee fan) in the 1997 edition of *Baseball Prospectus*: "Buck Showalter, one of the best managers in baseball, was coerced into resigning and Joe Torre, one of the managers in baseball, [was] hired."[6]

At that point, Torre had won one World Series; he'd win three more, plus two more American League pennants, and eventually was selected for the Hall of Fame by one of the institution's many committees. Sheehan was spot on—nobody thought at the time of the move that the Yankees had upgraded—yet Torre's legacy was completely altered by inheriting a roster that had four future Hall of Famers on it and several perennial All-Stars, to say nothing of the later addition of Roger Clemens. Maybe Torre learned something from his lack of success at three previous stops, or maybe he was the same manager he always was but benefited from managing the

best roster of his life. The Hall of Fame electorate is certainly prey
to outcome bias, too.

If the outcome does not appear to match the process, we may
also ask whether our evaluation of the process was itself sound.
Perhaps the decision-maker did not have all of the relevant
information, or we did not have all of the information the decision makers had. In July 2011, the Houston Astros traded their
best player at the time, outfielder Hunter Pence, to the Philadelphia Phillies for a package of four prospects led by infielder
Jon Singleton and Jarred Cosart, whom I then ranked as the
Astros' numbers one and two prospects right after the deal.
What was not known at the time was that Singleton had a longtime problem with substance abuse, eventually serving multiple
suspensions in the minors for testing positive for marijuana.[7] In
2014, after he was suspended for the second time, he entered
a rehabilitation program and referred to himself as "a drug ad-
dict." In January 2018, however, he tested positive for "a drug
of abuse" (MLB does not typically reveal the drug in question)
and was suspended for 100 games, during which the Astros
released him.

The deal was a complete bust for the Astros. They traded Cosart before injuries and a gambling scandal ruined his career, and
never got any value from the other players in the deal, Josh Zeid
and Domingo Santana; Santana was part of the trade for Carlos
Gomez and Mike Fiers, a deal that also went sour. If Singleton
was the key to the Pence trade, then how do we evaluate their
decision?

- If the Astros knew at the time of the trade that Singleton had
  a substance abuse issue—he hadn't been suspended by MLB,

and I was at least unaware of it as a member of the press—then the decision may have been flawed: they either ignored or did not adequately assess his addiction and its possible effect on his playing time and productivity.

- If they did not know, however, then they may have made a sound decision that had a bad outcome. Perhaps the Phillies were unaware of the extent of the problem, or knew it but didn't share it with the Astros. (I'm not accusing the Phillies of anything in this case, but there are other examples of teams trading players without disclosing key information like injuries or personal issues.) In that case, based on the information available to the Astros at the time of the trade, they may have made a good decision that had a bad outcome because of the information they couldn't get.
- Or, perhaps the Astros didn't investigate Singleton's history enough, or they did and found nothing. This would be a case of a specific process failure that fed bad or insufficient information to the decision-makers, who then made the right decision based on what they knew. There are many ways this disastrous deal—they traded their best player for an effective return of zero—could have been a good process/bad outcome decision, but in the sports world in particular, we default to the black-or-white framework of good trade versus bad trade, or success versus bust.

The Astros whiffed on the outcome of the deal, regardless of the truth behind the process, finishing that 2011 season with the worst record in baseball, then doing so again in 2012 and 2013. By 2015, however, their rebuilding efforts started to show up in the standings, as the team won a wild-card playoff spot; in 2017, they won the AL West division title and advanced to win the World Series for the first time in franchise history. They did so in spite of the Pence trade, not because of it, another good outcome that does not, in hindsight, make an unsuccessful trade into a successful one.

In a 2012 paper simply called "Hindsight Bias,"[8] Neal J. Roese and Kathleen D. Vohs discuss one evidence-based method to getting around hindsight or outcome bias, which has the clumsy but transparent name of "consider-the-opposite." They define it in simple terms: "In this strategy, the decision maker is encouraged to consider and explain how outcomes that did not occur could well have occurred." To return to Bob Brenly's bunt bumbling and bullpen blundering, imagine a scenario where Mariano Rivera closes out the ninth inning of Game 7—no throwing error, no excuse-me bloop single—and the Diamondbacks lose the Series. It's fairly easy to conceive this alternative outcome, especially if you watched the last game and saw how close the margin of victory was for Arizona. If you're an adherent of the many-worlds hypothesis,[9] you can see multiple points just in that ninth inning where the universe split into parallel ones, and in several of these, the Yankees held on and took the title, which would have been their fifth in six years.

If Arizona loses the series—and does so in spite of two herculean efforts by their top two starting pitchers, Randy Johnson and Curt Schilling—then the narrative after the fact would have revolved around how they managed to lose, and my choice of the word "managed" there was not an accident. All fingers would have swiveled to point at Brenly, and he gave us plenty to pick apart with his incessant bunting ahead of Luis Gonzalez and mishandling of Byung-Hyun Kim. If you reimagine the Series by changing just the last half inning of the last game, you should find it easy to see how Brenly's moves led to a different series outcome, and then how fan perceptions and media coverage would have focused on Brenly's managing.

Within the same paper, the two authors also examine whether subject-matter expertise is a defense against hindsight bias—in other words, if you know a lot about the subject, are you less prone to this particular bias? While in some circumstances, "expertise would seem to offset hindsight bias"—really, could you damn it with fainter praise, folks?—"Expertise in itself offers no blanket protection." If you're human, you are prone to this bias. They cite a meta-analysis, a study that looks at multiple studies on the same topic, from 2004 that found no correlation between expertise and reduced hindsight bias: "we may hypothesize that expertise reduces hindsight bias as defined in terms of the memory distortion level but at the same time increases hindsight bias as defined in terms of the foreseeability level."

In plain English, their hypothesis is that experts are less likely to misremember their own predictions or judgments, but that they're more likely to think they could have seen some event or outcome in advance—so being an expert on the subject doesn't give you immunity to hindsight bias, but merely changes the way that bias will show up in your musings.

Outcome bias comes up all the time in fandom as well, because it is just so easy to judge decisions—or the people making them—strictly by outcomes when the processes are often hidden from view. Just this off-season, the Giants hired Gabe Kapler as their manager after he managed the Phillies for two seasons in which the team didn't make the playoffs. Does that mean Kapler wasn't a good manager? Or do the players bear that responsibility? If you're a Giants fan, that distinction matters to you, both for your own opinion of the hire, and for your confidence level in the front office's choice of managers. The Pittsburgh Pirates hired Ben Cherington as their general manager, four years after he was forced out as GM of the Red Sox. With him at the helm, the Red Sox won the World Series in 2013, but finished in last place in 2012 and 2014. Does he get credit for the championship, blame for the last-place finishes, or some of both? What were the processes that he used to make key decisions on free agents, trades, or front-office personnel?

I'm on record as favoring both of those hires because I believe in the processes both Kapler and Cherington used in their previous roles, and in their capacity to learn from previous mistakes and be more effective the second time they're given the same responsibilities. Simply judging them on their outcomes doesn't give anyone a complete picture of their skills, their weaknesses, or, perhaps most important in this case, their talents.

# 4

## But This Is How We've Always Done It

### Why Groupthink Alone Doesn't Make Baseball Myths True

Falsehood flies, and truth comes limping after it,
so that when men come to be undeceived, it is too late.
—Jonathan Swift

Lineup protection is not a thing. If you read *Smart Baseball,*
you've seen my explanation—standing on the shoulders of
others who did the heavy lifting for me—of why this concept, that
a major-league hitter will perform differently based on who hits
behind him in the lineup, does not play out in practice. I mention
it here not to debunk the myth a second time, even though doing

so might be fun, but to explore why this falsehood and other baseball superstitions like it persist even in the face of contradictory
evidence.

The argument for lineup protection goes something like this:
Let's say our old friend Joey Bagodonuts is the best hitter on his
team and generally hits second in the lineup, which is where your
best overall hitter should be. (There's another baseball myth about
that, too.) Who do you bat right behind him? The hypothesis of
lineup protection says that if you put a weak hitter behind him,
opposing pitchers will pitch around Joey B., risking walking him
but avoiding the risk of a hard-hit ball, to get to the weaker hitter.
If you put a strong hitter behind Bagodonuts, however, pitchers
will have no choice but to pitch to the big guy, thus allowing
him to see more strikes, or maybe more fastballs, or some other
change that increases his chances to hit the ball hard and get on
base or knock in runs.

It's not true, at least not in the majors—I've never seen any data
on the subject in the minors or at the amateur level—and the fact
that it's not true has been public knowledge for at least twenty-
five years at this point. Baseball Prospectus's 2006 compilation
of essays, *Baseball Between the Numbers*, which I have seen on
bookshelves in front offices and even the occasional manager's
office, contained multiple essays that eviscerated the myth of protection. That hasn't stopped anyone, including many people who
should know better, from preaching the gospel of lineup protection just in 2019:

- Jim Bowden, former general manager of the Cincinnati Reds
  and Washington Nationals, wrote in August 2019 how Nick
  Castellanos "was buried on the Tigers, with little lineup protection."[1]

- Joe Maddon said of a decision to move Kyle Schwarber up from the fifth spot in the Cubs' lineup to the second spot that "I thought he deserved more protection right now."[2]
- A piece by MLB.com's Ken Gurnick was built entirely around the premise of lineup protection, saying that Cody Bellinger was being "pitched around" because of who hit after him in the Dodgers' lineup, then claiming that manager Dave Roberts adjusted the lineup "with David Freese and Max Muncy batting behind Bellinger for protection" in an article loaded with conclusions drawn from tiny samples.[3]
- Tigers infielder Miguel Cabrera, who is almost certain to end up in the Hall of Fame after he retires, blamed his offensive struggles in 2019, which were a function of his age (thirty-six) and physical breakdown, on a lack of lineup protection: "You know Prince Fielder? You know who's hitting behind me right now? That's a big difference, too."[4]

That's just a quick sampling from the season in which I'm writing this book, which still has a few weeks to go as I type. It's hardly limited to this particularly low moment in the history of American intellectualism. A 2015 post by David Laurila on Fangraphs included quotes from a dozen players and managers on whether lineup protection existed or whether it affected how they approached certain at bats. The replies varied, but Evan Longoria, Rick Porcello, and Mark Teixeira all came down hard on the side of protection existing, with Longoria ("I think that's a pretty silly question. It's a question that answers itself. If you have somebody like Miguel Cabrera behind you, you're going to get pitches to hit, as opposed to if it's a rookie without much big-league time") and Porcello outright dismissive about it ("I think anybody who watches the game knows protection exists"). Teixeira, now a game analyst for ESPN, was more measured, saying, "There are a lot of variables, but common sense tells you that if a stud is hitting behind you, you're going to see better pitches. In today's game, you have so many match-ups."[5]

While the viewpoint has faded from front offices, it's still pervasive throughout clubhouses, to the point that several managers have used it just this year, as Maddon did, to defend specific changes they made to their teams' lineups. (Maddon also cited protection in early June to explain why Javier Baez had two good games with Carlos Gonzalez hitting behind him.) We can infer from this that in at least some of those instances the managers used their belief in protection to inform how they structured those lineups. Ned Yost told reporters on August 20 that he'd moved Jorge Soler to the second spot in the Royals' lineup to provide him with protection[6] after Cheslor Cuthbert, who had been hitting behind Soler, had an 0-for-35 stretch that provided, in Yost's words, "zero protection." (Cuthbert's hitless streak eventually reached 40 at bats before he doubled on August 24.) Yost and Maddon both managed teams that won the World Series, and Maddon won the National League's Manager of the Year award in 2015—although you may know by now how little those things tell us about a manager.

So why does this myth persist? In part, it's because it's one line of the baseball gospels preached to players, coaches, scouts, and anyone else working their way up the hierarchy of professional baseball, whether on the field or as an employee out of uniform. It is true because everyone believes it to be true, and they tell two people, and they tell two people, and they tell two people, and baseball actually isn't a very big cluster of humans and it is certainly not the most diverse group of folks you'll ever see—you can swing a cat around by its tail in most MLB front offices without hitting more than one woman or one person of African-American descent—so the lie gets repeated even when the truth is public and easy to find.

W hy do we cling to untruths long after they've been disproven or lost their usefulness? Is it really just a matter of hearing something preached as true so frequently that our minds accept them not just as fact, but as the default perspective that must be actively dislodged by the jaws of life?

Yes, as it turns out. That's the illusory truth effect, and it is a real problem well beyond the sports world, especially in our current era of disinformation campaigns and social media.

Three researchers at Temple University and the University of Toronto first identified the illusory truth effect in a 1977 research paper, although they didn't give this cognitive illusion its current name. The authors found that test subjects who were told plausible statements of fact multiple times over several weeks were more likely to rate those statements as "true," regardless of their actual validity: "The repetition of a plausible statement increases a person's belief in the referential validity or truth of that statement."[7]

Think about that for just a moment: The more you hear something, the more you'll believe it's true . . . *regardless of whether it's actually true.* Now think about some patently untrue things you've heard repeatedly over the last few months or years. Evolution is "just a theory." (Misleading: A scientific theory has been proven by direct observation, as evolution has many times over.) There's a "five-second rule" for food you drop on the ground or an unclean surface. (Food picks up microbes from other surfaces instantaneously. By the time it's left your hand, it's too late.) Humans only use 10 percent of their brains. (Utter nonsense.) Eating spicy food causes ulcers. (A bacterium, *Helicobacter pylori,* is the real culprit.) Taking more vitamin C can prevent the common cold. (Disproven, repeatedly, yet vitamin C supplements continue to sell.) Food X, or nutrient Y, is increasing your risk of heart disease/cancer/diabetes. (These statements nearly always over-simplify the facts, and often vilify foods, like eggs, that are not harmful in most folks' diets.)

The original 1977 paper had a very elegant research method. Subjects were given three tests across five weeks, each comprising 60 plausible assertions on a variety of subjects, and were asked to rate the likelihood of each assertion being true on a scale from 1 to 7. One-third of the assertions were repeated on each test; the other 120 (40 per test) were unique. The subjects were more likely to rate the repeated assertions as more likely to be true on the third test of the three, even if the assertions were false, when compared to nonrepeated statements. Even hearing an assertion on a second test, two weeks after the first one, boosted the subjects' ratings of the assertion's likely validity.

More shocking is that knowledge in the subject does not seem to be an adequate defense against this effect. Another study published in 2015 in the *Journal of Experimental Psychology* found that "illusory truth effects occurred even when participants knew better."[8] The study cites earlier work that found that hearing something repeatedly makes it easier for your brain to "process" it, and that "people rate statements presented in high-contrast (i.e., easy-to-read) fonts as 'true' more often than those presented in low-contrast fonts."[9] So, say it loud, and say it in boldface, and you'll get people to buy in.

The study's two experiments found that subjects would use this ease of processing as a first cue, even ignoring their prior knowledge to do so. They found that study participants would sometimes ignore their previous knowledge under "fluent processing conditions"—that is, when the assertions they were given were repeated or otherwise easy to understand. One hypothesized reason for this is that people rarely do "source monitoring," considering where they learned some past information, when considering things they've learned in the past and must recall from their "knowledge bases," while it's easier to evaluate the source of something you're reading or hearing right now. A second hypothesis supposes that it is easier to accept something as true than to disbelieve it by retrieving contradictory information from our knowledge bases.

The authors also found that subjects were happy with a "partial match" between their stored knowledge and what was in the assertions. For example, they provide the question, "How many animals of each kind did Moses take on the ark?" and say that respondents will often answer the question as if nothing were amiss. That's because there's a partial match to our stored knowledge of this Bible story, that there were two animals of each kind on the ark, enough to make some people neglect their prior knowledge that it was actually Noah and not Moses on the boat.

This has particularly stark connotations today, as the developed world is fighting a wave of dangerous disinformation spread by people who offer false assertions against the safety and efficacy of vaccines—and are now taking their message to developing countries that lack the same infrastructure that has kept outbreaks of highly contagious diseases like the measles from turning into nationwide epidemics. If merely repeating a lie is enough to convince some people that it's true, or at least that it is slightly more likely to be true, then we need entirely new strategies for defeating those who spread such fictions.

I write this in September 2019, and so far this year there have been 1,241 confirmed cases of measles, a viral infection that is almost completely preventable with vaccines, in the United States alone. This comes just nineteen years after the United States declared it had eliminated the virus, and incidence dropped to below one case per one million residents. (Cases could still occur if someone traveled outside of the United States and contracted the virus elsewhere.) The primary reason for this resurgence in what might be the most contagious viral disease in humans is the spread of disinformation, which started with the publication of a fraudulent study in 1998 that claimed that the combined MMR (measles/mumps/rubella) vaccine could cause autism spectrum disorder in infants.

Let me be unequivocal about this before I go any further. The MMR vaccine does not cause autism; no vaccine causes autism, nor could any vaccine cause autism. Autism has a strong genetic component and signs of autism spectrum disorder are visible in a gestating fetus. People who say vaccines cause autism are wrong. They may be lying, or they may simply be misinformed, but they are wrong, and it is important that everyone who knows better—which now includes you—says so.

Andrew Wakefield was the primary author of the since-retracted study, and was very willing to spread this news that he'd discovered a potential cause of autism—not least because he'd received funding from a group of lawyers considering suing vaccine manufacturers over this matter. It turned out that Wakefield lied about the children in the study, as only one of the nine children he claimed had regressive autism had actually been diagnosed with the disorder, and he failed to disclose that several children in the study had developmental problems before they received the vaccine.[10]

In a rational world, this would have ended the matter, but it hasn't. A *Sunday Times* reporter named Brian Deer began to uncover the malfeasance in 2004, and the *Lancet* retracted Wakefield's study in 2010, the same year in which the United Kingdom revoked Wakefield's license to practice medicine. None of this has stopped the spread of the assertion that vaccines cause autism, which has been repeated so many times across so many channels—even to this day you will see stories in the media about the vaccine-autism "controversy," which implies there's still some doubt[11]—that there are still many parents who decline to vaccinate their children, against all medical advice. Data from the Centers for Disease Control estimate that over 200,000 U.S. kindergarten students in the 2017–18 school year had not received the MMR vaccine.[12]

Once a repeated myth is entrenched in someone's mind, whether it's "vaccines cause autism" or "lineup protection works," it's hard to dislodge it—even with facts. A 2017 study looking at three failed strategies to unseat anti-vaccine views in subjects found that showing these people correct information on vaccines "often backfire[d], resulting in the unintended opposite effect, reinforcing ill-founded beliefs about vaccination and reducing intentions to vaccinate."[13]

Yes, sadly, giving facts to people who believed falsehoods about vaccines only made them further convinced in the falsehoods.

The myth of the clutch hitter also earned a debunking in *Smart Baseball*, which, again, just built on the work of others who came before me. It has the same prion-like refusal to die; you could put the clutch hitter myth in an autoclave and it would still come out intact, ready to get that big hit with two strikes.

Writing for NBC Sports Philadelphia in 2019, Corey Seidman did a great job distilling the clutch hitter myth in a way even folks who don't follow baseball could grasp:

Not everyone believes in the concept of "clutch." People who have played and/or watched sports all their lives know it when they see it and usually think they have a good gauge on which players are and are not clutch.

But there are many who think "clutch" doesn't exist or at least cannot be properly quantified, that individual events in games are more random no matter how much of a narrative exists that a player "thrives on big moments."[14]

I'm firmly in the latter camp, as the evidence that certain hitters are better in the clutch simply does not exist. Seidman's piece argues that Bryce Harper had, to that date, been the most clutch hitter in MLB in 2019, but not that Harper himself has some sort of clutch gene or woo.

Beyond the Box Score's Patrick Brennan ran yet another analysis on clutch hitters in August 2019, looking at 434 hitters who had at least 300 PA in any two consecutive seasons between 2014 and 2019, and found . . . nothing. A player's "clutch" performance in one year doesn't predict his performance in "clutch" spots the next year. His conclusion is unequivocal:

No correlation, meaning being "clutch" isn't a repeatable skill. High leverage performance could not be any more inconsistent than it already is. To summarize, it's look [sic] to be as clutch is not a skill, as in general it is not repeatable. It's a random distribution of offensive production that messes with the perception of a player's performance. It can be a fun stat to look at, sure, but in no way should it be used in evaluation of performance.[15]

Oh, but it is used that way. When the Baseball Hall of Fame's "Today's Game" committee met in December 2018, they stunned the baseball world by selecting Harold Baines, a perfectly cromulent player who was never considered a Hall of Famer by contemporaries or after he retired, for enshrinement in the Hall. Tony La Russa, who served on that committee and managed Baines, defended the choice by repeatedly saying the magic word: "In Oakland, we were looking for a clutch hitter [in 1990] and that's when we got Willie McGee and Harold—Harold always had the ability to drive in a big run. . . . Remember in '92, after [Dennis Eckersley] had his save streak messed up by Gregg Jefferies, Harold hit a three-run homer in the bottom of the ninth to win it. He was a clutch, clutch hitter."[16] When retired slugger David Ortiz was shot and wounded in June 2019, the news wire story referred to how he "blossom[ed] into a clutch hitter in his 14 seasons with the Red Sox."[17] Players buy into the myth, too; when the Twins signed Marwin Gonzalez as a free agent in February 2019, his former teammate, Lance McCullers, tweeted that Gonzalez was "one of the most clutch hitters and best defenders around."[18] When Ortiz joins Derek Jeter in the Hall of Fame, you will hear ad nauseam how they were both such clutch hitters. They really weren't; they were both great hitters regardless of the situation, which means that they hit well in the "clutch" just like they hit well at all other times.

The 2016 NL Most Valuable Player, Kris Bryant, acquired the tag of being "unclutch"—an unwieldy way of saying a player is worse in clutch situations than in others—early in his career, in part because, in both 2016 and 2017, he was the worst clutch hitter in the National League according to Fangraphs' Clutch statistic, which weights performance in clutch situations by the game score and state. Detractors could say it had to be meaningful if the same player finished last two years in a row. It didn't last, of course; Bryant was well above average in the same metric in 2015, and as of September 15, 2019, he was the 12th most "clutch" hitter in the National League, still according to Fangraphs. Gordon Wittenmyer of the *Chicago Sun-Times* poked fun at the misconception in a column in August 2019, starting with a summary of

72                                    Keith Law

the criticisms of Bryant: "He doesn't have the clutch gene. Can't hit when it matters. Soft."[19]

The idea of certain hitters having some magical power to raise their games in clutch situations is appealing on an emotional level, contributing to the heroic stories we build around our favorite players, but the existence of such clutch hitters is not supported by data. The strongest refutation I've seen is in *The Book,* whose three authors found that if there is any clutch effect at all for certain hitters, it is extremely small, not enough to affect anyone's decision-making.[20] If it's there, it's not important—yet it's still cited frequently by managers, players, and media members when discussing the game and justifying decisions.

The reality is people rely on inaccurate information even when they have prior knowledge, have been warned that the information might be inaccurate, or have received correct information.[21] As long as the false information was easy to understand, subjects' brains had no difficulty processing—understanding and then retaining—this information, as they might have with accurate information that was told in an unclear manner or in more challenging language. The actual causes of autism are still under investigation, but it appears to involve dozens of different genes and to first manifest in utero; it's much easier to process a simple causal statement like "vaccines cause autism" even though there isn't an iota of truth to it. Explaining that hitters' performances are subject to normal random variation over the course of a season or even several seasons, and thus they might appear to have specific skills like superpowers in clutch situations because of statistical noise, requires a bit of understanding about statistics—notably that random distributions are not uniform. A true .300 hitter will not have 3 hits in every 10 at bats, or hit .300 in every month of the season. It's easier to believe that random variations have underlying causes or explanations.

The authors of the 2017 study about the three failed strategies to unseat anti-vaccine views propose several reasons why we hold on to misinformation even when we hear the truth, one of which seems especially apt for this discussion. They propose that once a person has established a belief in something, they will interpret new information in a way that fits their previously held belief—or reject the information entirely if it would force a contradiction. The human capacity to rationalize away evidence that undermines a tightly held belief is strong and crosses all disciplines.

Unfortunately, the authors found that repeating the falsehoods in attempts to debunk them, such as "myths vs. facts" presentations, only reinforced participants' belief in the myths because it "paradoxically amplifies the familiarity of that false claim making it seem even more believable and widely-shared . . . people tend to mistake repetition for truth, a phenomenon known as the 'illusory truth' effect."[22] It puts the truth tellers in a difficult position where repeating the lie to try to dislodge it from believers' minds only entrenches it further. Telling someone who believes fervently that his favorite player is not actually "clutch" can end up strengthening his belief through repetition, while he may try to concoct explanations to fit the facts you give him into his previously held views.

You can see this with sports fans and even members of the media who will rewrite definitions to preserve those beliefs. When Red Sox slugger David Ortiz announced he'd be retiring after the 2016 season, there was, again, a flood of coverage that referred to him as "clutch," including a list in the *Boston Globe* on "13 moments when David Ortiz defined clutch,"[23] another list on FoxSports.com with "10 times David Ortiz defined clutch in October for the Red Sox,"[24] and a MassLive story that simply dubbed him "Mr. Clutch."[25] Much of the justification revolved around specific hits he had in high-leverage situations, which is classic cherry-picking—you choose the data you like, you throw out the data you don't—or pointed to his exceptional performance in fourteen career World Series games while ignoring his other post-season stats and his clutch stats from the regular season. Ortiz is a beloved figure on and off the field in Boston, playing on three World Series champions for the Red Sox, giving an emotional speech on the field after the Boston Marathon bombings in 2013, and, in a very New England moment, appearing in a Dunkin' Donuts commercial with Patriots star Rob Gronkowski. He was a great hitter all the time, no better or worse in clutch situations, but the combination of "Ortiz" and "clutch" has been repeated so often that it has become the default belief across baseball.

The stakes are lower in sportsball, but in the world of medi-cine, the stakes are substantially higher, and research into more effective methods of fighting disinformation on vaccines, fake cures for cancer or autism, or charlatans selling pseudoscience to desperate patients and parents is ongoing. A 2015 Gallup poll, coming seventeen years after the fraudulent Wakefield study and five years after its retraction, found that 73 percent of respondents had heard at least "a fair amount" about the "disadvantages" of vaccines (pro tip: there are no disadvantages), and 52 percent of respondents said they were personally "unsure" if vaccines were a cause of autism (pro tip: they're not), beyond 6 percent who said that vaccines were a cause of autism (sorry, just banging my head on my desk now).[26] A 2018 poll by Research America, with support from the American Society for Microbiology, found 48 percent of respondents said they didn't "trust" the flu vaccine (the flu vaccine has never lied to me, and also it reduces your odds of getting the flu), and 29 percent said it wasn't "very important" that parents vaccinate their children (it is essential, unless you like children suffering needlessly from preventable diseases).[27]

Such misinformation is even harder to combat in areas without established infrastructure to allow authorities to disseminate correct information. The 2019 Ebola outbreak in the Kivu region of the Democratic Republic of the Congo, a poor country ravaged by more than two decades of nearly continuous civil war, has been exacerbated by false information and errant beliefs; one research survey found one in four residents believed the outbreak wasn't real.[28] The same study found levels of distrust in government authorities' ability to respond to the outbreak ranging from 70 percent for local authorities to 98 percent for national ones. The challenge of dealing with disease outbreaks is thus amplified by the challenge of fighting disinformation and a noncompliant public.

Countering the illusory truth effect in yourself is relatively straightforward, as long as you take an objective attitude toward your own opinions. When you hear information that contradicts your existing views, be open to the possibility that your views are wrong, or at least require modification. Consider the sources of the new information, and whether your existing opinions are based on information from reliable sources or merely information you've heard often—conventional wisdom, old wives' tales, even just outdated information that has been superseded by new insights. Bear in mind that your . . . uh, mind will always be biased toward information you've heard more often, even if it's wrong, and take the extra step to question those previously held beliefs. We all need to think like fact-checkers whose entire job involves reading drafts of books or articles looking for possible mistakes.

The greater challenge is to dislodge such entrenched information from the minds of other people whom you're trying to convince of some new idea—that lineup protection is a myth, that vaccines are safe and essential, that climate change is real, and so on. Existing research on combating "vaccine hesitancy," the catchall term for people who show some resistance to the recommended vaccine schedule for infants and young children, is mixed. Direct confrontations often backfire, causing the vaccine-hesitant to become more obstinate and more convinced of their errant views.[29] A 2015 paper by two European researchers in cognitive science found that eroding trust in authorities, especially scientific institutions, was a major factor in opposition to vaccinations and the associated resistance to factual arguments. Telling people that the Centers for Disease Control or the American Academy of Pediatrics have shown, with data, that vaccines are safe and effective will only work if those people already trust the CDC or AAP or similar authorities; otherwise, they will discredit the new information to conform with their preexisting views.

If I tell you the clutch hitter or lineup protection is a myth, you will be more inclined to believe me if you already find me a trustworthy source. (That's debatable, but let's go with it.) You may be more willing to accept this new input if it comes from, say, a current MLB manager or a former player. Another pervasive baseball myth is that of the "hot hand"—the idea that current streaks are predictive of future performance. Former Red Sox manager Alex Cora, whose team won the World Series in 2018 in his first year at the helm, has said he doesn't let the "hot hand" affect his choices on who to play and how to build his lineup, earning praise from Professor Daniel Drezner, a professor of international politics at Tufts University, during Boston's playoff run that fall because Cora "never succumbed to recency bias" and didn't merely try to ride the hot hand.[30] The appeal to authority—the idea that a claim is more valid because of the stature of the person who says it—may be a fallacy, but we can use that to our advantage by putting trusted authorities out there with important messages.

The second technique to combat the illusory truth effect is raising the stakes, or just showing people how high the stakes already are.[31] Vaccine hesitancy dropped dramatically in 2018–19 when several measles outbreaks hit Oregon, Washington State, New York, and Minnesota, among other regions; demand for the MMR vaccine jumped 500 percent year over year in Clark County, Washington, when measles went from a hypothetical threat to an imminent one.[32] Showing parents the potential harm of such diseases has also been effective; measles can cause deafness, brain damage, and death in around 1 in 1,000 patients, including death by a form of brain swelling known as SSPE, which occurs years after the initial measles infection.

Granted, the stakes are a bit lower in sportsball—build your lineup wrong and you might score fewer runs over the course of a season—but MLB teams are built to chase even small advantages, just like arbitrageurs in the world of finance, because those five extra runs could mean the additional win that puts you in the playoffs. Show people what they might stand to lose and they may be more receptive to new information.

Major-league managers often set their lineups based on simple choices: do I play Smith or Jones at second base today? Do I bat Jones third or sixth? There are data they should consider, such as how these players match up against the opposing starter—for example, if Smith is a left-handed hitter and Jones is a right-handed hitter, the manager might choose to play Jones on days when the opposing starter is left-handed, because Jones will have the platoon advantage. The risk you encounter with persistent myths is that they compete with data-driven decisions, or even cause you to discard data that doesn't agree with your predetermined conclusion: Smith might be "hot" at the plate in the manager's mind, and if that causes the manager to play Smith over Jones and cede the platoon advantage, it reduces the team's offensive potential for that game. Over the course of a season, it might not amount to much, but in the postseason the value of one additional win is enormous, and playing the wrong players or batting them in a suboptimal order could be the difference between winning or losing a playoff series.

# 5

# For Every Clayton Kershaw There Are Ten Kasey Kikers

## Base-Rate Neglect and Why It's Still a Bad Idea to Draft High School Pitchers in the First Round

*If you always do what you've always done,*
*you always get what you've always gotten.*

—Jessie Potter, in a speech delivered to the Woman to Woman conference in October 1981

If you ask any longtime scout or baseball executive what the riskiest category of player is in the MLB draft, the majority of answers will probably come down to high school pitchers. The industry regularly selects between two and ten such players—

teenaged pitchers who often throw hard, but are still growing physically and emotionally, and whose careers thus have a panoply of ways to go off the rails—in its first round, despite the long-held belief that such players are high-risk bets, because the belief is that the potential rewards justify the risks. Some front offices have eschewed the category almost entirely, including the Oakland A's of the era documented in *Moneyball* and the Blue Jays while I worked there, but such strategies have been short-lived; in 2005, just two years after that book was published, the A's had two second-round picks and used them both to select high school pitchers, neither of whom ever saw the majors. (The A's still haven't used a first-round pick on a high school arm since taking Jeremy Bonderman with an extra first-rounder they received in 2001.)

The truth of the matter seems pretty clear: high school pitchers selected in the first round have a higher failure rate than other categories (high school position players, college pitchers, or college position players), and do not offer higher upside. That's not to say that it is always wrong to take a high school pitcher in the first round, but that such players should be pushed down on draft boards to reflect the greater risk of them failing to reach the majors or produce first-round value once they get there. If you have two choices for your next draft pick in front of you, one a high school pitcher and one any other type of player, and you believe their value is about equal, you should take the other guy.

This information isn't necessarily new, although recent data seems to bear it out again. Yet teams continue to—in the vernacular of the industry—"pound" high school pitching in the first round. The data say that teams should be moving away from these players, but until the 2019 draft, which came close to historic lows for this category, there was no evidence that the industry as a whole was backing off high school pitchers.

Focusing on the individual case in front of you while ignoring the data you have on the more general category to which that case belongs is known as *base-rate neglect*. Base-rate neglect is the name for the phenomenon where you have a mountain of evidence saying one thing, but you choose to ignore it in favor of the specific case in front of you. You favor the information that stands out because it's more recent or it's more memorable or it's just the first thing you found, and in the process you forget or fail to check on the larger sample of data over a longer period of time. The former could be misleading, while the latter should be more predictive because of the greater sample size. You know high school pitchers flame out more often than other players do, but dangit, this here kid Joey Bagodonuts—you just know he's different, right? He's the exception that proves the rule,[1] or something. Your scouts are just sure he's the one kid who's different.

And sometimes there are indeed exceptions. The Royals took Zack Greinke with the sixth overall pick in 2002, and said at the time that they thought he was as advanced as a college pitcher even though he was just eighteen. They were right about that, and they were right about his upside; as of this writing, he's been the most valuable player drafted in 2002, and has enough of a margin over the second-most valuable player (also a high school pitcher, Cole Hamels) that he seems likely to retain that title. He really is an exception, though, and one Greinke don't stop no show. Taking a high school pitcher with your first-round pick remains a high-risk, medium-reward proposition, and we should see fewer such players taken in the first round.

Major League Baseball's draft differs from the drafts in North America's other two largest sports leagues (the NFL and the NBA) by allowing teams to select players who have finished high school but not yet matriculated at any college. To be eligible for the draft, you must have graduated from high school (or be about to do so), or have completed three years of eligibility at a four-year school, or have completed one or both years at a two-year school, or have turned twenty-one by the draft, or be about to turn twenty-one within forty-five days of the draft. That's a lot of rules, but for most players, the upshot is that you can sign right out of high school, or you can go to a four-year college and come back out after your junior year.

This presents major-league teams, from their individual scouts on up to the general manager, with the challenge of evaluating high school players who are typically seventeen or eighteen years old against college players who are twenty-one and occasionally twenty-two years old, a comparison that isn't quite apples to oranges, but more like red apples to green. They're similar, but you probably have different feelings about Fuji apples than you do about Granny Smith apples. (And don't get me started on Golden Delicious apples, which are not delicious, and turn to mush when you bake them.) It's not easy to decide whether the seventeen-year-old wunderkind you're watching is going to be a more valuable player in the long term than the twenty-one-year-old player who's not as exciting or athletic but who promises to get to the majors a year sooner, if not more.

With pitchers, the comparison is further complicated by perceptions that high school players are more likely to get hurt, because they're still growing and developing physically during the years they might be in college, and that going to four-year schools tends to thin the herd—whether just because of natural attrition or because there are still college coaches who'll overwork their pitchers in pursuit of soon-to-be-forgotten wins.

Thus major-league front offices are confronted by an epistemological question. The conventional wisdom in baseball has

long held that high school pitchers are higher risk than other categories, but that the higher reward justifies the risk. Clayton Kershaw was the best pitcher in baseball for a five-year stretch, and
he was a high school pitcher (taken 7th overall in 2006 by the
Los Angeles Dodgers). Greinke has been incredibly successful
since he was drafted, as has Hamels, as well as Matt Cain, also
taken in that same first round, 25th overall. (That draft yielded
six high school pitchers who were drafted in the first four rounds
and produced at least 20 Wins Above Replacement in their careers: the three I just mentioned, as well as Scott Kazmir, Josh
Johnson, and Jon Lester.) Partisans of prep pitching prospects
point to these players as proof of their proposition, and can invoke a baseball-centric FOMO argument: if you don't take high
school pitching prospects, you'll never get a Kershaw or a Greinke or a Roy Halladay.

Baseball-Reference has every draft in MLB history with players
linked to their career stats, which makes this a question we can
easily answer just by choosing our parameters. Does taking a high
school pitcher in the first round make sense? That is, is the *base
rate* for such a draft pick on par with those spent on other types
of players?

Of course it doesn't—otherwise we wouldn't be talking about
it. Yes, there are stars who come from the high school pitching
ranks, but such hits are infrequent enough to say that, in the absence of other information, spending a first-round pick on a high
school arm is a poor strategy.

I looked at every first round from 1985 through 2012, which
is the most recent first round to see any high school players accu-
mulate at least 10 WAR in the majors, and compared high school
pitchers' production to those in other categories. For example,
how frequently did players taken in the first round reach the 10
total career WAR threshold?

| 1985–2012 | Over 10 WAR | Total players taken | % |
|---|---|---|---|
| HS pitchers | 26 | 159 | 16.4% |
| College[2] pitchers | 59 | 240 | 24.6% |
| HS hitters | 57 | 219 | 26.0% |
| College hitters | 64 | 179 | 35.8% |

Pitchers have more ways to fall short of expectations or to bust completely than hitters do, thanks to higher injury rates, so it's unsurprising that both categories of pitchers fare worse than even the less successful category of hitters . . . but first-round high school pitchers are so much less likely to pan out that it's hard to believe they're still chosen there as often as they are.

What if we look just at the uppermost echelon, the top ten overall picks in the draft, where one would assume only the absolute best high school arms are taken, those who should have a lower failure rate while still carrying the same potential upside?

| 1985–2012 | Over 10 WAR | Total | % |
|---|---|---|---|
| HS pitchers | 10 | 47 | 21.3% |
| College pitchers | 29 | 92 | 31.5% |
| HS batters | 28 | 72 | 38.9% |
| College batters | 32 | 64 | 50.0% |

If you pick in the top ten and you choose a high school pitcher, you're the guy at the craps table betting on eight the hard way because it sounds cool to say it. You might hit big on your bet, but you're accepting a much higher risk that you get little to no return than you would by taking any other category of player.

As you might expect, some of the hits in that group of ten high school pitchers taken in the top ten picks of their drafts are enormous. Two are probably going to the Hall of Fame: Clayton Kershaw and Zack Greinke, inarguably great picks for their respective clubs (the Los Angeles Dodgers and the Kansas City Royals) where they were selected. Two others, Josh Beckett and Madison Bumgarner, racked up more than 30 career WAR each, and were both major contributors to World Series titles won by the teams that drafted them, with Beckett earning a second championship ring after a trade to Boston.

A fifth, Kerry Wood, is one of the great might-have-been stories in recent baseball history; as a rookie, he recorded what was at the time just the second 20-strikeout game in MLB history, then won the NL Rookie of the Year award. He blew out his elbow and missed all of 1999, but returned to post three seasons as an above-average starter, culminating in a 2003 season where he led the NL in strikeouts and was part of a Cubs team that came within five outs of reaching the World Series. Unfortunately, a long history of overuse that dated back to high school—he started both ends of a doubleheader just days after he was drafted—and ran through 2003, where manager Dusty Baker had him throw 120 or more pitches six times in seven starts to end the season, ended Wood's career as an effective starter after age twenty-seven. He's both a successful pick, taken 4th overall in 1995 and producing 27.5 career WAR within nine years of his draft, and a cautionary tale of the risks of taking high school pitchers (or any pitchers, really) with high picks.

The other 37 high school pitchers[3] taken in the top ten picks who didn't reach 10 career WAR, however, include a lot of names you've probably never heard before, or perhaps heard once on draft day and never heard again: Matt Hobgood, Chris Gruler, Clint Everts, Colt Griffin, Mike Stodolka, Matt Wheatland, Mark Phillips, Joe Torres, Josh Girdley, Bobby Bradley, and Kirk Presley combined for exactly zero major-league appearances.

Taking high school pitchers against these odds amounts to a bit of magical thinking: Yes, the failure rate for high school arms taken high in the draft is high, and the opportunity cost of those picks is also pretty high (you could have taken a position player who was more likely to return sufficient value for the pick), but we think this guy right here is the exception. This amounts, at least at some level, to saying that you believe that your group of evaluators, from the general manager to the scouting director on down, can figure out which players will be the exceptions to the base rate. That's quite possible—perhaps some teams or individuals have proprietary tools or ideas that allow them to sift through high school pitchers and find prospects with higher probability of success. Yet in the sample I examined, covering 28 first rounds, three teams drafted three high school pitchers each who met the 10 WAR threshold, and no team drafted four. Of those teams, only the Toronto Blue Jays, who took Steve Karsay in 1990, Chris Carpenter in 1993, and Roy Halladay in 1995, never whiffed on such an evaluation: They took five high school pitchers in the sample, those three plus two who didn't sign. If there's a way to distinguish these high school pitchers from one another, no team has found the secret.

I asked multiple front-office executives why they continued to take high school pitchers with first-round picks, or why they thought other teams did so. One simply called them "stubborn" but asked me "don't convince them otherwise." Another executive who has taken high school pitchers in the first round in the past said, "I think people still think they'll draft the exception. The logic has always been if you don't take HS arms then that means that you'll pass on guys like Kershaw, Bumgarner, etc. I've definitely learned my lesson."

The Major League Baseball draft is a somewhat controlled environment for teams to act on their predictions: they evaluate eligible players, today doing so with traditional scouts and with analytical methods, and predict their long-term potential as professional players, often considering both their potential returns and the likelihood of them achieving it. This remains the paradigm in baseball, and other sports, and the business world in general, despite mounting evidence that humans are really bad at making predictions—especially when there's no accountability, which is often the case for people who make predictions on television, radio, or now podcasts. (Speaking as a writer who makes predictions, I do face some accountability—it's easy for anyone to find my written predictions, and I acknowledge errant player predictions in a column every September—but am not at direct risk of losing my job if I have a bad prediction year, because my employer isn't investing money in my predictions. They sell my predictions, so to speak, for profit.)

Philip Tetlock, a political science and political psychology professor at the University of Pennsylvania, has written multiple books on predictions and forecasting, talking about how we're not very good at this as a species, although there are things we can do to make better predictions in the future. Writing in *Expert Political Judgment: How Good Is It? How Can We Know?* of a long-term experiment that asked experts to make more than 30,000 predictions on world events, he said that political experts "thought they knew more about the future than they did" and that, in the aggregate, the "experts edged out [a] dart-tossing chimp but their margins of victory were narrowed, and they failed to beat . . . experts making predictions outside their specialty."[4] (This has often been miscast in the media as a claim that experts were no better than a dart-tossing monkey, which is inaccurate.) Tetlock also found that automated forecasts that predicted the future would be just like the past, only more so, beat the experts' predictions. If you want to know what a player will do next year, look at what he did last year and the year before.

Tetlock's next book, *Superforecasting*, looked at the problem of predictions and forecasting from the other angle, asking why there are indeed some people who make consistently better predictions to determine what they do that the rest of us don't. In *Superforecasting*, he proposes a thought experiment by asking the reader to estimate the probability that a certain family, the Renzettis, might own a pet. A bad prediction would start with questions about the family themselves and work backward from there. A good prediction would start with what Tetlock calls the "outside view"—in this case, what percent of all families own pets? Or, what percent of families who live in the same type of house or apartment as the Renzettis own pets?

Starting with that outside view, which economists would call the "base rate," makes predictions better even if you don't refine it with new information. It also serves as an anchor for future estimates: once someone puts a number in front of you, even if the number has absolutely nothing to do with the question at hand, your answer will be skewed by that number. This is the anchoring effect I described in chapter 1, but used to our benefit, as we are starting with a number that is meaningful and should have more predictive value, which thus "anchors" future estimations.

Kahneman and Tversky discussed the base-rate fallacy[5] several times during their writing partnership, and are probably the ones most directly responsible for popularizing the term. In their 1973 paper "On the Psychology of Prediction,"[6] they write that "one is allowed to ignore the base rate only when one expects to be infallible." If you are omnipotent, then, yes, you can neglect the base rate. In God we trust; all others must have data.

Across multiple surveys, the two authors found that respondents would utilize the given base rate for a question if they had no additional information, but would default to making estimates based on the specifics of the inside view if they had it. In baseball terms, this happens all the time: Such-and-such eighteen-year-old right-hander has a mature body, a good delivery, throws his fastball up to 98 mph, and shows a major-league-caliber slider already, so we will rank him along with the other players in the draft rather than discounting him for being a high school pitcher. The probability of this pitcher becoming a viable major leaguer is lower than it is for college players, or for high school position players, so any projection of his future value should start there, with the outside view. It would make more sense, for example, to rank all of the high school pitchers against each other first, then discount the entire group before merging that list with the lists of players from other categories.

In no way does the base-rate fallacy tell us to avoid exceptions completely; it merely counsels us to avoid the sort of magical thinking that goes along with neglecting the base rate or outside view. When you ground yourself in the facts of the base rate for whatever category applies—baseball prospects, American households, world events—you improve the accuracy of your predictions from the outset, and set an anchor for any adjustments you'll make to try to be even more accurate. That means we will occasionally see major-league teams that adhere to this kind of rational thinking still reach for the exception, such as drafting high school pitchers in the first round.

The Astros are one of the most analytics-driven teams in MLB right now, and their former GM, Jeffrey Luhnow, and his former lieutenant (now Baltimore Orioles assistant GM), Sig Mejdal, were both devotees of Daniel Kahneman's book *Thinking, Fast and Slow*. Mejdal himself has a master's in cognitive psychology. But they did choose to take a high school pitcher in the first round twice during their joint tenure with the Astros, with Mike Elias as the scouting director for those drafts. One of those was Forrest Whitley, a tall right-hander from San Antonio, Texas, who was the top pitching prospect in baseball a year and a half after he was drafted. The Astros saw what they felt was a rational reason why he would be an exception to the base rate for high school pitchers: even as a teenager, Whitley had an unusually high spin rate on his four-seam fastball.[7] As of this writing, Whitley hasn't reached the majors yet, and has been slowed by a shoulder injury, so we don't know if the Astros were correct to go against the base rate for this decision, but their process here was sound: they started with the base rate, so they were disinclined to take a high school pitcher, and then established reasons why Whitley was dissimilar enough from the class that they might consider him anyway. (The other high school pitcher they took in the first round under Mike Elias, Brady Aiken, failed his post-draft physical due to an inborn malformation in his elbow, and probably isn't a useful example in any direction.)

Magical thinking is everywhere in baseball; teams see what they want to see, when they want to see it, especially when the pressure to win now is present. It comes up in the majors as well, from managers saying a player is "due" to teams thinking they're just a player away from contention. Teams giving long-term deals to free-agent relievers is a longtime bugbear for me, as I think most executives understand on a rational level that reliever performance and health is among the most difficult things to forecast in baseball, but they still hand out three- and four-year deals to relievers because that's what the market asks.

The Colorado Rockies, for example, have given three-year deals to four separate relievers over the last three off-seasons, guaranteeing them a total of $125 million. As of this writing, the first contract, given to left-handed reliever Mike Dunn, is halfway through its final year; the other three contracts, for Wade Davis,

Jake McGee, and Bryan Shaw, are all at their midpoints. The Rockies have received a total of 0.7 Wins Above Replacement from the quartet, with about $70 million spent to this point, and all of the positive value has come from Davis (1.2 WAR). That is, the Rockies would have been better served grabbing three decent triple-A pitchers off the baseball scrap heap and paying them the major-league minimum than paying Dunn, McGee, and Shaw to pitch no better than these so-called replacement-level pitchers would have. Even Davis has performed below expectations, and below what a team should expect for that kind of salary. In 2018, the Rockies spent more than $41 million on these four relievers and got close to no return on them . . . and in 2019, they did it over again, with about the same results.

The track record of relievers given long-term deals is pretty dismal, even with some slight improvement in the most recent batch. There have been seventeen four- or five-year deals handed out to relievers this century, and only one of those deals, an extension Mariano Rivera signed with the New York Yankees before the 2001 season, was an unqualified success: Rivera was good and healthy for all four years of his deal, missing a little time in 2002 to minor injuries, and racked up 12.4 Wins Above Replacement, which is still the highest for any reliever on a four-year or five-year contract. Several deals were modestly successful, and at least seven were outright disasters, including the still-current four-year deal Brett Cecil signed with the Cardinals, during which he's been worse than replacement level.

I looked at all relievers from 1990 through 2018 to see just how bad the idea of giving a reliever a long-term deal was, based on how likely it was for a reliever who'd been good in a particular season (usually the one before someone chooses to give him a big pile of money) to do so again the next year. Measuring a reliever's performance is a little tricky because their stats don't always do a great job of reflecting their value—they may allow runners to score that are charged to preceding pitchers, or leave the game with runners on base only to have subsequent relievers let those runners score, and the small samples inherent in relief seasons mean one or two bad outings can really mess with a season line. One possible definition of a "good" relief season I used set a minimum of 50 innings pitched—60+ is typical for a full year, but I wanted to set the bar a little lower to account for minor injuries— and a FIP (Fielding Independent Pitching)[8] of 3.00 or lower.

In the sample, I found 627 individual relief seasons that matched those two criteria by 340 different pitchers. Only 28 pitchers managed to produce four such seasons at all, consecutively or not, and only 14 pitchers did it in four consecutive years. Of course, some of those years would come before any decision on whether to offer the pitcher a long-term deal, and there's always the risk with any professional athlete that his best years may be behind him when you give him a lucrative new deal. Mark Melancon had 50+ innings and a sub-3 FIP every year from 2013–16, after which the Giants gave him a four-year contract, only to see his streak end immediately.

In fact, a pitcher who met these two criteria was less than 50 percent likely to do so again in the subsequent season. Out of those 627 pitcher-seasons that met the criteria, only 181 were followed up with a second qualifying season the following year. The majority of relievers who had such a season either never had another one or had at least one "off" year between them. A quarter of these relievers posted ERAs over 4 in the season following their sub-3 FIP—this, even though FIP is a better predictor of future ERA than ERA itself is—and 7 percent of them posted an ERA over 6 the next year.

I did a similar, simpler study when I still worked for the Blue Jays, when the team was considering signing closer B. J. Ryan, coming off three straight qualifying seasons (his FIP was under 2.60 in all three years; after throwing 50 innings in 2004, he threw 70+ the next two years). At the time, I found that full-time relievers who had above-average seasons handling a full work-load, set at 60 innings, were about 50/50 to repeat it the following year, and that multiple years of above-average performance didn't improve the odds in a significant way.

This seems to still be true; of the 627 seasons in my sample, only 305, or just under half, were followed by a season with 50+ innings and an ERA under 3. The odds were worse with FIP, and even worse with Wins Above Replacement (WAR). You can move the thresholds around and change the probabilities somewhat, but the odds stayed at or under 50 percent. Even if we just look at relievers who met some standard for "good" for two consecutive years, the probability of them repeating it for a third year remains a little under 50 percent. This held true using ERA thresholds of 3, 3.50, and 4; the odds approach 50 percent as you raise the bar but don't pass it until roughly an ERA of 4.10 (using that level for all three years).

(The median ERA for the following year was 3.01, which would be a great outcome for the signing team . . . but one standard deviation was 2.12.)

The base-rate fallacy might be the most persistent cognitive bias in sportsball, because so many decisions either happen in real time (managers or coaches choosing what players to use or what plays to run) or involve competitive decisions where you might look for reasons to do something (for example, why you should sign that closer you already wanted to sign). Ignoring the base rate is a recipe for making decisions that aren't just bad, but are bad in an expensive way, especially if you're in any environment where some of your competitors are paying attention to the base rate. If most of the teams bidding on a free agent use projection systems to put a value on the player's future performance, and you as a general manager don't use one, the value you put on the player's output will be highly skewed by other, less predictive factors, like what the player did most recently, or what he did against your club in games you happened to see personally. The pitcher who threw a shutout against your club in September will seem especially enticing; the shortstop who failed to make two routine plays in another game you saw will seem overrated. A manager might play the hitter who "sees this pitcher well" or "hits good pitching"—which, by the way, nobody hits good pitching, otherwise it's not good pitching—because he ignores the hitter's overall production in favor of thinly sliced samples or scattered memories. Base-rate neglect is pervasive in baseball and just about everywhere else we have to make decisions, and the solution—finding and using the appropriate data or information for the base rate—is right there in front of us.

# 6

## History Is Written by the Survivors

### Pitch Count Bingo and Why "Nolan Ryan" Isn't a Counterargument

Making robberies into larcenies. Making rapes disappear. You juke the
stats, and majors become colonels. I've been here before.
—Ronald "Prezbo" Pryzbylewski, *The Wire*, episode "Know Your Place"

In the chapter on base-rate neglect, I talked about major-league
teams' continued insistence on taking too many high school
pitchers in the first round of the draft despite clear and compelling evidence that this is a bad idea: the failure rate of that demo-
graphic group is higher than any comparable category, and the
team also faces the opportunity cost of that pick—the value they
could have gotten by taking a high school hitter or a college player.

Of course, there have been exceptions to the base rate—high school pitchers taken high who turn out to be good choices because they turn into successful major leaguers or become valuable pieces for trades—but their existence is built into the base rate itself: the argument is not so much that teams should never take high school pitchers, but that, on the whole, teams do it more often than the hit rate (pun intended) of high school pitchers can justify. If you're a scouting director for a major-league baseball team, or perhaps a general manager, then you should be less inclined to take a high school pitcher in the first round . . . but open to the possibility. That could mean requiring more information or beginning the process with a more skeptical attitude toward taking such a player.

The power behind the continued desire to take high school pitchers high in the draft comes from the big names who became exceptions to the "rule." Clayton Kershaw's name is usually the first one mentioned by anyone arguing in favor of taking high school pitchers, for good reason. The 7th overall pick in the 2006 draft class, Kershaw made his major-league debut less than two years after he was drafted, and was a league-average starter for the rest of 2008 at the age of twenty. Since then, he's won three Cy Young Awards and finished second two other times, been the most valuable pitcher in the National League in four seasons, and accumulated about 68 career WAR[1] through late August 2019. He's been the best player from the 2006 draft class, a few wins ahead of Max Scherzer, whom the Diamondbacks took 11th overall out of the University of Missouri.

Kershaw is the most commonly cited example of a high school pitcher taken in the first round who worked out, at least in my experience, but not the only one. Madison Bumgarner is another popular name for advocates of this drafting approach; while his career total of 36 WAR isn't at Kershaw's level, he performed extremely well for the San Francisco Giants, who took him 10th overall in 2007, in three separate World Series, all of which the Giants won. Tampa Bay took Blake Snell 52nd overall, with a compensatory pick between the first and second rounds, in 2011; he won the American League Cy Young Award in 2018 while posting the sixth-lowest ERA by any starter in the 2010s, at 1.89. Of the 15 pitchers who have racked up at least 30 career WAR in the 2010s so far, six were drafted out of high school, with all six in the first two rounds. (And two of the seven college pitchers came from the same school—not a powerhouse like Vanderbilt or LSU or UCLA, not even a school from the SEC or ACC or Pac 12, but Stetson, a mid-major university in Deland, Florida.)

But you know who you probably didn't remember? Kasey Kiker, the second high school pitcher drafted in 2006, five picks after Kershaw. Kiker never saw the majors, and neither did Colton Willems (22nd overall), while Kyle Drabek reached the majors but finished his career right at replacement level. Bumgarner was drafted one pick ahead of Philippe Aumont, twelve picks ahead of Tim Alderson, and fourteen picks ahead of Michael Main, all high school pitchers who never saw the majors, with two more reaching the majors for very short careers that saw them finish with less than two career Wins Above Replacement.

A number of different biases come into play when it comes to the ongoing affinity for taking high school pitchers with high picks in the draft, including base-rate neglect and the related availability bias, but it's also an example of a logical error known as survivorship bias.[2] In any sample where members tend to drop out over time, we tend to remember the survivors and forget everyone else. This shows up in population studies that don't account for people in the original group who die, or disappear, or for any other reason vanish from the studies, skewing the results toward the people who did "survive," literally or figuratively, to be counted at the end of the research. Our memories work the same way: we remember the people who survived, not those who never made it. In other words, taking a high school pitcher in the first round seems like a less risky proposition if you can only remember Clayton Kershaw and you forget all the other ones who didn't work out.

In that 2006 draft that gave us Clayton Kershaw, the first round, including compensation picks, saw seven other high school pitchers selected, six of whom either never reached the majors or did so but were just "replacement level," meaning their production was no better than that of the typical triple-A (minor league) pitcher available to teams for free. We can name Kershaw, and I would guess some serious fans would identify the other high school pitcher in that first round who has had a successful career, Jeremy Jeffress, if they followed the draft at all. Most fans have probably never heard of the high school pitchers in that draft who never reached the majors: Kasey Kiker, Steve Evarts, Colton Willems, and Caleb Clay. Because they never spent even a day in the major leagues, they're forgotten, when they should serve as cautionary tales—in this draft, the high school pitching crop in the first round included one superstar, one good reliever, and six guys who produced no real value for any team, including four who didn't make it out of the minors at all. Their names no longer ring any bells for us, or even for many people in the industry: unless you were involved in drafting Kiker or Willems, they're just names on someone else's draft list.

Survivorship bias is a specific form of the subject of chapter 2, availability bias. The latter is when we overemphasize the examples we can remember, those that are more readily available in our memories, because they're more recent or more memorable for some irrelevant reason. The former involves overemphasizing the examples we can remember because other examples didn't "survive" to the end of the time period or the study. History is written by the survivors because the dead have very little to say.

In his 2005 book, *How Not to Be Wrong: The Power of Mathematical Thinking,* Jordan Ellenberg describes survivorship bias in terms of mutual fund performance metrics. He cites a report from Morningstar, a financial services company that provides research and recommendations on mutual funds, that showed that mutual funds in its "Large Blend" category earned an average annual return of 10.8 percent per year during the decade from 1995 through 2004—a solid rate of return that exceeds the S&P 500's annual rate of return for the same time period. The problem, Ellenberg notes, is that the 10.8 percent is itself the result of an approach that only includes the survivors:

> Think again about how Morningstar generates its number [the 10.8 percent rate]. It's 2004, you take all the funds classified as Large Blend, and you see how much they grew over the last ten years. But something's missing: *the funds that aren't there.* Mutual funds don't live forever; some flourish, some die.[3]

Including the mutual funds that went out of business during that decade drops the rate of return over the ten-year period to 8.9 percent, which is well below the S&P's annual return from 1995 to 2004 of 10.4 percent. Everybody lives if you don't count dead people.

Whether a deliberate omission or an innocent oversight, ignoring the nonsurvivors in any sample skews your results toward the survivors and thus gives you larger results—usually on the positive side, since the survivors in the sample likely did something well enough to make it to the time of measurement.

Baseball writers, myself included, often point to a player as the worst qualifying hitter or pitcher in some statistical category in a given season, where "qualifying" means they garnered enough playing time (usually 503 plate appearances or 162 innings) to show up in the rankings. That ignores all the players who were worse, enough so that they lost playing time or even were demoted to the minors. Thus discussions of the worst qualifying player always need to bring the caveat that there were worse players who lost their jobs, so to speak, and that the worst *qualifying* player isn't actually the worst overall player.

Gary Smith said much the same thing in a different milieu in his 2014 book, *Standard Deviations,* in which he argues that "many observational studies are tainted by survivor bias," saying that "this problem plagues the entire genre of books on formulas/ secrets/recipes for a successful business, a lasting marriage, living to be one hundred, and so on and so forth, that are based on backward-looking studies of successful businesses, marriages, and lives."[4]

Smith gleefully undercuts the sort of business book that looks at successful companies and tries, post hoc, to determine what made them successful, often glamorizing the companies' leaders in the process. He cites Jim Collins's mammoth bestseller *Good to Great,* which looked at eleven companies whose stock prices outperformed the market as a whole over a forty-year period and tried to isolate what made them such outliers, highlighting, among other things, "Level 5 leaders" at their helms. Smith points out, however, that Collins juked the stats: he looked at the *end* of the forty-year period, plucked out eleven companies that did especially well—ignoring more than 1,400 other companies in the sample that did not fare as well, including declining stock prices or even bankruptcy—and decided after the fact which variables contributed to their successes.

Smith's proof is in the results that came after Collins's book. These eleven companies didn't continue to outperform the market, because Collins's hypotheses on why those companies were successful in the earlier period were not sufficiently tested on companies in the sample that had the same characteristics (like "Level 5 leaders," which I assume is like reaching Operating Thetan Level V) but did not see the same stock price appreciation. Five of the eleven companies outperformed the market in the subsequent sample; six did not, with one, Circuit City, going bankrupt, and another, Fannie Mae, nearly doing the same while losing 98 percent of its stock price value.

Survivor bias is everywhere in our media, including in advertising. Companies that advertise enormous customer satisfaction rates or rates of repeat business often do so by excluding or ignoring customers who didn't respond or weren't asked (for example, because they didn't return for another visit). Health surveys often exclude patients or members who died during the course of the study.

Poker players are familiar with the term "royal flush," the most valuable hand in the card game, where a player has the top five cards (ace, king, queen, jack, and 10) in a single suit. (It's a variety of a straight flush, which means any five consecutive cards in a single suit, that includes the five highest-valued cards.) The odds of getting one of the four royal flushes with your initial five-card hand in a traditional game of poker are 0.000154 percent, or 1 in 649,740. Most poker players would go a lifetime without ever seeing a natural royal flush.

The odds of getting a royal flush before the deal are minuscule, but if you've been so fortunate as to receive a royal flush, the odds have then condensed to 1. Once it has happened, it is no longer the unlikeliest of card draws; it has happened, and therefore the probability of it happening is 1. Predicting an outcome before the time period or triggering event might be useful; predicting the outcome after it's already known is akin to telling your readers that water is wet or Mike Trout is good. You should never pay for such post hoc predictions, but that is exactly the sin that Jim Collins committed in *Good to Great* and Tom Peters and Robert H. Waterman did in *In Search of Excellence:* they identified companies that had survived the wars, called them "great," and assumed that common factors among those companies explained the greatness. (Peters and Waterman's highlighted companies didn't fare any better than Collins's, but both books were massive bestsellers anyway.) They picked the companies that had drawn straights and flushes while ignoring the companies that drew less valuable hands of 8 high or maybe a pair of 3s, even though the two sets of firms may have had key variables in common that would have helped isolate what factors, including plain old luck, made certain companies go from good to great.

There are real consequences to the effects of survivorship bias, even in the world of scientific research itself. In a widely cited 2005 paper published in the peer-reviewed, open access journal *PLoS Medicine,* John P. A. Ioannidis argued right in the title that ". . . Most Published Research Findings Are False."[5] Nobody wanted to hear this, but Ioannidis's argument was both supported by evidence and well argued, pointing out how multiple biases, including survivorship bias, influence not just what results researchers find, but what papers get to publication in the first place.

University of Pennsylvania professor Uri Simonsohn has popularized the term "*P*-hacking" to describe a phenomenon in the academic world where professors are largely judged on their ability to produce and publish research. P-hacking is the research equivalent of throwing shit against the wall and publishing what sticks; in Simonsohn's own words, it entails "trying multiple things until you get the desired result."[6] Given large data sets, researchers can tweak their inputs to try to drop a single (yet insufficient) measure of statistical significance called the $P$-value to the desired threshold, usually 0.05 or lower. They might drop a condition to lower their $P$-value, or sift through a lot of potential relationships between variables to see which relationships just happen to have low $P$-values, even if there's no plausible causation between the two. This one trick produces papers that might get published but often can't be replicated by other researchers because the results are spurious or show false positives.

$P$-hacking blew up into a massive scandal that hit the mainstream news in 2018, when independent researchers exposed widespread data manipulation by Cornell professor Brian Wansink, who directed the school's Food and Brand Lab and had previously headed the U.S. Department of Agriculture's Center for Nutrition Policy and Promotion from 2007–2009. Wansink was a favorite of mainstream media outlets for his eye-catching conclusions, including claims that telling people to think of exercise as "fun" made them less likely to eat an unhealthful snack afterward, that pricing at all-you-can-eat buffets affects how full and how guilty diners feel after eating, and that veterans who'd experienced combat trauma were less brand-loyal and less sensitive to advertising. (The latter two studies have since been retracted.)

*BuzzFeed* investigative reporter Stephanie M. Lee documented many of Wansink's misdeeds, with the help of numerous emails he exchanged with members of his lab, in a piece published in February 2018.[7] In it, she quotes Wansink specifically telling a researcher to "tweek" (*sic*) variables to get a specific paper's $P$-value below 0.05, and cites multiple instances of Wansink telling students in his lab to sift through large data sets to find any possible correlations. Real science starts with a hypothesis and looks for data to support or disprove it. Wansink started with the data, looked for connections, and then cooked up hypotheses after the fact so he could publish them and garner mainstream attention.

This is survivorship bias in a white lab coat. Most of these correlations couldn't hold up when other researchers tried to replicate them, because the initial correlations were based on faulty samples, involved changing variables to get better $P$-values, or were just out-and-out flukes. It worked for some time; Wansink appeared on *60 Minutes* and *CBS This Morning*, spoke in multiple documentaries on healthful eating, and was cited in more than two dozen articles in the *New York Times* before his fall from grace, such as a 2012 post that was entirely dedicated to one of his research papers on how to get kids to make better snack choices.[8] Wansink figured out how to publish more papers from existing data, and how to market those papers and himself to improve media coverage. If you put any large data set through a sieve, something will fall through, even if there's no meaning to the correlations you think you've found. Mainstream writers— often from good, reputable publications—who covered Wansink's findings failed to ask key questions about his methods, and weren't sufficiently skeptical of how often he found interesting results. Stephanie Lee's piece tipped the scales against him, however; in late 2018, Cornell announced their internal investigations had found multiple instances of academic misconduct, at which point Wansink "resigned," effective June 30, 2019. As of this writing, more than thirty papers he authored or coauthored have been retracted.

Getting back to the baseball world, survivorship bias is easiest to spot whenever there's a discussion of the pervasive mention and use of pitch counts—simply counting the number of pitches a pitcher has thrown in a game. Higher pitch counts are associated with greater risk of arm injuries, although the exact nature of that relationship is still not clear. If you say "pitch counts" three times in front of a computer, however, a Grumpy Old Man will appear to tell you how "back in my day" pitchers threw 200 pitches a game and never got hurt. Never was survivorship bias so clear.

The link between overuse of pitchers and injuries is well established, with several peer-reviewed papers on the subject; one notable one, published way back in the Dark Ages of 2002, noted that in a study of 476 youth pitchers, "there was a significant association between the number of pitches thrown in a game and during the season and the rate of elbow pain and shoulder pain."[9] Major League Baseball teams have caught on to this, and since they have very strong incentives to keep their young pitchers healthy, all teams limit pitchers' workloads in single games and over the course of full seasons. Limits vary by organization and pitcher, but one common if arbitrary threshold is 100 pitches—if a team is trying to protect a young pitcher's elbow and shoulder, that pitcher will probably be limited to 100 or fewer pitches in every start. That's the upper boundary because, as far as I can tell, it's a nice round number that's on the conservative side of things, but if you think about it for a moment, you'll realize that particular limit is just a function of humans having ten fingers.

Professional organizations have, by and large, gotten away from high pitch counts for young pitchers, often referred to as overuse or abuse. Amateur coaches, however, have not, and the worst offenders in North America 2019 are college coaches.[10] Several high-profile college pitchers have broken down recently after overwork in college. Left-handed pitcher Anthony Kay from the University of Connecticut faced 36 batters in a complete game in March 2016, despite his team holding a 17-run lead. Two months later, he threw 101 pitches in his first start of UConn's conference tournament, then returned on shorter-than-normal rest to throw another 90 pitches. The Mets took him in the second round that June, but in his post-draft physical the team found a torn ulnar collateral ligament in his elbow, requiring the operation now known as Tommy John surgery. Kay lost about $800,000 of the signing bonus to which he'd originally agreed and didn't throw another pitch until April 2018.

Oregon State went a bit further in June 2018, using freshman Kevin Abel, just nineteen years old at the time, three times in a six-day span, asking him on June 23 to throw 95 pitches, 23 in a relief appearance on June 27, and then 129 pitches—in and of itself an excessive total before we consider that he did it with zero days of rest—on June 28 in the clinching game of the College World Series. Major League Baseball's PitchSmart guidelines, created in consultation with leading experts in sports medicine, recommends a maximum of 120 pitches in any single game for a nineteen-year-old, and that assumes the pitcher is working with regular rest. The Beavers won their championship, but Abel's elbow blew out early in the following season.

I often point out on social media cases where college or even high school coaches abuse their pitchers by asking them to throw too many pitches and/or throwing them with insufficient rest, and when that happens, we get to play Pitch Count Bingo. The center square on your bingo card is Nolan Ryan, whose name is certain to come up in any attempt to discuss the limits of the human body to throw a projectile at 95 mph repeatedly over a three-hour span. For just one example, an Oregon State fan responded to my criticism of Oregon State coach Pat Casey when he overworked Abel by sending this tweet:

Let's see you get the ball out of Nolan Ryan's hand after 100 pitches. He could go over 200 and he had what some would say was an ok pitching career! How the hell can someone so ignorant on pitch count write a book about baseball. Old adage those who can do those who can't teach

Nolan Ryan was a physical marvel, and an extreme outlier when it came to durability, although most discussions of the latter ignore the part where he missed 1967 and 1968 with persistent arm trouble. Ryan did things we will probably never see again, not now that pitchers throw harder than ever and play more than ever as kids, while teams work to keep their most gifted pitchers healthy until they reach the majors. Among Ryan's most incredible feats was a 13-inning outing on June 14, 1974, where he threw **235 pitches**,[11] facing 58 batters, walking 10 and striking out 19. His opponent, Luis Tiant, worked into the 15th, facing 56 batters, before he gave up the winning run. Baseball-Reference's Play Index database includes pitch count data back to 1988, and the highest single-game pitch count they show was 173 by Tim Wakefield, who, as a knuckleballer, expended far less effort on each pitch than traditional pitchers do.

Nolan Ryan is the ultimate survivor, the survivor *ne plus ultra,* the übersurvivor when it comes to survivorship bias. Yes, Ryan defied anything we know now about pitch limits, and shouldered (pun intended) workloads that no MLB team would ever allow a pitcher to carry in 2019, whether in individual games or entire seasons. As of September 2019, the last time any MLB pitcher pitched into the tenth inning was Cliff Lee on April 18, 2012, in a 102-pitch, 10-inning complete game. Nolan Ryan pitched into the tenth inning 17 times in his career, doing so for the final time in 1990 when he was forty-three years old. No pitcher has made 39 starts in a season since knuckleballer Charlie Hough did so in 1987; Ryan did it four times in five years in the 1970s.

He is, however, an outlier, a great exception—not one that "proves" the rule, but one that causes many people to discard the rule. Most pitchers can't handle the workloads that Ryan did; they would break down and suffer a major injury to their elbow or shoulder, or they would simply become less effective as a result of the heavy usage, and thus receive fewer opportunities to pitch going forward. Teams did try to give pitchers more work for decades, well into the early 2000s, but you don't know the names of those pitchers *because they didn't survive*: they broke down, or pitched worse, or some combination of the above.

Mets fans may want to skip ahead a few paragraphs, as their "Generation K" trio of pitching prospects was a shining example of how not to handle young pitchers—and, as it turns out, the specific examples that first alerted me, by way of my then-colleagues at Baseball Prospectus, to the possibility that teams were actively contributing to the ruination of their own prospects. The three prospects were Paul Wilson, Bill Pulsipher, and Jason Isringhausen, all of whom were allowed to throw far too much in the minors, and all of whom suffered injury-plagued careers, with only Isringhausen finding success thanks to a move to a relief pitching role.

Pulsipher's overuse was the most striking; in 1994, at age twenty, he threw 201 innings for the Mets' double-A affiliate in Binghamton, enough to lead the Eastern League by 23 innings, even though he was one of the league's youngest pitchers. He missed all of 1996 due to injury and spent the rest of his career bouncing around various organizations, throwing just 200 major-league innings after he returned with an ERA of 5.89.

Wilson's overuse started in college; in 1994, the year in which he was drafted first overall by the Mets, he threw 149 innings for Florida State under coach Mike Martin, then threw another 49 innings in the minor leagues after he signed, a total of 198 innings at age twenty-one. He threw 186 the next year, reached the majors in 1996, and then suffered tears to both the labrum in his throwing shoulder and the UCL in his left elbow, costing him most of the next three seasons. He returned to the majors in 2000 with Tampa Bay but finished his career with a 4.86 ERA in 941 innings, never coming close to the promise that had made him the first overall pick.

Isringhausen was also worked very hard by the Mets: 193 innings at age twenty-one, 221 innings at age twenty-two, 171 less effective innings at age twenty-three, after which the wheels started to come off. He missed most of 1997 and all of 1998 to injuries, including the first of what would eventually be three Tommy John surgeries. The Mets traded him to the Oakland A's, who converted him to a full-time reliever, after which Isringhausen had a ten-year run of success for Oakland and St. Louis, throwing 676 innings from the trade to the end of his career.

That's just a few examples from one organization from one period of time. Public research on minor-league pitch counts is limited, although work going back to Rany Jazayeri and Keith Woolner's calculations of "pitcher abuse points," assigning greater weight to pitches above 120 in a game, has demonstrated a consistent correlation between high pitch counts and future injuries/ decline in performance. New papers appear regularly on various hypotheses for the high rate of elbow ligament tears in youth pitchers; one presented at the American Orthopaedic Society for Sports Medicine in 2018 found that, for pitchers aged 7–11 years, "elbow pain was significantly associated with more than 200 pitches per week," as were counts of more than 50 pitches per day or more than 70 games per year.[12] Other studies show that fatigue leads to biomechanical changes, which can in turn increase the risks of injuries. We know this, because study after study shows it: throw too much and you increase your odds of getting hurt.

Yes, Nolan Ryan seemed to be able to pitch forever, in a game, in a season, in a career, until eventually it was Father Time that got him rather than excessive workloads. Bob Gibson didn't pitch quite as long, but threw over 3,800 innings in 16 seasons, crossing 300 innings twice, still pitching effectively at age thirty-seven and at least pitching a lot at age thirty-eight. Pitchers prior to integration pitched even more, and if you go back to the nineteenth century they often pitched every other day; a dapper gent and pitching deity known as Charles "Old Hoss" Radbourn started 73 games for the Providence Grays in 1884 and threw 678.2 innings, but survived to pitch another seven years beyond that. The game itself has changed dramatically in the last few decades, with pitchers throwing harder than ever, and hitters bigger and stronger than ever, but those outliers were even outliers in their own times—and they should not distract us from what we see from looking at all pitchers, not just the ones we can remember.

The good news is that avoiding survivorship bias is straightforward, at least compared to some of the other biases and illusions I cover in this book. Always check your data sources, or those behind the papers/articles you're reading, to ensure that they did not omit data from people, groups, or companies that did not survive to the end of the study, whether due to death, bankruptcy, or some other reason. Start with your hypothesis and then look at the data to see if the relationship holds true, rather than gathering data and shaking it aggressively to see what relationships might fall out.

And stop saying "Nolan Ryan" like it's some mic drop.

# 7

---

# Cold Water on
# Hot Streaks

## Recency Bias and the Danger of Using
## Just the Latest Data to Predict the Future

This may not be true anymore, but there was a time in the not-too-distant past where all a player needed to secure a lucrative five-year deal was a good season and a great catch.

Gary Matthews Jr. entered the 2006 season as a fairly well-established backup outfielder, not good enough to play regularly but a fine addition to any team in a reserve or bench role. He'd played in 728 major-league games to that point, appearing for six different teams across eight seasons, and his performance was unremarkable: a career .249/.327/.397 line, 59 career homers, 9.6 career Wins Above Replacement, a good chunk of which came from his superior ability on defense. He was thirty years old, and thus past the typical peak age for hitter performance, which historically has been around age twenty-seven, plus he was at least reaching a point where you'd expect him to slow down and lose some defensive skill as well.

Then came his age-thirty-one season, which was rather a surprise. Matthews hit .313/.371/.495 for the Texas Rangers, setting career highs in all three marks, with 19 homers, also a career best; 58 walks, also a career best; and 5.2 WAR, also—wait for it—a career best. He made more contact than he'd ever made before, with a career-low strikeout rate, and did a lot more when he did make contact. It was a career year so precise it could serve as the dictionary definition of the term.

And then there was . . . the Catch. The Rangers were playing the Houston Astros, with Matthews playing center field and Mike Lamb at the plate. Reliever Mark Corey threw a pitch he almost immediately wanted back; you could see his posture give out when Lamb crushed the ball to center field, as Corey clearly suspected Lamb had homered. So did the announcer, who said, "Looking for the single, instead he's got . . ." just as Matthews stood at the base of the wall and timed his jump perfectly. Matthews' feet appeared to be at least six feet off the ground when he caught the ball over the fence, and his shoulders were above the yellow line that marks the top of the fence and delineates the boundary between home runs and balls still in play. The announcer moved away from the mic, but you can hear him shout "Oh my God!" before he returns to say, "What a catch by Gary Matthews, Junior!" His colleague followed up with, "You may not see a better catch than that all year—maybe for a decade." It was an incredible play, one that very few players could make, and thirteen years later I'd still say it's among the five best outfield catches I've ever seen.

Matthews was very fortunate to hit free agency after that season; even if teams were concerned about his age, his most recent performance was the best he'd ever posted, and nobody was going to forget that catch—which, in that case, seemed merely to support defensive metrics that also agreed he was a good center fielder—anytime soon. He had two offers for five years and $50 million, choosing to sign with the Angels over the Giants so he could be closer to his son, who lived in the greater Los Angeles area.

When the Angels signed him, then-GM Bill Stoneman said that "[g]uys learn at different times in their careers. . . . Gary's coming into his own. In addition to his outstanding play in center field, he has the versatility to lead off or hit deeper in the lineup." (This last bit was especially strange, as Matthews's 2006 season was the only year he played full-time and posted an on-base percentage that was even league-average.)

The deal went sour before Matthews played a single game in an Angels uniform when law enforcement officials raided a Florida pharmacy that was suspected of distributing steroids and human growth hormone. Matthews's name was leaked to the press as one of the pharmacy's customers.[1] Stoneman declined to "speculate or comment on" whether Matthews's outlier 2006 season may have been aided by the use of banned substances. The leaked information alleged that Matthews had received human growth hormone (HGH) from the pharmacy in 2004, but Matthews denied ever taking it at any time, and said publicly that no law enforcement agency had accused him of or was investigating him for doing so.

A year later, Stoneman stepped down as Angels GM, and whatever pixie dust the baseball gods had sprinkled on Matthews had long washed away. He hit .252/.323/.419 in his first year with the Angels—very close to his career line prior to the 2006 outlier, .249/.327/.397—and experienced a noticeable decline in his defensive prowess. He was even worse in 2008, lost his starting job during 2009, and was eventually traded to the Mets along with enough cash to cover all but $2 million of the salary remaining on the last two years of his deal. He played in 65 games for the Mets, who released him five months after the trade, ending his major-league career.

This disaster was easy to foresee if you weren't the Angels (or the Giants). I wrote a short reaction to the deal the day it was signed, November 22, 2006, saying:

If the Angels believe that Gary Matthews, Jr., is the .313/.371/.495 hitter he was in 2006, I could almost understand their willingness to hand him a five-year deal. If they believe that, however, they are wrong. Before he put up those gaudy numbers in 2006, Matthews was a career .249/.324/.397 hitter in over 2,400 major-league plate appearances. At age 31, he had a fluke season where his core indicators (particularly his walk rate and isolated power) were right in line with where they were in 2005, but his batting average spiked to .313, the first time in his career he has ever hit over .275. The problem for the Angels is that they've committed to him in time and money as if he is legitimately a .313 hitter, against overwhelming evidence that he's not. When you also consider that they've signed him for his age 32–36 seasons, and that even today he only has fringe-average range in centerfield, this contract is likely to turn south for the Angels sooner rather than later. This looks like the Willie Blair contract of this offseason.

This brings us to Willie Blair, another journeyman player who parlayed a good "walk year"—baseball jargon for a player's last year entering free agency, a tacit acknowledgment that teams tend to overvalue performance in that final season—into a lucrative free-agent deal. Blair pitched for five teams in seven years from 1990 to 1996, posting a 4.73 ERA over that span (a 90 ERA+, meaning he was about 10 percent worse than league average over that span, adjusting for the parks in which he pitched), never getting his season ERA below 4, and ending that period with a career won/lost record of 25–41—significant in a time when most teams still compensated pitchers as if won/lost record were a real indicator of performance or underlying talent. (It's not.)

The Padres traded Blair to Detroit in December 1996, and Blair responded with his best season, although some of it was obviously a mirage. Blair's ERA was 4.17, and his ERA+ was 110, marking him at roughly 10 percent above league average, although his inability to strike many hitters out was a potential red flag going forward. What stands out even today about his 1997 season is his won/lost record: Blair went 16–8, thanks not to his own performance but to the best run support any offense had ever given him in his career, going from about 3.3 runs per game started before 1997 to 5.2 runs scored for him per start in that walk year. Had modern analytics existed at all in the off-season between 1997 and 1998, Blair probably wouldn't have found great demand for his services, but the brand-new Arizona Diamondbacks—who have handed out many, many bad free-agent contracts in their relatively brief history—gave Blair a three-year, $10.5 million deal to pitch for them during their inaugural season of 1998.

It was a fiasco from the start. Blair started the second game in Diamondbacks history, giving up 5 runs on 12 hits in 7 innings, and was mostly terrible for the team, with a 5.34 ERA in 23 starts over four months before they dumped him and his contract on the Mets for Bernard Gilkey's bad contract and Nelson Figueroa. The Diamondbacks, having learned nothing from history, chose to repeat it a few years later, signing Russ Ortiz to a four-year deal after some similarly fluky performances in 2003–04, and released him a year and a half into that contract.

What all of these instances—and many, many more—have in

common is that the decision-makers were blinded by what had just happened. More recent occurrences tend to stand out in our memories and take on undue weight in our mental decision processes, a phenomenon known as *recency bias*. In the sports world, recency bias is almost automatic, because those of us who evaluate players as part of our jobs are quite used to seeing players change as they age, or grow, or learn new skills, so we can't simply hand-wave away a new level of performance as a fluke—yet neither can we accept an outlier season (or half season) as evidence of a new baseline level when handing out a new contract or choosing to make a trade. Understanding that the new thing might be the old thing in new clothes is one of the keys to making rational choices.

We often think our memories are infallible—I mean, mine is, but yours may not be—yet they're obviously not, not even when it comes to remembering similar types of information. Your memory will overemphasize information or events that you heard or that occurred more recently than the same stuff that happened before it, even if the separation in time is small. This phenomenon, known as recency effect or recency bias, is so stark that psychologists have demonstrated its existence even in cases where the information is given to test subjects one item after another.

One of these tests is called a "memory span experiment," in which recipients are given a series of items to remember, like numbers, and are asked to recall them all, in order, after hearing the list just once. The purpose of the test is to measure "serial recall," which is just what it sounds like: how well people remember items given to them in an ordered list, including their ability to recite them back in order. If you plot the accuracy of responses, you get a U-shaped curve: people remember the first item in the list most strongly, which is called the "primacy effect" (more on that later), and also are more likely to remember the last item on the list more than all of those in the middle,[2] which is called the "recency effect." In other words, you remember the first thing you heard about something and the last thing you heard. While this probably sounds obvious, it has the additional advantage of being true.

(Psychological research on working memory, and the associated processes that can impede our memory, affects lots of areas of our regular lives. One such effort, conducted in the 1960s by Bell Labs researcher Roger N. Shephard, later a professor at Stanford and National Medal of science winner, showed that consumers would remember phone numbers more easily if we switched the three-digit exchange and the four digits that follow—so 867–5309 would instead become 5309–867. Bell rejected the proposal as too cumbersome.)[3]

The recency effect becomes recency bias when it affects your decision-making: in recency bias, the most recent information you received has greater bearing on your judgment than other available information.[4] When you make a decision, you weigh the information you've received, consciously or subconsciously, to try to inform the decision. In an order bias, like primacy or recency biases, the order in which you received the information affects how much weight you put on the information. It's not about whether the information is better, or more relevant, but whether it was the first thing you'd heard on the topic, or the last thing you've heard, or somewhere in the middle. It isn't rational, but it is a natural function of our brains—it's easier to recall the first or last items we learned about a subject, so we tend to put more weight on those items when using them.

You're prone to this bias because you're human. There's no natural way around it, no untraining your brain to forget your recency bias. Since sports in general and baseball in particular now generate a lot of data to fuel decision-making, there's one solution from the sports world that may help us find a way around recency bias: letting the data determine how heavily to weigh newer information than older.

Every MLB team and many independent analysts and websites produce player projections—estimates of a player's future performance, based on his past performance and other variables (age, height, weight, injury history), going forward one year or perhaps several years. If you want to know how much to pay Garry Matthews Jr., and for how many years, you first need some kind of estimate of his production going forward—how good will he be, and for how long. In the case of a player like Matthews, who was already past age thirty and thus likely to decline over the course of a long-term deal, a projection would give you an estimate of when his salary might exceed the value of his output. (The actual answer, of course, was "the moment the ink dried," but the Angels didn't know that.)

Dan Szymborski has been publishing his ZiPS player projections for at least a decade now, most recently on the essential site Fangraphs.[5] His projections start with a baseline that incorporates the player's last four years of statistics, and then adjust from there for factors like age. For example, a hitter's strikeout rate, which has the strongest correlation to the previous year's rate of any statistic in the ZiPS hitter forecasts, is 53 percent a function of last year's strikeout rate, 22 percent of the rate from the year before that, and the remainder from the previous two years. Those weights, called coefficients, are the result of linear regression analyses that Dan ran over thousands of players to determine the optimal baseline rates for all players, which he could then adjust based on other work showing the effects of factors like age. (This also matters for players so young they don't have enough existing data, such as players who reach the majors now at age nineteen or twenty, and for players at the tail ends of their careers, when their strikeout rates might rise quickly because they are losing bat speed.)

Harry Pavlidis, director of R&D for Baseball Prospectus, oversees that site's PECOTA projection system, originally developed by Nate Silver (now of FiveThirtyEight.com) and upgraded regularly by Pavlidis and his team. Harry gave a similar response to Dan's when asked how they decide the weights for statistical measures from previous years: "We do indeed derive the weights by 'regression,' for each specific item we project. So, the weights themselves vary by item but, as you described, they do put more emphasis on recent years. I think the method we have now is one I put in place a few years ago, or at least based on it. Since putting that in place, we do tend to put more emphasis on recent seasons than prior versions of PECOTA did."

Ehsan Bokhari became the director of research and development for the Houston Astros after the 2018 season, and prior to that spent several years in the R&D department for the Los Angeles Dodgers. Speaking in general terms about how he approaches building projection systems, he said, "The weights are typically determined empirically, meaning whatever weights provide the best fit within some constraints. What combinations of weights give us the best predictions, given that the weights typically need to be less than 1 and greater than 0, and they need to be decreasing as you go further back in time. It makes sense for the weight to be monotonously decreasing toward zero as you look further back in time. Weights are usually the same for all players." You'd expect the most recent year of performance to have the highest weight in a projection for the next year, but you also expect previous years to have nonzero weights attached, going down as you move farther backward from the present date.

Bokhari also pointed out some issues that analysts have to consider when building such forecasting models. "Some players make legitimate changes that warrant higher weights on more recent data and ignoring less recent data (J. D. Martinez is one example)." Martinez was below replacement level for Houston over three seasons, so the Astros released him in the spring of 2014. He retooled his swing, and has produced 25 WAR in seven seasons since that time. Such swing changes are becoming far more common; the Dodgers alone have turned Max Muncy and Chris Taylor from afterthoughts to everyday players by improving their launch angles, meaning the angle from the ground at which batted balls leave those hitters' bats, and turned Will Smith from a light-hitting catcher with a good glove into a legitimate 20-homer threat. Scouting reports and video work could help analysts decide in such cases whether to remove or deemphasize older data.

Bokhari continued, "Determining what is real and what is noise is extremely challenging but worth trying to solve. The second issue is that age should factor in how far you go back in time. The third is when environmental changes occur (e.g., the ball). This is especially important this season because of the implementation of the ML ball in AAA (not to mention whatever is happening to the ML ball itself). We want to update our projections to capture the current run environment but that environment is dramatically changing every year, or at least it has the last three or four years."

In other words, the way you decide how much weight to give more recent data—or any data, from any point—is through analysis, not instinct. Your brain will tell you to give the most weight to the first thing you heard (primacy bias) and the last thing you heard (recency bias), and probably too little weight to everything that came in between.

Primacy bias comes up in baseball as well, in slightly more subtle ways. All-Star Game voting, the process for which has changed six times since I started writing this paragraph, has always been a weird function of recency bias, because of the belief that it is simply a reward for first-half performance, rather than an attempt to get the game's stars into one exhibition (regardless of how they've played in the first two to three months of the season). In practice, however, the fan voting starts so early in the season—usually in early to mid-May—that the voting often just rewards players who had the best April.

Bryan LaHair was a twenty-nine-year-old minor-league veteran who came into the 2012 season with only 195 career at bats in the majors. He played in 45 games for the Mariners in 2008, then was outrighted off their 40-man roster after the 2009 season and signed with the Cubs as a minor-league free agent, spending two years in triple-A for the Cubs until resurfacing in the majors late in 2011. He started the 2012 season on the Cubs' major-league roster and had the greatest month of his life that April, hitting .390/.471/.780 with 5 home runs in just 20 games, including a comically high .600 BABIP[6] that should have tipped people off that LaHair's performance was a stone fluke. He hit two more homers in the first two games in May, and by May 15 had 10 homers . . . and then the pixie dust wore off. LaHair hit .220/.278/.341 until the All-Star break, .211/.274/.323 from May 16 to the end of the season, striking out in 35 percent of his plate appearances.

NL manager Tony La Russa, no friend to analytics or anything that doesn't reek of man sweat and tobacco spit, selected LaHair as a reserve for the NL All-Star team that season—even though by that point LaHair was no longer the Cubs' starting first baseman, having lost that job to Anthony Rizzo, with the Cubs using LaHair as a platoon right fielder starting in mid-June. LaHair did get into the All-Star Game, grounding out on the only pitch he saw. It proved the high point of his career; after homering in his final game in October 2012, LaHair never appeared in the majors again.

Outfielder Derek Bell managed to parlay one good, wildly out-of-character month into a two-year, $10 million contract with the Pirates in the winter of 2000–01, one factor in the Pirates' decision after the next season to part ways with General Manager Cam Bonifay. The Astros had traded Bell to the Mets after 1999 in a trade that paired his bad contract with star pitcher Mike Hampton—you can have our good player if you take this bad player and we can save more money—and then started off his Mets tenure with a bang, hitting .385/.449/.567 in April, light-years above anything he'd done previously in his career. Of course, it didn't last; he hit .238/.325/.391 for the remainder of the 2000 season, much closer to his 1999 performance (.236/.306/.350), and likely a better indicator that, going forward, he was no longer good enough to play regularly. Bonifay, whose tenure as Pirates' GM covered eight and a half seasons, none of which involved the team winning more games than it lost, gave Bell that two-year deal despite a preponderance of evidence that Bell wasn't going to produce enough to justify it, and Bell went directly into the tank, hitting .175/.287/.288 in 46 games around injuries. The next spring, new GM Dave Littlefield indicated that there would be a competition for the right field job, to which Bell responded by saying he'd begin "Operation Shutdown," choosing not to play rather than compete for the job he'd lost via poor performance. The Pirates released him a few weeks later, ending his major-league career.

One quirk of baseball stats is that a great performance to start a year can color views of your entire season in a different way that exactly the same performance later in the season won't do. Bell's April made its impression in two ways: he was atop leaderboards for much of the first half of the season, and even five months of mediocre performance only dragged his overall season line down to just a shade below average (a 98 OPS+, where 100 is average).

At the All-Star break, it still looked like Bell was having a good season (.318/.398/.498, a 126 OPS+ for the half), even though he'd stopped hitting anywhere near that level two months before then.

Recency bias also comes up in the day-to-day decisions a manager must make when setting the lineup or choosing which pitchers to use in a game. Managers in 2019 have started to get away from this kind of thinking, buoyed by support from analytics departments, but for most of the game's history, the belief that certain players were just "hot" or "cold" was conventional wisdom.

Writing in 2014 for the *Washington Post,* James Wagner had no trouble finding players and coaches just within the Nationals' clubhouse to tell him the hot hand was real. Their hitting coach at the time, Rick Schu, said, "Hot streaks are real. Totally. One hundred percent." (Hot streaks exist, but they are not meaningful or predictive.) Their right fielder at the time, Jayson Werth—who later blamed analytics for the end of his career—said, "That's a real thing. It's been talked about over and over." (That's the *argumentum ad populum,* or the appeal to popular opinion. Just because people believe something is true, that doesn't mean that it is true. This is one specific example of the illusory truth effect, covered in chapter 4, where something is repeated often because many people believe it, even though the evidence or data don't support it.)[7] Orioles outfielder Nelson Cruz, then in the midst of an atypical, late-career hitting surge that saw him remain a productive hitter for average and power into his mid-thirties, said, "It matters a lot mentally if you've been successful in your last at-bats. Your confidence definitely goes up and you're more likely to get a hit in your next at-bat."[8] You've probably heard announcers or writers or managers referring to "riding the hot hand" to defend certain decisions on when or how certain players were used.

Cardinals team president John Mozeliak told the Athletic in 2019 that manager Mike Shildt would "try to find the hot hand" when setting his lineup.[9] Mets infielder Todd Frazier, discussing his dwindling playing time that September, defended his manager's choice to use other players instead of him by saying "You've got to go with the hot hand."[10] Nationals manager Dave Martinez seems to invoke the hot hand frequently, from defending his use of a specific reliever in April 2019 to describing how he'd cope with an injury to closer Sean Doolittle that August. Managers may speak less about protection and clutch because they're aware that their front offices and many fans no longer believe in such things, but the hot hand myth seems alive and well.

The very idea of the hot hand seeped into the realm of academic research in a very widely cited 1985 study by Thomas Gilovich, Robert Vallone, and Amos Tversky[11] that argued that this was merely pattern-seeking within random data. Looking at basketball shots, they found that a "streak" of successful shots did not predict a greater likelihood of the shooter making his next shot, whether looking at field goal attempts or undefended free throws. If you'd like to get your paper mentioned in the mainstream media, claim you've disproved these authors' conclusions; journalists seem happy to give plenty of play to such studies, even if they don't hold up under scrutiny or change certain definitions from the original paper.

This conventional wisdom has persisted throughout baseball since well before I was born, but it's magical thinking—the idea that a hitter, independent of some physical change, can raise his game almost at will, or can acquire a new ability to "see the ball" better that can vanish as quickly as it came. It's a popular subject for academic studies; every year or so there's a new paper that claims the hot hand is real, but none of these has held up under subsequent scrutiny.

Russell Carleton, a clinical psychologist who wrote many insightful pieces for Baseball Prospectus before joining the New York Mets' front office after the 2018 season, wrote an essential debunking of the hot hand theory in 2010 for the BP site called "Going Streaking." In it, he found that a hitter's recent performance, whether we define "recent" as 10 plate appearances, 25, or 100, was no match for the hitter's overall performance for predicting the outcome of a subsequent plate appearance. The recent data was statistically significant in one category, on-base percentage, but the difference would only show up about once every ten thousand plate appearances—roughly the career total for Chili Davis or Buddy Bell. As Carleton wrote of the then-superstar for the Yankees, "It's OK to walk Alex Rodriguez when he's on a hot streak, but only because he's A-Rod, not because of the streak."[12]

The hot hand fallacy is the inverse of the gambler's fallacy, which says, in essence, that if a flipped coin has come up tails ten times in a row, then it is "due" to come up heads, even though the probability of the next flip being heads remains 50 percent. (Unless the coin is rigged, of course.) These fallacies are both false, which is why they're called fallacies in the first place, but it should also be apparent that it would be impossible for them to both be true: if you wish to believe one, you must choose your illusion.

In May 2016, John Oliver, the host of the Emmy-winning HBO series *Last Week Tonight,* discussed the media's breathless coverage of scientific studies as his main topic for one episode, criticizing the way news outlets handle studies and saying science "deserves better than to be twisted out of proportion and turned into morning show gossip."[13] He identified a series of reasons why the media does this to scientific studies, including news sites' bias toward novel or striking results, press releases by schools or institutions that exaggerate the results, and journalists further embellishing those results without explaining the studies' limitations or looking at possible flaws. It may be intrinsic to the nature of the business of news, but it's problematic and leaves readers worse off in the end. It's happened twice just around the topic of the hot hand in sports in the last five years.

A paper by professors at Stanford and the University of California, Berkeley claimed to show evidence that the "hot hand" existed in baseball, at least for hitters. The paper[14] was first posted online in 2014, then revised and published in 2017. It was presented at the Sloan conference for sports analytics, held every March on the campus of MIT. Their results received unquestioning coverage in the *Washington Post,* the *Boston Globe,* and the *New York Times,* even though the same afternoon that the paper was posted in 2014, a commenter on analyst Tom Tango's sabermetrics blog[15] pointed out that the authors had discarded crucial data before and after the evaluation samples they called the "streak at bats."[16] Throwing out data that would otherwise be useful is a huge red flag for any study. As Gary Smith wrote in *Standard Deviations:* "The best rule for readers is to be wary of studies that discard data. Ask yourself if anything is really clearly wrong with the omitted data. If not, be suspicious."[17] Journalists writing about studies should apply the same standard.

Similarly, a 2015 paper by Joshua Miller and Adam Sanjurjo[18] claimed to find evidence of the hot hand in basketball, a direct refutation of the seminal 1985 paper by Amos Tversky et al. that found no evidence of the hot hand in that sport. Miller and Sanjurjo used a bit of statistical sleight-of-hand to try to show that the hot hand was real, although it doesn't even hold up under a common-sense evaluation, let alone a more rigorous look. The authors of this new paper used in-sample prediction—essentially looking for a needle in a stack of needles—to argue that, once you started with a given, *finite* sample of basketball shots, there is "significant evidence of streak shooting, with large effect sizes."[19] Their argument says that the baseline expectation for players in the initial study was too high, and they use the principle of restricted choice, used in analysis of the card game bridge and useful in many other card and board games, to demonstrate it. The distilled claim is that, within any finite sample of N shots, there will be X successful shots and N-X misses. The odds of any shot being successful, chosen at random, should be X/N. If you look at streaks of successful shots within the sample, however, the odds of the next shot being successful are reduced because the successful shots in the streak are no longer available for the numerator; if the streak has three successful shots, therefore, the odds of the next shot being successful are not X/N, but (X-3)/N. That means the bar a player would have to clear to show evidence of a "hot hand" is lower than the one the authors of the original 1985 paper used. This is correct in the most technical of senses, but players do not enter games with a finite supply of successful shots for the night, and I would hope that last bit is obvious on its face without delving into the arcane statistical argument Sanjurjo and Miller used. Common sense should tell you that a baseball player doesn't start each season with a tank full of hits that he can parcel out over the course of the year, and once that's exhausted, he's out of hits—but that is essentially what this study's authors claimed.

Again, the media was ready to tout the new finding. Ben Cohen wrote about it twice in the *Wall Street Journal*;[20] it received coverage from the *New York Times*,[21] *New York* magazine's The Cut,[22] and my employer at the time, ESPN.com;[23] and Miller and Sanjurjo were even given space to describe their claims on *Scientific American*'s website.[24] Rebuttals or rejoinders were given nowhere near that level of coverage and received little or no mention in the articles about the paper; the *New York Times* article that extols the new paper gives the 1985 paper's author Tom Gilovich a mere two sentences and dismisses his concerns by saying he is "with-holding judgment."

So, no, the hot hand isn't really a thing, but my point here is a broader one: The very nature of modern journalism means surprising, unusual, or outright contradictory research findings get significant coverage, often without sufficient vetting, and subsequent retractions or debunkings get little to no air time to try to correct the earlier view. Journalists have an obligation to their readers and to the public to present information that is accurate and properly couched, and in these cases, several major media outlets ran with great headlines that they likely knew would get attention rather than considering the validity of the research papers they were touting. It's just sportsball, so there were no consequences to these lapses in judgment, but it's easy to see how similar bombshell headlines on health, nutrition, or the environment could have serious and long-lasting consequences for the public.

One example comes from the food world, as media outlets have been trumpeting the latest research on diets and foods deemed "unhealthful" since before I was born. One of the most famous magazine covers of my lifetime was *Time*'s March 26, 1984, edition, with the headline "Cholesterol: And now the bad news . . ." with two sunny eggs and a strip of bacon shaped to make a frowning face on a plate. As I write this today, the new enemy is sugar, and research after that *Time* story has shown little to no relationship between dietary cholesterol and either heart disease risk or overall longevity. Food journalist Tamar Haspel wrote in 2016 that the media's obsession with oversimplifying research on diets leads to articles that say, "'All you have to do is not eat that, and you'll be fine.' The fatal flaw in such advice is that it's much too easy to do that one thing and still eat badly."[25] Thirty-five years later, I still remember seeing that issue of *Time* in the magazine basket at my house, but the histrionic headline didn't hold up after further studies, and I'm still eating eggs with impunity.

In addition to the data showing that the hot hand isn't real for hitters, I've also offered an argument based simply on the logic that in baseball, there's someone trying to get the hitter out. If a hitter shows he can make quality contact against a fastball in a certain location, opposing pitchers will stop throwing that pitch in that spot. Coaches and pitchers are now armed with reams of data to help them choose what pitches to throw, to where, in what counts. And hitters don't get to face the same pitchers over and over while they're "hot"—the key variables will change; they'll regress to the mean.

Streaks are real, of course. Joe DiMaggio's 56-game hitting streak in 1941 has been the longest in major-league history for seventy-eight years as of this writing; the existence of the streak is not in question. We may even see the streak as evidence that DiMaggio is a great hitter, which he was even if we throw the streak out of his statistical record; from 1942 through the end of his career in 1951, with three seasons lost to military service during World War II, DiMaggio hit .304/.389/.533, with an OPS+ of 150, or 50 percent above the league-average hitter. Hitters hit, as the late Tony Gwynn, himself quite a hitter, liked to say, and when you hit as often as someone like DiMaggio or Pete Rose (who had a 44-game hitting streak in 1978) does, those hits will cluster into streaks; a true .300 hitter does not get exactly 3 hits in every 10 at bats, but given 1,000 at bats will probably get pretty close to 300 hits.

What a streak does not prove, or even demonstrate, is that a hitter is "hot." A hitter who's had a hit in each of his last thirty games is no more likely to get a hit in his next game or his next at bat than he was before the streak. Just because the roulette wheel came up red six times in a row doesn't mean you should bet it all on black. (You probably shouldn't bet on it at all, as the roulette wheel is random and if you bet on it you should expect to lose money.)

The manager, therefore, shouldn't change his thinking about how to use a player based on what he's done in the last few games or even weeks. If Joey Bagodonuts has had twelve hits in his last five games, he's had a nice week, but the manager shouldn't put Bagodonuts in the lineup or move him to a higher spot in the lineup just because Joey is "hot." He should disregard this more recent data in favor of more substantial data over a longer term, whether that's the entire current season or even data from previous seasons. If Bagodonuts doesn't hit lefties well in general, and tonight's starter is a lefty, perhaps he should start the game on the bench—assuming the presence of an alternative player on the roster—even though he's on what looks like a hot streak.

Mike Matheny was the manager of the St. Louis Cardinals for six and a half years until he was relieved of his duties in July 2018, and was often criticized by his own fans for his overemphasis on recent performance—even taking hits from Randal Grichuk, an outfielder who was traded to the Blue Jays after the 2017 season. Grichuk called out Matheny in a radio interview with Bernie Miklasz on 101.1 ESPN in St. Louis, saying "they like to play the hot hand a lot. If you struggle a couple of games, you might be sitting a couple of games," and told Toronto media that "[s]ometimes in St. Louis, me and the other OFs thought we would have to get two hits, or two hits and a walk, to be in the lineup the next day, and that's not good for anybody."[26]

Matheny often discussed this as a rationale for decisions, like his choice not to use Shelby Miller, the Cardinals' best starter in the 2013 season, in their postseason rotation that October;

Miller threw one inning the entire month as the Cardinals won their first two series but lost the World Series to the Red Sox. He justified playing thirty-five-year-old journeyman Dan Johnson in 2015, saying "we're not afraid to play that hot hand," because Johnson had had four homers in his last ten games in AAA before his recall. (Johnson went 3 for 21 for the Cardinals, after which he was outrighted off the forty-man roster. He never played in the majors again.) Coverage of the Cardinals during Matheny's tenure frequently refers to his tendency to play the "hot hand"; VivaElBirdos, a long-running Cardinals blog, wrote of Matheny in 2016, "One of Matheny's most consistent traits has been to play the hot hand," and spoke of the possibility that then-hot Aledmys Diaz might regress to his own mean (which he did) that "you just have to hope that, once he cools off, Matheny moves on to trying to find another hot hand."[27]

The belief is becoming less pervasive among managers and front office personnel. Former Mets manager Mickey Callaway dismissed the idea of the hot hand on the 7 Line's *Orange & Blue* podcast in December 2017, saying, "Hot handedness is something that is probably just an illusion. It's such a small sample size that it might not make much sense to do because a guy is going to get cold at some point." Not long after Jeff Luhnow became GM of the Houston Astros after the 2011 season, he told Tyler Kepner of the *New York Times* that "if you end up changing your strategy based on hot or cold tendencies, more often than not, you're chasing your tail and you're actually destroying value rather than sticking to what you know is right based off the data over a longer period of time," while conceding that executing on-field strategies based on that long view was a challenge.[28]

Playing the "hot hand" is a relatively pure example of recency bias in action, colored slightly by the conventional wisdom of a baseball culture that resisted new ways to think about the game for over a half century. We certainly want to believe players are heroes, capable of raising their games at will, rather than seeing them as immensely talented athletes whose performance will still vary over the course of a season or a career. Former Red Sox manager Alex Cora, who was the bench coach for Houston manager A. J. Hinch when the Astros won the 2017 World Series, said early in his tenure with Boston that he was more interested in setting match-ups—such as playing more right-handed hitters when the opposing starting pitcher was left-handed—than going with the "hot hand," which is a textbook case of taking the larger sample into account and ignoring the noise of recent data. It takes a bit of mental discipline to deemphasize the most recent information that our brain tells us is more important, but when you have more data for your decision, you should use it all.

Ultimately, baseball coverage is suffused with recency bias, an unfortunate intersection of the human mind's tendency to fall into this trap and the mortal fear announcers (and producers) have of silence during game broadcasts. Mentioning when a hitter is oh-for-his-last-umpteen at bats is almost rote at this point, even though hitless stretches are going to happen to every hitter given enough playing time. Hall of Famer Tony Gwynn, one of the best pure hitters for average of his generation, had an 0-for-19 streak across seven games in 1998, a season in which he still posted a .321 batting average and struck out only 18 times in 505 trips to the plate. I doubt the Padres considered benching Gwynn during that ice-cold week, but it's a good thing they didn't do so: after it ended, he hit .338/.357/.588 the rest of the season. He was the same Tony Gwynn he'd been before the oh-fer.

The pernicious effects of recency bias can show up across the sport. It can affect how we value a player, including whether a manager or GM thinks a player is capable of helping the team right now or if he needs to be replaced. Recency bias and general availability bias can work together when the player in question is a recent call-up; the major-league staff probably didn't see the player do well in the minors, but if they see him struggle in the majors in a small sample, they might then conclude that he's not very good, or just not ready. A nineteen-year-old outfielder made his major-league debut in 2011 and hit .163/.213/.279 in his first three weeks in the majors, playing in 14 games, so his employers sent him back to the minors. He was already better when he returned twenty-two days later, and the following season, he was the most productive player in the American League. Was Mike Trout really that much different after barely three weeks in the minors? Or did the Angels overrate what they saw most recently and undervalue what came before that in the minors, out of their direct sight? Recency bias plays right into our emotions, and emotional decisions are usually going to end up worse than rational ones.

Just as financial advisers and economists tell you not to look at your 401(k) or retirement account balances too often, because short-term fluctuations are normal, sports executives shouldn't lose sight of the big picture just because a player has an especially good or bad week. Even fantasy sports players could fall for this; if you're obsessively following the players on your team, and one has a brutal stretch, of course you're going to want to drop him and pick up someone else. This is natural, but it's emotional, and not how humans make good decisions in any endeavor.

# 8

## Grady Little's Long
## Eighth-Inning Walk

### Status Quo and Why Doing Nothing
### Is the Easiest Bad Call

A good manager can win you a few extra games over the course of a year with his tactics on and off the field, but a bad manager can end your season with one poor decision.

Perhaps no managerial blunder of my lifetime—which started in 1973, at least according to Wikipedia—has been more discussed and derided than Grady Little's choice to leave Pedro Martinez in Game 7 of the 2003 American League Championship Series after a mound visit that appeared to be a precursor to a pitching change. Little had relievers warmed up and ready even after the first batter of the eighth inning; Pedro, who was handled very carefully by the Red Sox, talked his way into staying in the game, and two batters later, the Red Sox' 5–2 lead was gone.

The Red Sox started the eighth inning with a 91 percent win probability—a calculation based on the score, the number of outs, and the number and location of men on base—that rose to 94 percent after Pedro retired the first batter. He'd thrown 107 pitches to that point, above his season average and median but not excessive by comparison to his regular workload. He was working on four days' rest, standard for most starting pitchers, but not for him; 16 of his 29 starts that year came on four days' rest, as the Red Sox tried to give him an extra day of rest whenever they could to protect his arm. More critically, he had just started his fourth time through the Yankees' lineup when he retired Alfonso Soriano to end the seventh inning, and we know now that pitchers fare worse each additional time they face a hitter over the course of a game, with the fourth time through a particularly perilous jump in hitter effectiveness.

Pedro retired the first batter, Nick Johnson, a left-handed hitter, with the left-handed Alan Embree and the right-handed Mike Timlin warming up in the bullpen, which boosted that win probability to 94 percent. Little left Pedro in to face the right-handed hitting Derek Jeter—a match-up of two future Hall of Famers—rather than going to Timlin, and Jeter doubled on the third pitch he saw. (In baseball, hitters fare better against pitchers who throw with the opposite arm, meaning left-handed hitters much prefer to hit against right-handed pitchers, and vice versa, so managers like to "play matchups" late in games, such as bringing in a left-handed reliever specifically to face a good left-handed hitter.) After Jeter, the Yankees' lineup had five straight batters who either hit left-handed or were switch hitters, meaning they could bat from either side. Martinez did not have significant trouble getting left-handed batters out in his career thanks to a devastating changeup, but this was his fourth time through the order, and Little had a left-handed reliever ready and available to face any of the five hitters coming up, and a right-hander available for any of the switch hitters.

The next batter, Bernie Williams, was a switch hitter who was slightly better against lefties in his career, and Little left Pedro in to face him as well rather than calling on the right-hander Timlin. Williams singled to center on a 2–2 pitch, scoring Jeter to cut Boston's lead to 5 to 3. This is the point where Little went to the mound, with Pedro at 115 pitches, which was already his seventh-highest total of the year; he'd left a game at 116 twice, and two of the other outings came with an extra day of rest, which this start did not. You might also consider that this game came on October 16, six and a half months into the season, by which point every player is feeling at least some fatigue from a full year's workload, and as good as Pedro was on the whole, he hadn't been dominant in his three previous starts that postseason.

The story came out after the game that Little went to the mound to ask Pedro if he had enough left in the proverbial tank to get the next batter, even though with just one out and a runner on, the question was probably more whether Pedro could get two more batters to end the inning, barring a double play. There's still a bias within baseball toward letting starting pitchers finish innings rather than going to relievers, which might be better for the fan experience—even as a lifelong fan, I will admit that nothing makes me want to claw my own eyes out as much as a pointless mid-inning pitching change—but is often counterproductive when the goal is to win the game.

I was on the phone with my boss at the time, Toronto Blue Jays GM J. P. Ricciardi, and we were just watching the game and commenting back and forth, which was part of my ongoing education in the sport as a second-year employee who was still learning about things like scouting or in-game decision-making. When

Little went to the mound, we both assumed that this was the end of Pedro's day. When Little turned and went back to the dugout, Ricciardi sort of laugh-shouted into the phone, "No, Grady, no!" not for any affinity for the Red Sox but because he believed in real time that Little was making the wrong decision.

Ricciardi was right, and Little blew it. The next batter was MLB rookie Hideki Matsui, who had just come to the United States that season after a successful career in Japan's major league, known as NPB. In his first year with the Yankees, which would see him win the American League Rookie of the Year award, Matsui was worse against left-handed pitching than right-handed pitching, a gap that was significant enough that it should have pushed managers to bring in left-handed relievers to face him in critical or high-leverage spots. Rather than call on Embree, the lefty warming up in the pen, Little left Pedro in to face Matsui, who hit a ground-rule double on the third pitch he faced, pushing Williams to third base, which in turn meant that the tying runs were now in scoring position (on second and third). Five pitches later, the switch-hitting catcher Jorge Posada—who hit left- and right-handed pitching equally well over his career—hit a broken-bat flare to center that scored both runners and finally ended Pedro's day at 123 pitches. The game was tied and would remain so until Aaron Boone hit a home run in the bottom of the eleventh inning to send the Yankees to the World Series and extend Boston's championship drought by one more year.

In the fall of 2018, Pedro still said in an interview on TBS[1] he "still believe(d) it wasn't (Little's) fault," even though Little had told Pedro he would only have to get one more batter in the eighth, leadoff hitter Nick Johnson. Pedro even pointed out that the tying hit was on a broken bat, which is a fair point—we do judge decisions by outcomes rather than by process, as discussed in chapter 3 about "outcome bias," but I don't think that applies here. But he said of Little's decision to ask him if he could continue pitching, "You don't ask a warrior to lay down his sword." Little should have simply removed Pedro from the game, rather than asking a proud, immensely talented pitcher who was full of adrenaline to admit he needed to hand over the ball to a reliever.

What was Grady Little thinking? In this case, I think he fell prey to the cognitive bias known as *status quo bias,* the preference for the way things are over any potential change. A 1988 paper by William Samuelson and Richard Zeckhauser[2] looked at data from psychological experiments and found that "[i]n choosing among alternatives individuals display a bias toward sticking with the status quo" across a wide variety of arenas, from public policy to brand loyalty to consumer searching. We like what we know. Our minds become anchored on the familiar—in this case, Grady Little already had Pedro Martinez, one of the best pitchers of his generation, on the mound. Making a change seemed to open up the possibility of loss, one that Little perceived as greater than the possibility that Pedro would perform so poorly that a change would be the correct decision.

Had Little weighed both options, he would have seen that even in qualitative terms, there was a better case to go to the bullpen than to leave Pedro in the game. Martinez was on his fourth time through the order. He was likely fatigued, both from the long season and from a pitch count that was above his norm. The upcoming batters were left-handed or switch hitters, and Pedro, a right-hander, was not the ideal pitcher for that sequence. But Pedro was *already in the game.* Going to the bullpen represented an affirmative decision: Little would have to actively make that change. It would have opened him up to substantial second-guessing had it failed—"Why didn't you just leave Pedro in?"—

although, as we know now, Little was going to be second-guessed either way.

Little wasn't the first Red Sox manager to fall prey to status quo bias in a postseason game, although the manager in the previous incident largely escaped blame for his blunder, which instead went to the player whose fielding error led to the loss of the game and the series—even though that player shouldn't have been on the field in the first place.

The Red Sox' World Series drought began in 1919, the year after they won what would be their last World Series title of the twentieth century. They did so with the help of a twenty-three-year-old two-way player named Babe Ruth, who made 19 starts and posted a 2.22 earned run average while leading the American League with 11 (yes, eleven) home runs in 95 games played. Red Sox owner Harry Frazee would sell Ruth's contract to the New York Yankees after the 1919 season; Ruth became a star in New York, as the Yankees would win six pennants and three World Series in the 1920s alone, while the Red Sox didn't even return to the Fall Classic until 1946. Their championship drought was often referred to as the Curse of the Bambino, referring to Ruth's nickname and the idea that there was some sort of "curse" on the franchise for selling their best player, a fun story until you remember that curses aren't real.

Between 1918 and 1986, the Red Sox won the American League pennant just three times, and in all three instances lost the ensuing World Series in the maximum of seven games. Their 1967 season was known as the Impossible Dream, which turned out to be accurate when they lost the Series to the Cardinals. Their 1975 loss to the Cincinnati Reds, a team known as the Big

Red Machine, is better remembered for the dramatic Game 6 win when Carlton Fisk homered in the bottom of the twelfth for a dramatic walk-off victory.

In 1986, however, they were one pitch away from ending their drought. The Red Sox were ahead in the series 3 games to 2, and were winning Game 6 by a score of 5–3 as they entered the bottom of the tenth inning at Shea Stadium, then the home of the New York Mets. Reliever Calvin Schiraldi retired the first two batters, so the Mets were down to their final out, and Boston's win probability was at 99 percent. The next two batters singled, so the Mets had the tying runs on base, but there were still two outs and Boston's win probability was 92 percent even after the second hit. Schiraldi got ahead of the next hitter, Ray Knight, with strikes on the first two pitches, so the Mets were quite literally down to their last strike—and the Red Sox were a single strike away from their first World Championship in sixty-eight years.

Then everything went pear-shaped. Knight singled to score one run and advance the trailing runner to third base. Manager John McNamara went to his bullpen to replace Schiraldi with Bob Stanley, a curious decision since Stanley had just had the worst year of his career and was already in clear decline. Schiraldi had faced 16 batters by this point and may have been too tired to continue to pitch effectively, but Stanley, also a right-handed pitcher, was somewhat vulnerable to lefties, and the next hitter, Mookie Wilson, could bat from either side.

That's not the McNamara decision that still gets Red Sox fans—now with four more championships under their belts—furious, though. Bill Buckner was Boston's starting first baseman, but he was thirty-six and hobbled, having pulled an Achilles tendon in the previous series while still receiving cortisone shots from an ankle injury he'd suffered that April.[3] Even for a position that asks little range of its fielders, Buckner was not very mobile at all. So, of course, the ball found him.

Before the ball found Buckner, though, Stanley threw a wild pitch to the backstop, allowing the tying run to score from third and moving Knight up to second base. Three pitches later, Wilson hit a ground ball to Buckner that the first baseman bent over to try to field, only to see the ball trickle through his legs, letting Wilson reach first safely and Knight score the winning run. The Mets then won Game 7 in a rout, taking their second-ever World Series title and extending Boston's drought for what would be eighteen more years of self-loathing.

Buckner took the blame, but the gaffe was McNamara's. He had Dave Stapleton on the bench, and if Stapleton wasn't there to serve as a defensive replacement for Buckner late in games, he had no purpose being in the ballpark without a ticket. The 1986 season would be Stapleton's last, as he was thirty-two and had just 144 at bats in the previous three years, but he could fill in around the infield and even in the outfield corners in a pinch, coming in as a defensive replacement at first base twenty-four times in that season. He was there, and ready, and McNamara chose not to deploy him, leaving Buckner in the game in the vain hope that his most vulnerable fielder would not be exposed. The baseball gods do not look kindly on such taunting. Indeed, Stapleton was still angry when he spoke to writer Mike Sowell for Sowell's book on the 1986 postseason, *One Pitch Away;* the chapter on Stapleton is titled "I Knew I Should Have Been in There."

He's right—he should have been in there, standing at first base to make the play that Buckner couldn't, or perhaps to receive a throw from an infielder. He should have started the inning there, as the Red Sox, with a two-run lead and a win probability well over 90 percent, could reasonably expect that Buckner's lineup

spot would not come up again in the game, since that would require seven more Red Sox hitters to bat first.

McNamara had used Stapleton as a defensive replacement for
Buckner throughout the postseason, so his decision not to do so in
Game 6 was peculiar in addition to just being wrong. McNamara
would later defend his inaction by saying he wanted Buckner to be
on the field when the Red Sox clinched, as some sort of honor to
the veteran.[4] What he was actually thinking is known to him and
him alone; what is beyond dispute, however, is that he chose the
status quo rather than the active change, and from his comments
years later it's clear that he thought using Stapleton—who he said
was nicknamed "Shakey"—would expose the team to some unknown risk of a miscue. Doing something trumped doing nothing, because McNamara overweighted the risks associated with
the action, bringing in Stapleton to play first base, and under-
weighted those associated with inaction, leaving Buckner and his
manacled legs on the field instead.

Individuals have a strong tendency to remain at the status quo[5]
because of what behavioral economists call "loss aversion," the
intrinsic belief that a loss of some amount is more painful than
the gain of the same amount would be pleasant. In other words,
you would be more upset to lose $100 than you would be happy to
gain $100. This bias impacts everyday decision-making, because
we tend to prefer inaction to action—we see taking no action as
safer, even though, as music fans know, if you choose not to decide you still have made a choice.

McNamara and Little both chose *not* to make a change: Little
left Pedro Martinez on the mound, McNamara left Buckner on
the field. Little even went to the mound to ask Martinez if he had
enough left to get the next batter, a question to which he likely already knew the answer, as "wanting the ball" is ingrained in baseball culture, and rare indeed is the pitcher who is willing to be

pulled from a game without the use of heavy chains and a truck with a high towing capacity. McNamara's post hoc rationalization implies that he feared putting Stapleton in and seeing the replacement fielder bobble or misplay a ground ball, but that he likely did not accurately assess the probability of Buckner doing the same. The consequences were swift for Little, who was relieved of his duties shortly after the series ended. He managed the Dodgers for two years after the Red Sox let him go, but that was the end of his professional managerial career. McNamara managed the Red Sox for another year and a half before the team fired him at the All-Star break in 1988, and then had one final stint as a manager for Cleveland, lasting a year and a half before he was fired again, marking his last job as a permanent field manager.

**B**ut the status quo bias exists independently of the human aversion to loss: We fear change, and we overvalue what we already have.

Daniel Kahneman and Richard Thaler, both of whom would eventually win the Nobel Prize in economics (I know, that's the fake Nobel, but just go with it, they're both pretty smart), ran an experiment along with Jack Knetsch at Cornell in the 1980s where they gave mugs, priced at $6 in the campus bookstore, to half of the participants in a study, and then the researchers designated the other half of the participants as buyers. In a series of test trials, they had the buyers and sellers (mug owners) negotiate over these mugs, expecting to see the market settle around $3, as it had in similar tests where the mugs were replaced by inherently valueless tokens to which the researchers had assigned some arbitrary values.

That didn't happen: the mug owners valued their mugs too highly, and very few sales took place in the trial runs or in the final

run, after which the researchers executed the negotiated sales. The
mug owners asked for prices over $5, tied to the price of the mugs
in the bookstore—but likely unconnected to any personal value
they'd place on a mug they'd just been given for free.

There's a name for this illusion that what we already have is
somehow worth more than its actual value to others: the endowment effect. In other words, getting something makes our brains
increase our instinctive belief in that thing's value. It's even more
true for goods that are typically not traded or sold, but it exists
even for regular goods, like the way MLB teams treat their own
players.[6]

MLB history is replete with stories of trades not made, and
how one side should be relieved that they didn't take an offer,
or that the offer they made wasn't accepted. The Expos of the
1990s pop up in several of these stories, as they had built a powerhouse by 1994 thanks to the work of GMs Dave Dombrowski and
Dan Duquette, but penurious ownership, the 1994 strike, and a
laissez-faire attitude from the league led to a selloff of top talent
akin to that of the 1970s Oakland A's. The 1994 Expos, who were
in first place on the day the season ended due to the labor action
that eventually wiped out the World Series, had two future Hall
of Famers on their roster and three perennial all-stars in their
outfield. By the start of 1998, four were gone, two as free agents
and two in trades, so the Expos had been left with very little to
show for what they'd built up.

One future Hall of Famer was Pedro Martinez, who was an
All-Star in 1996 and won the NL Cy Young Award in 1997—
which makes him the only Expo to ever win that award—after
which ownership decided he was too expensive to keep and put
him on the market. Martinez was just twenty-five in 1997 and was
worth 9 WAR (Wins Above Replacement) thanks to a season that
saw him lead the NL with a 1.90 ERA in 241 innings with 305

strikeouts (second best in the league). He was a top four pitcher in all of baseball at that point, if we're conservative, and I'd argue he was the most valuable pitcher for a team to acquire, since Greg Maddux and Roger Clemens were already highly paid, and Randy Johnson was thirty-three years old, so it would have seemed at the time that Johnson was likely to decline rather than improve. (That was wrong; he won four straight Cy Young Awards for Arizona in 1999–2002 and came in second in the voting in 2004.) If you were the GM of a contending team with some prospect capital to trade for a starter, Martinez was the best target: he was young, he was already great, and his team was motivated to make a deal because he was one year away from free agency.

If you're reading this, you know by now that the Expos eventually traded Martinez to the Red Sox. They only did so, however, after Cleveland GM John Hart turned down an offer from Montreal that would have altered the future of his franchise. He could have acquired Martinez for two of his own top pitching prospects in Bartolo Colon and Jaret Wright. Hart decided that this was too much to pay for one guaranteed year of Martinez's pitching, and declined the offer. I believe it is safe to say now, twenty-plus years later, that this was a mistake: Colon had a nice career, with a 4-WAR season in 1998 and over 22 WAR before Cleveland traded him for prospects in 2003, but Pedro became Superman, with a 7-WAR season in 1998 and a total of 54 WAR over his seven years in Boston. The trade and subsequent contract extension that kept Pedro in Boston for all of his peak years helped the team win their first World Series in eighty-six years in 2004.

The holdup wasn't Colon, though; it was Wright. Hart has said in interviews since 1997 that he doesn't regret declining the offer, because of the promise Wright in particular held after his half-season debut that summer and fall, culminating in a Game 7 start in the

World Series against Florida. Wright turned twenty-two that off-season and certainly had the pedigree of a top pitching prospect: he was the tenth overall pick in the 1994 June draft out of high school in Anaheim, California, and had recorded plenty of strikeouts at three different levels in the minors, although to modern eyes his high walk rates stand out as red flags. Wright was above average in 16 starts for Cleveland in 1997 and the team had his rights for six more years, so trading that must have felt significant to Hart when the return was just a single year of Martinez.

What Hart didn't seem to consider, however, is the risk involved with young pitching prospects. Wright was indeed a top prospect; the publication *Baseball America,* the only major public prospect-ranking outlet in the 1990s, had Wright as Cleveland's number one prospect going into 1995 and again into 1997, ranking him second before 1996 after Colon. They had him as the No. 22 prospect in all of baseball before 1997, the last time he was eligible for their list, although somehow he was behind Colon (14th) on the overall list while ranking ahead of him on the team list.

Wright pitched a full season in 1998—what would turn out to be his highest innings total in any season in the majors—but didn't improve, and in 1999, the injuries began. After 1998, Wright threw 689 innings over the rest of his major-league career, qualifying for the ERA title[7] just once more, and he finished his career with a 5.09 ERA, meaning he was a well below-average major-league pitcher. He was worth scarcely more than a typical journeyman triple-A starter.

There are two rationales behind Hart's decision not to pursue the trade for Martinez. One is actually quite rational: Martinez was scheduled to reach free agency after 1998, so the acquiring team was only getting one year of his services, as well as the negligible value of the right to negotiate an extension with him before he hit the open market (an exclusive window). Trading

Colon and Wright meant giving up six years of team control of each pitcher—the amount of major-league service time required to attain free agency—for one year of Martinez. For most teams, this would be a terrible trade-off—dealing what turned out to be more than 25 wins of future value from Colon and Wright for 7 wins of Martinez's value in one season. For Cleveland at the time, however, they were at the peak of their cycle, coming off a near victory in the World Series, a season in which falling short of a championship would be a disappointment; adding Martinez to lead their staff and potentially start multiple games across the postseason would have increased their odds of returning to the World Series and potentially winning it by a significant enough margin that the deal may have made economic sense for them and only them.

The second rationale, the more interesting one for our discussion here, is the irrational one, where Hart did what so many GMs have done and will continue to do in trade discussions: he overvalued the assets he already had. Colon and Wright were in-house already; they had already been acquired, Colon as an international amateur free agent and Wright in the draft, so there was no additional cost required to let them go. Wright was a high draft pick too, taken tenth overall; in my experience in the industry, I have at least seen enough anecdotal evidence to believe that teams particularly overvalue their own first-round picks, because they spent so much time and energy scouting those players, and then subsequently invested so much hope in them after they signed. (When you work for a team, especially one that's building through its farm system, you start to live and die with the nightly box scores from your minor-league affiliates. Watching a player develop over time in your system can increase your affinity for him, and you may start to envision future lineups or rotations built around that player if it looks like he's going to be a star.)

This is another instance of the *endowment effect*. First identified by Richard Thaler in 1980 as a subcategory of the loss aversion effect, he explained it as the perception that the loss from giving up, say, your former first-round pick is greater than the gain from getting a Cy Young winner who immediately becomes your number one starter. (I'm oversimplifying here just to explain the concept.) The effect seems to be stronger the longer you own the thing, called the "duration of prior ownership effect," under which the value you place on something before losing or selling it is higher the longer you've owned it up to that time.[8]

So now put yourself in John Hart's seat. You've just won the AL pennant and come within a few outs of winning a World Series. You have two of the ten best pitching prospects in baseball, both of whom are ready to help your major-league staff. One of them was your first pick, high in the first round, and you've had him in your system for three and a half years. The other signed as a free agent out of the Dominican Republic and has been in your system for four years. You've had both for quite some time and have watched them develop to the point where you're about to see your investment produce a return, perhaps a very strong return, in the upcoming season.

You can value the potential contributions of all players involved in this deal—preferably with ranges, since the performances of players, especially pitchers, are still volatile even when predicting the short term—but when it came to Hart making an affirmative choice to lose the two prospects and gain an ace for his rotation, increasing his odds of winning in 1998 at some cost in future years, he chose not to act because he put too much value on Wright.

The endowment effect comes into play with baseball prospects all of the time because of the emotional attachment executives form with those players—not so much as people, but as ideas.

We took this kid at age eighteen or age twenty-one, watched him grow over time, and now you want us to trade him away? In some sense, it's easier to trade a player right away, as the Padres did with Trea Turner a few months after drafting him, leading to a rule change that has allowed teams to trade players five months after the draft, than to trade a player you've had in your system for years who is about to reach the majors.

When I worked in the front office for the Toronto Blue Jays, we got off to a miserable start in 2003. After an ugly loss on April 30, the team's record was 10–18, we were in last place, and we were already 12 games out of first. Our twenty-six-year-old ace, Roy Halladay, had been one of the best pitchers in baseball in 2002, but couldn't get himself going in April, posting a 4.89 ERA in the month and allowing batters to hit a composite .304/.351/.522 against him in six starts, with nine walks and eight homers, both uncharacteristically high for him. (We couldn't know this at the time, but every one of those numbers would be his worst of any month in that season, other than the .317 batting average he allowed in August.) My boss at the time, General Manager J. P. Ricciardi, had two simultaneous concerns about Halladay: that he might not be as good as we thought he'd be after his very good 2002 season, and that if he were actually that good we'd be unable to retain him for the long term because he'd leave as a free agent in a few years or even become too expensive in arbitration. Because of those fears, he called Brian Sabean, the GM of the San Francisco Giants at the time, to offer him a deal: the Giants could get Roy Halladay in exchange for their top three pitching prospects: Jerome Williams, Jesse Foppert, and Kurt Ainsworth.

Sabean said no, and the rest is indeed history. Halladay turned his season around and won the AL Cy Young Award in 2003, then eventually signed an extension that kept him in Toronto until

2009, after which he was traded to the Phillies to finish a Hall of Fame career before his untimely death in 2017. He generated over 21 WAR in just the next four seasons, and 55 for the rest of his career. The three Giants pitchers didn't quite do so well; Williams had two solid seasons, producing a little under 4 WAR, before he was traded to the Cubs, and ended up out of baseball before a comeback in his early thirties, while Ainsworth and Foppert were both below replacement level (posting negative WARs) for their careers.

The Giants passed on an incredible buy-low opportunity for the same reason Hart passed on the Pedro deal: they overvalued their own players. All three were seen as top prospects; *Baseball America* ranked Foppert as the best pitching prospect in baseball before 2003, putting him fifth overall, with Williams 50th and Ainsworth 64th, so it wasn't strictly a function of the team liking its own guys. But they were all high draft picks, taken in the first or second rounds, and had been in the organization for several years—Ainsworth and Williams since 1999, Foppert since 2001. Halladay had just about four years left to free agency at that point, and even if he'd just repeated his 2002 performance he would have been the Giants' second-best starter in 2003. His addition could have helped them beat the Marlins in the playoffs in 2003, or win the NL West in 2004 when they lost it by two games, while they ended up with little value from the three guys they kept, eventually trading Williams and Ainsworth in minor deals.

I do think that at that time teams didn't adequately discount the future production of young pitchers, given what we knew then and know now about their attrition rates due to injury. It's possible that the Giants simply thought they had three mid-rotation or better starters in those three guys and couldn't fathom giving up all of that future value for one pitcher. Or maybe they just didn't think Halladay was all that good—I suppose they could have had a scout see him that April and sound an alarm that something was amiss. We do know with hindsight that they made the wrong decision, and that the Blue Jays were fortunate they did so, as Halladay would make five All-Star teams and have five top-five finishes in Cy Young voting while wearing a Jays uniform, becoming one of the most beloved players in team history.

Fighting the endowment effect and the associated status quo bias is difficult, in part because it's tied to our emotions. There is some research, however, showing that our overvaluing something we already have may also be a function of our failure to update our expectations; research by Campbell Pryor, Amy Perfors, and Piers D. L. Howe in 2018[9] found that the strength of subjects' endowment effect could be altered by altering their prior expectations. Thus one possible solution for the decision-maker is to reassess your valuation of whatever it is you already have, or what the status quo option is, by reconsidering your reference point for your current valuation: What makes you value the current option so highly in the first place? Is it because the player was a first-rounder, or has been in your system so long?

In the general case, when presented with multiple options, one of which is to leave things as they are or simply keep the thing you already have, bear in mind that you will probably overvalue the status quo, because everybody does. Ask yourself what the actual value is of staying with what you already have—or, in Grady Little's case, what the cost is of sticking with it—just as you would ask for the value of any new asset or strategy before choosing it.

# 9

---

# Tomorrow, This Will Be
# Someone Else's Problem

## How Moral Hazard Distorts
## Decision-Making for GMs,
## College Coaches, and More

Over the 120-plus years of the history of professional base-ball, major-league owners have tried just about everything to avoid paying players any more than they absolutely had to. They've locked the players out. They've colluded, violating their collective bargaining agreement with the players' union with pre-dictably disastrous results, got caught, and colluded some more. In 2003–04, however, they sank to something of a new low: they threatened to eliminate two of MLB's thirty teams, a bluff I don't believe they ever remotely intended to execute, in an ill-advised plan to create leverage in their negotiations with the union by creating the potential for the loss of fifty union jobs.

The two teams targeted for contraction were the Minnesota Twins, whose billionaire owner, Carl Pohlad, was scheming for a new, taxpayer-subsidized stadium, and the Montreal Expos, which was owned by MLB itself at the time as a result of some swift self-dealing by the league that put former Expos owner Jeffrey Loria in control of the then-Florida Marlins. The contraction threat went nowhere; the Twins were ordered by a court to finish their lease at the Metrodome and eventually landed a new stadium, while MLB sold the Expos to a new ownership group that moved the team to Washington, DC, and renamed them the Nationals.

In the interim, however, the Expos were a lame-duck team. The mere specter of contraction, combined with ownership by a league that clearly wanted to dispose of the franchise in any way possible, was enough for the team's management to change the way it approached the roster. So when the Expos had a fluky start to the 2002 season, they decided to go for it right away, because tomorrow wasn't promised at all.

The Expos weren't actually that good in 2002, but weird things happen in small samples, and an eight-game winning streak in early June put their record at 39–33, good for second in the NL East and five games behind the wild-card leading Dodgers, which meant that as of that date they were not in position to win a playoff spot. They'd played a bit above their heads at that point—they'd been outscored on the season—but it was enough for their general manager at the time, Omar Minaya, to look to bolster the big-league team to try to keep them in position to make the postseason.

That's all well and good—they're hardly the only team in history to try to turn an unsustainable start to the season into real contention by addressing the team's flaws—but the 2002 Expos were different because of the possibility of contraction. Like all MLB teams, the Expos had an extensive farm system with a few hundred minor leaguers under contract, several of them prospects of real promise, but their future potential had little to no value to the Expos if they were going to cease to exist as a franchise. This wasn't a certainty, but there was enough of a chance it might happen that it changed the way the MLB-appointed front office executives approached their season and their farm system.

The result was one of the most obviously lopsided trades in MLB history, derided at the time as such and playing out over time as a franchise-altering trade for two clubs. The Expos traded for Cleveland starter Bartolo Colon, who was headed for free agency after the 2002 season, for Montreal's three best prospects at the time. The deal was strictly a rental for the ninety games left and, if they qualified, for the playoffs, which would mean about eighteen regular-season starts from Colon. The Expos traded the No. 20 prospect in baseball (according to *Baseball America*'s preseason rankings), shortstop Brandon Phillips, who had yet to reach the majors, to get Colon, which in and of itself would have been a significant overpay and one that made little sense given the Expos' position in the standings.

But that's not all! The Expos also included their No. 3 prospect at the time, outfielder Grady Sizemore, whom they had selected in the third round of the 2000 draft and offered a $2 million bonus, which at the time was high first-round money, and was more than the Expos had paid their first-rounder the year before. Sizemore was just nineteen at the time of the trade, but had already performed exceptionally in the low minors, with a .373 on-base percentage for his career at the time of the trade, even though he was very young for every level at which he'd played. A former football star in high school, Sizemore was seen as a high-upside prospect who'd come into power as he got older.

We're not done, though, because neither were the Expos. They also included left-handed starter Cliff Lee, their fourth-round pick from 2000, ranked 11th in their system by *Baseball America* coming off a 2001 season that saw him strike out 129 batters in 109.2 innings with a 2.79 ERA, all in the high-A level of the minors. Lee was the closest to major-league ready of the three prospects the Expos traded for Colon—yes, I'm done now, they didn't trade any more prospects in this deal—and was busy dominating double-A at the time of the trade. Cleveland sent him to double-A Akron for a few starts, then to triple-A, and he debuted in the majors that September.

That's three prospects ranked in the team's top eleven—even considering that Lee was probably ranked too low, since he wasn't an especially hard thrower—traded for a bit more than half a season of Colon, who was very good at the time and in the midst of his best season to date, but who wasn't going to be enough to make the Expos a contender. The team had been outscored on the season, which indicated that they were likely to see worse results going forward despite their winning record; teams that don't outscore their opponents over long periods nearly always lose more games than they win. (Yeah, citation needed. Just trust me on this.)

Colon was good for the Expos, albeit not as good as he'd been for Cleveland prior to the trade; he had a 2.55 ERA for Cleveland, producing 4.7 WAR in just half a season, when he was traded, but posted a 3.31 ERA for Montreal even though the National League has lower run scoring because they lack the designated hitter, and produced 2.4 WAR for the Expos the rest of that year. And the Expos did indeed regress after the deal, going 44–46 for the rest of the season, finishing 13 games out of the wild-card spot and 19 games behind division-winning Atlanta. Colon left after the 2002 season as a free agent, and Major League Baseball did not allow the Expos to offer him salary arbitration, so they didn't receive an extra draft pick in 2003 as compensation for his departure.

Cleveland, on the other hand, made out like bandits. Sizemore was the least-known prospect at the time of the trade, but ended up the most valuable part; he debuted in the majors in 2004, was a regular for all of 2005, and produced 27.7 Wins Above Replacement (WAR) from his debut through 2011, when injuries caught up to him and effectively ended his career at age twenty-eight.[1] Lee pitched parts of 2002 and 2003 in the majors, became a full-time starter for Cleveland in 2003, and produced 17.3 Wins Above Replacement for the team before they traded him to Philadelphia in 2009, including winning the Cy Young Award in 2008, when he led the American League in ERA. Phillips turned into a very valuable big leaguer too, but not for Cleveland, who dumped him in a nothing trade just to clear a roster spot in April 2006. Cleveland's hitting coach at the time, Hall of Famer Eddie Murray, didn't like Phillips, and the team barely used him in 2004 and 2005. Phillips thrived after the team traded him to the Cincinnati Reds, where he became a frequent All-Star and fan favorite who produced 14 WAR in his first five years, roughly approximating the time he would have still been under Cleveland's control if they'd retained him.

The Expos gave away at least 55 WAR of future value in the trade for Colon, which netted them about 2 WAR before he left as a free agent and did nothing to advance them toward the playoffs in the one season in which they had him. It also set the franchise back for years; they dropped to fourth place in the NL East in 2003, last place in 2004, and then moved to Washington, where they finished in last place in five of their first six years (hurt further by more poor decision-making by the Nationals' first GM, Jim Bowden, who was later fired after revelations of bonus-skimming in the team's international scouting department). Cleveland's fortunes went the other way; they won 93 games in 2005, then 96 in 2007, coming within a victory of winning the AL pennant that year, and later traded Lee in another veteran-for-prospects deal that brought the team starter Carlos Carrasco.

Teams make these future-for-present trades all the time—less often today than they did twenty years ago, certainly, but they still do so, because it can be rational to value additional wins in the present year, such as in the case where you have a legitimate chance to reach the playoffs, more than you value the potential for even more wins several years down the road. In the Expos' case, if Minaya and his group believed there was a sufficient chance that the team would cease to exist after the season, it may have been rational to trade all that future value for more short-term help—in fact, you might argue that they didn't go far enough, and should have traded all of their prospects for players who'd help them in 2002.

Of course, there was still a chance that the Expos would not be contracted, and would continue as a going concern into 2003 and beyond—I argued at the time that contraction was a feint, that MLB never intended to eliminate any teams and would likely have faced threats from the federal government and affected states or cities if they'd tried. Expos management should have weighed this probability into their decision to trade three of their best prospects—in the next two off-seasons, Phillips, Lee, and Sizemore would all appear on *Baseball America*'s rankings of the top fifty prospects in baseball—for short-term help, because doing so would harm the franchise substantially in the long run if they were not contracted. Indeed, they were not, and were shipped off to Washington, where they became doormats in the NL East for long enough that, thanks to a rule change, they became the first team ever to hold the first overall pick in the draft in two consecutive years.

Minaya and his group, however, had a second variable affecting their perspective that doesn't apply to most general managers.

Major League Baseball's ownership of the team was always designed to be temporary; if they didn't contract the team, then they
would sell it to new owners who would, most likely, want to hire
their own front office personnel after taking control of the team.
Minaya was long seen as a GM-in-waiting, so his ascension to that
post with the Expos was neither surprising nor undeserved, but
it was not a typical general manager's job. One way or another,
he was unlikely to hold that position for very long, which meant
no matter the eventual outcome for the team's ownership, he had
a very strong incentive to make decisions to improve the team in
the short-term—including the potential to show off his skills as
a GM so that he'd be better positioned to assume the same role
for another team in the future. (While the Nationals' new owners
chose not to retain Minaya after 2004, the Mets hired him immediately to become their new general manager, a role he then held
for six seasons.)

Aligning a leader's incentives with those of the company they
run is a problem in any industry, although in baseball there are
two positions, the general manager and the (field) manager, where
firings are so frequent that this problem is easier to spot and call
out, if not quite so easy to solve. This particular problem faced
by sports team owners is known as *moral hazard,* which sounds
dangerous, and I suppose on some level it is: these executives are
allowed to make moves that, if they go sour, will leave messes
for someone else to clean up, because the contract might go on
well past the point where the general manager has been fired or
reassigned.

The term "moral hazard" did not appear until the late nineteenth century,[2] but the concept predates the phrase by as much
as two hundred years, appearing in discussions of the insurance
industry in the mid-1600s. Moral hazard, or the risk of it occurring, is especially pertinent to insurers because of the perverse

effect insurance can have on human behavior: You may make riskier choices if you know that your losses will be mostly or entirely covered by another party. You may drive a little faster because your insurance company will pay to repair your car if you have an accident; banks make riskier loans because they believe the government will bail them out if those loans go bad. (And they're right. The government's response to the mortgage-lending crisis in 2008–09, propping up banks that were teetering on the edge of insolvency, made it clear to future lenders that offering high-reward loans to high-risk clients is smart business, because that high risk is shared between the bank and the government—if the bank takes any of the risk at all.)

Robin Pearson, a professor of economic history at the University of Hull in the United Kingdom, described moral hazard in the insurance industry as "the possibility of unfavorable features of a risk arising from the character of the insured," and says it was recognized, albeit not named as such, before 1850.[3] Insurers used the term and concept to include more than what we now think of as the subjective choices of morality, and included not just changes in behavior, but broader ideas such as the increased desire to purchase insurance among those more likely to need its benefits—much as U.S. residents have heard that some people may wish not to purchase health insurance because they believe they are unlikely to utilize it. (As someone who assumes every headache is a brain tumor and every heart flutter is cardiac arrest, I do not understand these people.) In the intervening years, economists have co-opted the term as a core tenet of the economics of choice. People will take on more risks if they know someone else will foot the bill if things go wrong.

There may be no better contemporary example than the Albert Pujols contract, which has fast turned into one of the biggest albatrosses in any U.S. professional sport. Jerry DiPoto was the general manager of the Los Angeles Angels of Anaheim in the winter of 2011–12 when Pujols, who had put together one of the best ten-year stretches of any hitter in MLB history to that point, became a free agent. The Angels signed Pujols to a ten-year contract—more on that in a moment—that still had more than seven years to go at the time that DiPoto resigned his post as GM during the 2015 season.

The Pujols deal itself was problematic from the start, with just about everyone pointing out the extreme improbability that the deal would end well for the Angels given its length, Pujols's age at the time of the signing,[4] and the track record of position players like him as they reached their mid- to late thirties. Pujols was thirty-two for his first season with the Angels, which meant that the deal would run through his age-forty-one season, an age by which most position players have been forced out of the league due to declining production. But Pujols had already started his decline in 2011, the last year before he became a free agent, which was his worst major-league season to date by any measure—5.3 WAR by Baseball-Reference's method, 3.9 by Fangraphs' method. Whichever WAR calculation you use, Pujols never reached his 2011 level again, and by 2017 was the worst everyday player in the majors. Through the middle of 2019, Pujols had produced less value in seven-plus seasons as an Angel than he did in his three worst years before signing with the team.

DiPoto had been hired by Angels owner Arte Moreno, who certainly pushed for the team to sign Pujols, that same winter, after the 2011 season, and was given a four-year contract with an option for 2016 that the team later exercised. That means that DiPoto signed Pujols for the four years DiPoto was under contract *plus* the six years beyond that. This is hardly uncommon in sports—I can't find any baseball general manager who gave a player a ten-year deal but was himself under contract for that same length of time—or in the business world in general. We expect government officials to make arrangements that can last for decades, even though those officials would likely long be out of office before such deals are finished.

The very nature of the job of a sports team's general manager entails moral hazard at its most general definition: that the person making the decision doesn't bear some or all of the risk entailed in that decision. In other words, if the decision goes wrong, someone else will have to clean up the mess. GMs hand out contracts that run to eight and nine figures to players through free agency and contract extensions, but it's not the general manager's money in question—it's the owners'. If you own a baseball team, or any sportsball team, you hire a GM to decide how to spend your money on players. If the GM makes a series of terrible decisions, the most he can lose is his job, while you will lose (or, more precisely, get insufficient return on) tens of millions of dollars. You bear nearly all of the risk of your GM's decisions, and your only recourse, firing the person responsible for the bad choices, is really no recourse at all—and then the replacement you hire gets to deal with the consequences, such as a limited payroll for future moves because so much money is committed to a decline-phase Albert Pujols.

The Angels' case is worse than just the one deal, and a bit more complicated because Moreno pushed DiPoto to make larger, splashy moves that were unwise from the start. The same day they announced the Pujols contract, they also announced they were signing left-hander C. J. Wilson to a five-year contract worth $77.5 million, a deal that saw him have one good season for the Angels, produce just 5.5 WAR in total, and miss the entire final year of the deal due to injury. A year later, the Angels, in this case very much pushed by Moreno, gave former AL MVP Josh Hamilton a five-year, $125 million deal, even though he was also

thirty-two to start the contract; it went bust immediately, and after two unproductive, injury-plagued years, the Angels handed
him back to his former team, the Rangers, primarily just to get
him off the roster. His career ended after 2015 due to recurring
knee problems.

These moves were all bad enough on their own merits, but
they're worse in context, because starting in 2011, the Angels
also had the best player in baseball, and one of the best in MLB
history, on their roster, earning at or just above the minimum
salary. Mike Trout debuted in 2011, became a full-time regular
in 2012, and led all AL position players in WAR for five straight
years, producing about ten wins above a replacement-level player
each year all by himself. The Angels made one playoff appearance in that span, winning the AL West in 2014, but didn't win
a single game in their lone playoff series against the Royals. As
of this writing, that's the only playoff appearance of Mike Trout's
career, as the first set of mistakes has limited what the Angels'
front office, now helmed by GM Billy Eppler, could do with the
remainder of the roster while working around the commitments
to Pujols, Wilson, and Hamilton.

There are copious examples in baseball just in the last twenty
years, but there's one other one that sticks out because of how
the careers of the GM and player in question went after the giant
contract was signed. The Detroit Tigers hired Dave Dombrowski
to serve as president and CEO before 2002, and a week into that
season he fired the team's general manager and assumed that role
himself, beginning a nearly fourteen-year tenure that included two
American League pennants and three other playoff appearances
for a team that hadn't seen the postseason since 1987. During the
MLB winter meetings in December 2007, Dombrowski pulled
off an epic trade, acquiring infielder Miguel Cabrera and right-
handed pitcher Dontrelle Willis from the Florida Marlins for a

six-prospect package. None of those six prospects produced as much as 3 WAR for the Marlins, but Cabrera continued on a Hall of Fame trajectory for the Tigers, producing 36 WAR from 2008 through 2013, thanks to a hilariously good .327/.407/.588 triple-slash line along with 227 homers in those six seasons.

In the spring of 2014, Cabrera still had two years left on his contract, but the Tigers gave him an additional eight-year extension to increase their guaranteed commitment to him to $292 million over ten years. Dombrowski, however, was gone before the extension even kicked in; the Tigers fired him on August 4, 2015. Within two weeks, he had assumed the same role with the Boston Red Sox, a team that had a few albatross contracts of its own but also had a young, productive, and very inexpensive core already in place. Dombrowski was aggressive, as usual, in free agency and in the trade market, and he combined that with the players he inherited to build a roster that won the American League East in his first three years with Boston and took home the team's fourth World Series title in a sixteen-year span with its win in 2018.

The term "moral hazard" is often a misnomer, because there isn't any morality built into these decisions—if anything, it's an amoral question: you'll do the best thing for yourself, like just about every person ever would do. There are cases, however, where the agent in question faces a decision with rational and moral components, where the choice that is most rational for the agent may be harmful to someone else. This comes up regularly in amateur baseball, where amateur coaches will work pitchers too hard because they have zero investment in the pitcher's long-term health.

The worst example of this I've seen since I first started working in baseball came on May 31, 2009, in a postseason game between the University of Texas, then coached by Augie Garrido (who died in 2018), and Boston College, then coached by Mik Aoki (who left BC to become Notre Dame's head coach in 2011). The game came during the four-team regional that also included Army and Texas State; the winner of the Texas-BC game would move to the championship game, while the loser of the game would have to play Army in an elimination game.

The game was tied 2–2 entering the seventh inning, when Garrido called on reliever Austin Wood, who'd mostly been used that spring in one-inning relief outings. With one out in the ninth inning, Aoki called on reliever Mike Belfiore, who was a significant prospect in that year's draft and hadn't thrown more than three innings in any one game that entire spring. The game remained tied for sixteen more innings until Texas scored in the twenty-fifth, and both coaches decided to ride those two particular relievers as long as they could—Wood threw 13 innings and 169 pitches, Belfiore 9 ⅔ innings and 129 pitches, both of which would be an excessive one-game workload for an experienced starter working on full rest. But both Wood and Belfiore had thrown two innings in relief the day before, so they threw more than a starting pitcher typically would while doing so on zero days of rest.

College coaches already have little formal incentive to care about players' health or performance once those players leave school. Some coaches will argue that they have a moral incentive, and care about their players, and while I am sure that is true in some cases, it certainly doesn't trump the power of the incentive to win games in the short term—especially in a playoff game. Both Wood and Belfiore were eligible for that year's MLB draft, which was held ten days after this game, and were expected to be drafted high enough to end up signing pro contracts, so both Garrido and Aoki had reason to believe that they were going to lose their pitchers after that season. Only one team wins each regional, so both coaches were aware during the twenty-five-inning game that at least one of them would see their season end that weekend. (Boston College lost its elimination game to Army, ending their season; Texas defeated Army, won its super-regional series the next weekend, and eventually advanced to the finals of the College World Series, losing in three games to LSU.)

The industry was already aware in 2009 that overuse of pitchers increased the risk of serious arm injuries, to the point where pitchers in the minor leagues rarely threw over 100 pitches in a game even on full rest, and major leaguers rarely went past 120 pitches. There were only 9 starts in 2008 where a major-league pitcher threw at least 120 pitches, led by Tim Lincecum's 138 on September 13. Major-league teams saw pitch counts for young pitchers, like Belfiore's and especially Wood's, as deleterious to the players' long-term health. Garrido and Aoki seemed to see the pitchers as expendable resources who'd leave in a few weeks and be replaced by the incoming freshman class.

Wood was a fifth-round pick of the Detroit Tigers but missed nearly all of 2010 after shoulder surgery and never reached the majors. (He told Mike Finger of the *Houston Chronicle* in 2011 that he didn't regret the way Garrido used him in that game.)[5] Belfiore was selected with the 45th overall pick by Arizona, but was never the same pitcher again after the long outing, reaching the majors for one inning in 2013 before his professional career ended after the 2015 season.

Moral hazard is inherent in human activity; it's not something you can simply eliminate by thinking about it or trying to hold yourself to a higher standard of morality. People respond to incentives, so to change behavior, you have to change the incentives to try to get your general manager to consider the long-term impact of any decision they might make, whether it's handing an older free agent a long-term contract or trading away top prospects to get short-term help for the major-league roster.

The Texas/BC pitcher abuse story provides an easy way to see how some simple incentives could change coaches' behavior to mitigate their natural (if rather gross) tendency to use pitchers like they're disposable diapers (okay, that was more gross) rather than considering their long-term futures, which may include substantial earning potential in professional baseball. (I've also written many times that overusing players with no professional future is still unconscionable. The ulnar collateral ligament in your elbow or the labrum and rotator cuff in your shoulder don't know that you're not getting drafted. They can still suffer tears, causing pain and maybe requiring surgery.) Individual colleges, which employ the coaches, or the industry's overarching cartel, the NCAA, could set mandatory pitch limits for pitchers based on age and days of rest, such as using the limits created by experts in concert with MLB for its PitchSmart program.

The players themselves pay the largest cost when they're overused by college or high school or youth baseball coaches, and it would behoove more parents to understand why experts recommend pitch limits and sufficient rest. Greater awareness of which college programs overuse pitchers and which never do should, in time, affect recruiting, although disseminating such information to parents is difficult, and, in my experience covering the sport and calling out pitcher overuse, coaches deny they've done anything wrong.

Major League Baseball, however, also pays a cost for this kind of pitcher usage: it means fewer healthy pitchers are available to teams, and that some players enter pro ball with undetected damage to their arms and fail to fulfill their potential after they're drafted. It would be easy for MLB as an entity to put a stop to such overuse in colleges by exerting its leverage over the NCAA, either offering to fund additional scholarships in the sport if the NCAA agrees to mandatory limits, for example, or changing the CBA to make players draft-eligible after their freshman or sophomore years rather than forcing them to wait until their junior year to turn professional.[6] Such a move would acknowledge that coaches have no direct disincentive to working pitchers until their arms fall off, and have every incentive to try to win more games in the current season (to keep their jobs, to get a raise, to get a more lucrative job at another school). You accept that people are just people, and you set up a framework that prohibits them from doing the thing they'd like to do but that works against your greater interests.

Solutions to mitigate moral hazard—to prevent someone from taking on too much risk in a situation because they will not bear the full costs if something goes wrong—are not always this clean; one reason you see sportsball examples come up in academic studies so often is that they often give us artificially simple conditions to look at behaviors. Also, talking about sportsball is more fun than, say, talking about banking . . . but moral hazard in the banking industry is how the U.S. economy ended up diving into a recession in 2008–09, as major banks issued increasingly risky mortgages in search of short-term profits from bundling and selling the loans, knowing that they would transfer much of that risk to investors buying those bundles (called CMOs, collateralized mortgage obligations), with the federal government always happy to step in and bail out large banks that might be "too big to fail."

In a 2009 paper looking at moral hazard and bank bailouts, William Poole wrote:

> Instead of more regulators with more power, we need to change the incentives under which firms operate. Our firms got into trouble because they had too much leverage and too much

of their debt was short term. They were subject to too little market discipline. Finally, we need a market-based method for forcing large firms to scale back their operations in an orderly way when they get into trouble. These issues can be addressed by changing the incentives under which firms operate.[7]

Poole goes on to outline four major problems that regulators and markets would have to address to either reduce decision-makers' ability to take on additional risk or reduce the benefits of doing so, and proposes market-based solutions like making debt more expensive for companies to use relative to equity by eliminating the tax deductibility of interest on corporate debt. The point is that to address moral hazard, you accept that you can't change people, so you change what they can do, or you change the incentives around what they can do. If college coaches knew they'd be fired for overusing pitchers, or were given mandatory pitch limits, that would solve the problem. If they were judged or compensated on the health or professional success of pitchers, they might alter their behavior. If—and I think this is inevitable—a player sues a coach or school for misuse that may have led to a catastrophic arm injury, that will certainly change behavior as well.

Similarly, MLB teams could change the incentives for general managers by spreading out or deferring compensation, or signing executives to longer deals with variable compensation that's tied to on-field results, so that executives have more skin in the game if a large player contract goes sour. You can't exactly ask a GM to cover the cost of a disastrous free agent signing—whew, I just lost half of my friends by even writing that—but ensuring that there's more reward for a GM who succeeds in the long term, and that said GM will likely be around to clean up any mess he might make, can at least help you avoid getting stuck with the five worst years of Albert Pujols's career.

# 10

## Pete Rose's
## Lionel Hutz Defense

### The Principal-Agent Problem
### and How Misaligned Incentives
### Shape Bad Baseball Decisions

When the Atlanta Braves signed their twenty-two-year-old second baseman, Ozzie Albies, to a seven-year contract in April 2019, the industry burst into flames. The deal, which covered four years when he would have been under team control plus two years of potential free agency, guaranteed Albies $35 million, and included two club options for additional years at $7 million apiece. I doubt any contract extension has prompted such an immediate and incendiary reaction before or since.

*Sports Illustrated*'s Jon Tayler wrote that "Albies got scammed" and said the offer was "insultingly low."[1] The Ringer's Michael

Baumann said "Albies got taken to the cleaners" and the contract's terms were "nothing short of shocking."[2] ESPN's Jeff Passan tweeted that "the Ozzie Albies extension might be the worst contract ever for a player. And that's not hyperbole." He followed that up with a column, after speaking with other agents and club executives, writing that "the overall dollars stunned the industry" and that "giving up four free-agent years . . . felt egregious."[3]

Within that column, Passan also hinted at one of the biggest problems that players can face when negotiating contracts with teams, whether as free agents or as players already under contract seeking extensions to their current deals. Albies was represented by an independent agent, David Meter, who runs a small shop compared to the largest agencies in the business—the Scott Boras Corporation, Creative Artists Agency, Excel Sports Management, and others—and Passan pointed out how the priorities for agent and player might differ:

> At 5 percent commission, a $20 million extension means $1 million for an agent. The incentive, then, to do an extension can be strong for smaller shops—Albies employs one in agent David Meter—which also fear client-poaching from larger agencies. Even among the larger agencies, the concern over losing a client—and a commission—can compel extensions.[4]

The sports agent business is cutthroat; players can switch agents on a dime, for any reason or no reason at all, and owe their previous agents neither loyalty nor a share of any earnings from future contracts. (An agent still receives commission on contracts they already negotiated for players.) I've covered baseball for more than thirteen years now and have heard no end of stories from agents about rivals stealing their players, offering cash or other incentives to players to switch (which is forbidden), or making unworkable promises to players about future income. Agents will approach prospects when they're freshmen in high school in the United States, or when they're as young as eleven or twelve in countries outside the purview of the draft, such as the Dominican Republic. These agents will invest time and money meeting with the players and their families, going to their games, following them to events, helping get them equipment . . . and the player can choose at any point to drop their agent and hire another. It's the accepted way of the business, one of the few aspects of the baseball industry that are favorable to the players.

Albies's deal was indeed a terrible one for the player when compared to reasonable projections for his earnings had he simply gone year-to-year, as many players do. Major League Baseball players receive close to the minimum salary until their third or fourth year of service time in the majors, after which they enter a period of eligibility for salary arbitration until they have accumulated six years of service, making them eligible for free agency. One rival agency ran internal projections for Albies's likely earnings through one more year around the minimum salary, three years of salary arbitration, and two years of free agency, and came up with a total of $61 million, 75 percent more than the contract Atlanta gave Albies would pay him. Long-term contract extensions may come at some small discount to compensate the team for guaranteeing that money, and because the player takes the smaller guaranteed payment in exchange for financial security. A discount of this magnitude, however, might have no precedent in baseball, certainly not in recent memory.

Why would any player sign a deal this far below his market value? Albies himself would say that he didn't care about the dollars, telling the Athletic's Dave O'Brien that "I took it because I want my family to be safe" and that "I want to be a Brave for the rest of my life." This could all be true, but Atlanta would likely have been willing to pay him quite a bit more than they did, given what Albies's production is worth, and what Atlanta would have had to pay him had he declined their offer and chosen to go year-to-year. If that rival agency's projections were correct, then Atlanta should have been willing to offer Albies up to around $60 million on the same deal, since such a contract would still have saved them money and locked him in for two years beyond when he could have left the team as a free agent. Instead of pushing for more money, however, Albies and his agent took an offer the entire industry, both agents and team executives, felt was far too low.

An agent may appear to have the same incentives as the players they represent, but that's not exactly true. If an agent fears that he's about to lose a player to another agency, he has a strong incentive to negotiate the best contract extension he can get right then for his player, locking in commissions for himself, even if the optimal strategy for the player is to defer signing a long-term deal until some date in the future. (Perhaps the player has been hurt, or is coming off a disappointing year on the field.) The funnel-shaped nature of baseball salaries, where compensation increases exponentially when the player first hits salary arbitration, and takes another large jump when the player hits free agency, means that the players who are good enough and stay healthy enough to get to those inflection points are always better off financially, at least in hindsight, by going year-to-year and getting to free agency rather than signing long-term extensions while they're still new to the majors. That's worse for the agent in two ways: his own compensation is still variable and tied to the player's ability to perform and avoid injuries, and he may lose the player as a client to another agency before getting the largest commissions.

That misalignment of incentives is known as the *principal-agent problem* in economics, and it happens to regular folks like us, not just to professional athletes or actors.[5] If you've ever bought or sold a house, you've probably used a Realtor to represent you in the transaction, helping you set the price and collecting offers if you're the seller, helping you look for houses and decide how much to bid if you're the buyer. A Realtor representing a buyer has conflicting incentives: they represent someone who wants to pay as little as possible for any particular house, but their own commission is a percentage of the sale price and thus increases if the buyer pays more!

There are multiple reasons why you might have to use an agent (or lawyer or other go-between) in a transaction; it may even be a requirement depending on the field or where you live. It's usually the right choice—few people choose to buy a house without using a Realtor or having a real estate lawyer review paperwork, for example, and if you do so, you assume the risk that you'll miss something critical in the process that someone with experience would catch. However, anytime you employ someone as an agent, as professional athletes nearly always do to handle contract negotiations with teams, you run the risk that your incentives and those of your designated agent won't quite line up, and that the agent will recommend choices that serve the agent better than they serve you.

Players can also be on the other side of the principal-agent problem; teams pay players to perform for some fixed period of time, but the players' own time horizons will almost invariably differ from those of their employers. As I write this, Anthony Rendon, the somewhat unheralded star third baseman for the Washington Nationals, is a few weeks away from hitting free agency. He's completing his sixth full year in the majors, and it is his best to date: His average, on-base percentage, and slugging percentage

(.330/.414/.622) are all career highs, as are more advanced measures of his total production like wOBA and wRC+. He has already set career bests in several counting stats, including hits, home runs, RBI, and runs scored, and needs one more double to match his career high in that category. With his usual excellent defense, this adds up to the best WAR total of his career—7.1 on Fangraphs, with 11 games remaining in the season for him to boost it.

Is it a coincidence that Rendon, always a great player anyway, is having the best year of his career as he enters free agency? And does that imply that, once he signs a long-term contract this winter as a free agent, his performance will regress as he "shirks" once he has a guaranteed deal and is no longer playing to impress his potential suitors?

Three economists examined this issue in a 2002 paper published in the *Journal of Sports Economics*[6] and found that the answers are yes . . . and no. Players do some things better in "contract years," the industry jargon for the last year of a player's contract before he enters free agency, but the authors did not find evidence of shirking—that players would in any way "take it easy" once they'd gotten that cushy new deal.

Joel Maxcy, Rodney Fort, and Anthony Krautmann looked at 1972 player-seasons in the post-free-agency period of Major League Baseball to assess whether either of these axioms was backed by empirical evidence: did impending free agents up their games or play through more injuries? Did newly signed free agents malinger once they were on Easy Street? Their answers were yes . . . and no. The data showed that players did play more in their contract years: such players are "less likely to end up on the disabled list and playing time is higher in the period immediately preceding contract negotiations."[7] The effect was small but statistically significant, and held whether the authors looked at playing time or at days on the disabled list (now called the injured list as of 2019). They hypothesized that players in their contract years might be trying to play through injury to improve their performance or avoid any implication that they might be "fragile," or that managers might use such players more because they're aware the player might leave after the season.

They did not, however, find any evidence of shirking: "Even though management continues to claim that long-term contracts adversely affect motivation and performance, our results simply do not support these allegations."[8] They found that players in their first years of new contracts played more and were on the disabled list less often, saying that "this may be explained by recognizing that management ultimately decides on playing time. As such, managers may be under pressure to use their new long-term commitments more intensively."[9] There's no evidence to support the contention that players take it easy in their new deals, at least in terms of their willingness or ability to play.

An article written a few years later by Dayn Perry in the book *Baseball Between the Numbers*, looking just at whether players played more or fared better specifically in contract years, found similar results: players were more likely to peak in their walk years—consistent with Maxcy et al.'s findings—and much more likely to play more in their walk years than in the years immediately preceding or following those. Perry points out that the structure of free agency in baseball, described earlier in this chapter, means that many players don't become eligible for free agency until they have already passed their prime seasons, generally held to peak around age twenty-seven for hitters.[10]

Players who push themselves harder in their contract years, playing through injuries that might otherwise push those players to take a few days off, are rational actors working in their own self-interest. Their teams may benefit from the extra effort . . . or they may not, if the player plays at 70 percent of his production, or aggravates a minor injury to the point that a stint on the injured list is necessary. The interests of the player and the team are similar, but not perfectly aligned.

The principal-agent problem is a specific class of problems that fall under the broader economic term "moral hazard," which, as discussed in the previous chapter, refers to the more general case of anyone who takes on additional or excessive risks because they would not directly bear the costs of failure. For example, drivers may drive less carefully, or be more cavalier about defending their car against theft or damage, if they know that insurance will cover some or all of their losses.

The 2008–09 financial crisis was itself the result of extensive moral hazard throughout the mortgage industry, while the U.S. federal government had to consider whether bailing out insolvent lenders would only increase moral hazard and encourage other banks to increase their leverage even further. The existence of a secondary market for "collateralized mortgage obligations," or CMOs, allowed banks to bundle together mortgages that shared some common attributes and sell those bundles, in pieces called tranches, to other investors, thus offloading the risk that these mortgages would fail—aided by credit ratings firms that helped the lenders understate the probability that the mortgages would bust. After the crisis began, the federal government chose to bail out Bear Stearns, even though federal protection did not previously extend to investment banks,[11] yet then declined to do the same for Lehman Brothers, allowing the latter to fail "as a warning to other financial firms that they needed to rein in their risk taking."[12]

The principal-agent problem was first identified in the 1970s, although it is unclear who first gave the problem its name; one of the earliest descriptions, at least, was a 1976 paper by Michael Jensen and William Meckling that states the problem succinctly as, "If both parties to the relationship are utility maximizers, there is good reason to believe that the agent will not always act in the best interests of the principal."[13]

Solving this problem—so agents will act consistently in the interest of their principals, instead of maximizing their own utility—has been the subject of substantial academic work over the last forty-plus years. One important 1983 research paper by Sanford Grossman and Oliver Hart argued for "breaking up the principal's problem into a computation of the costs and benefits accruing to the principal when the agent takes a particular action,"[14] which means you have to know ahead of time what actions the agent might potentially take in any given situation, solves this problem of misaligned incentives. Imagine having to construct a sizable spreadsheet every time your designated agent needed to make a significant decision on your behalf!

Another solution, called the "first-order solution," predates the Grossman/Hart paper, and doesn't apply in most cases, but was "more mathematically tractable"[15]—easier to solve, even if it doesn't work. Other academic papers that have proposed solutions to the principal-agent problem include "Solving nonlinear principal-agent problems using bilevel programming," "Deterministic versus stochastic mechanisms in principal–agent models," and "On dynamic principal-agent problems in continuous time." In other words, this problem has been studied for more than four decades, and even the application of mathematical methods beyond most people still hasn't adequately solved it. It is baked into the nature of any principal-agent relationship: the agent's interests might look like they're the same as yours, but they're going to be slightly different. That Realtor should push the sellers to agree to a lower price for the house, but she gets a slightly higher commission if the sellers don't agree, and maybe she won't push as hard.

Pete Rose retired from his playing and managing careers as the "Hit King," with more hits than any other player in major-league history, having limped past Ty Cobb to set the record at a point when Rose probably shouldn't have been playing as much as he was. Of course, he was his own manager at the time, too, and kept putting his name in the lineup so he could break Cobb's record—which, for the record, was a pretty exciting moment for baseball, too.

Rose played his last MLB game in August 1986, and his legacy lasted all of three years before the commissioner's office announced in August 1989 that Rose had been hit with a lifetime ban from the sport for betting on games in which he was involved as a player and/or manager. This is the sport's one Eternal Sin: in the wake of the 1919 "Black Sox" scandal, where multiple Chicago White Sox players (including "Shoeless" Joe Jackson) conspired to lose the World Series in exchange for payments from gamblers, the league cracked down on any such threat to the game's integrity. Rose wasn't the first player banned under the new rules, but by far the most prominent, and the punishment led to years of denials from Rose, claims that the stress of the investigation led to the death by heart attack of Commissioner Bartlett Giamatti, and, inevitably, Rose's attempt to profit from his own duplicity by writing a book confessing that the charges were true.

One of Rose's few consistent claims over the ensuing three decades was that he only bet on his team, the Reds, to win games—never betting on them to lose—as if this were some sort of mitigating factor. If he had bet on the Reds to lose, the story goes, that would have been the greater crime, as he might then have chosen to manage those games differently to try to increase the odds that the Reds would lose and he'd profit from his bets. Advocates for Rose's reinstatement, or merely his enshrinement in the Hall of Fame, often tout this claim: Yes, he bet, but he only bet on the team to win, and don't you want your manager to always try to win? Isn't it just a perverse sign that Rose believed in his team's potential to win every night?

The shortest answer is that Major League Baseball Rule 21(d)(2) does not specify whether the bets had to be against a player or coach's own team; betting on a team in which you are playing, coaching, or managing is forbidden and punishable by baseball death:

> Any player, umpire, or club or league official or employee, who shall bet any sum whatsoever upon any baseball game in connection with which the bettor has a duty to perform shall be declared permanently ineligible.[16]

So bets for your own team still violate this rule; Rose did that, without question, and received the statutory punishment.

The reason this is still a Very Bad Thing, however, is best explained by the principal-agent problem. Think of the team—its owners, or the team president, or perhaps its stakeholders as a collective unit—as the principal, and the manager as the agent. The principal has asked the agent to handle all aspects of in-game management, including lineup construction, player usage, and tactics, as well as key aspects of managing the personnel on the team. The principal's primary goal is to win a World Series, perhaps more than one, while also maintaining a competitive team that is likely to be profitable in the long term, which generally entails winning more games. (There's a strong positive correlation between winning and revenues in baseball, with a big boost if a team gets to the postseason.) In some situations, the manager may also be asked to simultaneously help develop young players who are new to the majors. The principal hires the agent-manager to achieve these goals.

The manager's goals, however, might differ slightly from those of the team's owners or stakeholders. The manager's contract is probably short in duration, so he will want to show more success in that short term so he either gets a contract extension or is more attractive to other teams that might employ him in the future. He might choose to use a known quantity in a veteran player more than a less reliable or simply less known young player who could be better or whose development depends on getting more playing time. He might choose to use a great pitcher more in the short term, even though there's a risk of fatigue and future injury from overuse. The manager may figure any such injury will happen after the manager's contract is over, so by that point, he'll either have a new contract or will be working elsewhere.

In Rose's case, this disconnect—which economists would call *misaligned incentives*—was exacerbated by his betting. Rose had the incentive to try harder to win the games on which he'd bet on the Reds, and on nights when he did not bet, he could just ease up on the throttle and not be as aggressive. He could work pitchers harder in the games on which he'd bet, knowing that he could decline to bet on the Reds if that pitcher looked tired or was hurt in a later game. If he hadn't bet on a game, perhaps he'd manage more passively, failing to pinch-hit a right-handed batter for a lefty in the late innings, or "forgetting" to put a defensive replacement in the field for another player, taking advantage of the fact that such nonmoves are less likely to attract attention than active choices.

Most observers wouldn't think much of this managing style; to outsiders, and even to most insiders, it would look like Rose was pushing harder to win games he thought the Reds could win. At worst, maybe it would seem like he was conceding losses a little too easily, but if the team won enough games, this would be an unlikely criticism or dismissed as a specious one. Rose may not have been thinking rationally when he risked his career by betting on baseball, but once he'd placed those bets, the rational course of action for him was to floor the gas pedal on games where he'd bet on the Reds to win, and coast in the other games.

There are two fundamental problems with the manager acting in this way, both of which justify the maximum penalty baseball imposes on people who violate Rule 21(d)(2). The first is that a manager who only bets on his team to win specific games is tacitly signaling to others, such as the bookmakers taking his bets, that he believes his team has less chance to win the other games, and might do less to win those games as a result of his failure to bet on them. Attorney Ryan Rodenberg said as much for the *Atlantic* in a 2014 column:

> First, when Rose did not bet on the Reds, his inaction was a signal to his bookies that he wasn't very confident in that game. Those bookies may have used this inside information to place a bet against the Reds. This doesn't mean the game was fixed, but is reflective of Rose's state of mind. He was compromised. Second, his wager on certain games, but not others, may have influenced the way he made decisions as a manager.[17]

Rodenberg goes further with his first point, saying that Rose could even have signaled his confidence level to bookmakers through the varying sizes of his wagers on individual games.

This pattern was made very clear years later when details of Rose's betting were made public through paper betting slips and a diary Rose kept of his own bets. Rose stopped wagering on the Reds on nights when pitcher Bill Gullickson was the team's starter; in 2007, the *New York Times*' Murray Chass wrote of these new revelations that "if Rose bet on his team to win other games but didn't bet on Gullickson's games, he was sending a signal to the bookies he was betting with that he, as manager of the team, didn't think much of his team's chances in those games." Rose bet on the Reds to win in just two of Gullickson's last eight starts for the team in the summer of 1987, until the team traded the pitcher to the Yankees that August.[18]

The second, less-discussed problem with Rose's actions is that such management does not align with the interests of the people who hired him, and may even work at cross-purposes. Sure, both principal and agent here want to win, but in baseball, a win tonight may come at some cost to your chances of winning tomorrow night, or in the future, because of how a manager might use his players. A relief pitcher who works two innings to win tonight's game will probably be fatigued if he is asked to pitch tomorrow, which would make him less effective, and maybe not available to pitch at all. A pitcher who's truly overworked in one game or over a period of several games may get hurt and be unavailable for some future period of time, and, in rare cases, may no longer be an effective major-league pitcher.[19]

A manager trying to win more games in the short term, whether due to betting or simply the desire to preserve his job, may also choose not to use younger players who need playing time to continue to develop. Rose had twenty-four-year-old outfielder Paul O'Neill on his roster for part of 1986 and almost all of 1987, but barely used O'Neill, giving him just 181 plate appearances in total in those two seasons, even though O'Neill was a significant prospect who'd performed well in double-A and triple-A through the 1985 season. O'Neill's career arc is an unusual one, as he didn't have his first league-average season at the plate until he was twenty-six and had his first All-Star appearance (justified by his performance) at twenty-eight, eventually blossoming in his thirties with the New York Yankees after a trade. It is an unanswerable question, but did Rose's refusal to use O'Neill beyond a bench role slow the player's progress and cost the Reds some of O'Neill's production in the years right after 1987? Given how late O'Neill peaked, it seems plausible.

The team wants to win now and to win in the future. That balance may shift over time—a team could decide to sacrifice some future value and trade prospects to gain more short-term value by trading for major-league talent. The balance is always there, however. Every MLB manager, and probably every professional sportsball manager, is subject to the biases of this principal-agent problem, but in the case of Pete Rose, the conflict between his own interests and those of his employers was exacerbated by his betting, essentially doubling down on his own incentives to win now.

(There's an ironic twist to Rose's gambling habits, however. Rose was still a player while he was managing the Reds and betting on the team to win, and for most of 1985 he was chasing Ty Cobb's all-time career hits record of 4,191. Rose put himself in the lineup regularly, playing 119 games and getting 501 plate appearances, in pursuit of the record . . . but by doing so he reduced his team's chances of winning. Rose was barely above replacement level in 1985, mostly because he slugged just .319, then the fourth-worst full-season slugging percentage for any first baseman since World War II. In 1986, he played much less, but was also substantially worse, and ended the year below replacement level. In both years, the Reds had superior alternatives at first base, including Nick Esasky, and in both years the Reds finished in second place in the National League West, missing the playoffs by six games

in 1985 and ten games in 1986. Rose's decision to play himself
didn't cost them those playoff spots, but it did put them further
away—and may have cost him some money, too.)

You can easily imagine how these misaligned incentives can
distort the way front offices try to build their teams, or the results
they get from what they think will be an optimal roster. There's at
least some evidence that players play more, likely playing through
small injuries, in their last years before free agency, and thus a
player just signed as a free agent might play fewer games because
he's more likely to ask for a day off here or there. The same incentives may apply to players heading into salary arbitration, a
process that is almost entirely stats-driven and is still more determined by traditional stats than advanced ones, although I haven't
seen any evidence on this class of players. Stories abound of
players calling an official scorer, angry about a play ruled an error
or ruled a hit, because of how it might affect those players' individual stats. (MLB changed the appeal process in 2012 to avoid
such confrontations.) Teams sign players under the assumption
that they will expend their full efforts all the time, and will play
whenever they are able, which is mostly true but seems to slip on
the margins. Players who've just signed guaranteed deals seem to
take more days off, while those approaching free agency seem to
play through more ailments (even though it might be better for
the team if the players rested).

There are no simple solutions for the principal-agent problem,
but modern companies have certainly tried to find partial solutions
to at least increase the incentives that executives and managers
will act in the companies' best interests. Apple instituted a rule in
February 2013 that executives must hold triple their base salary in
Apple stock.[20] Thus, what's good for the company becomes good

for the executives, and the executives should shift their decision-making to choices that most benefit the company—or, at least, its stock price. This is superior to the previous attempt to tie executive behavior to share prices by giving executives stock options, which provide benefits to the executive if the stock price rises past the options' strike price but are costless to the executive if it doesn't.

There are other confounding factors that make solving the principal-agent problem more difficult, regardless of the industry or field. One worth mentioning here is called *information asymmetry,* which means what it sounds like: the principal and the agent do not have the same information, with the agent holding information that they use to make decisions that the principal lacks. This gives the agent substantial latitude to defend their decisions after the fact if the principal questions them—for example, imagine a (baseball) manager saying he didn't use a specific reliever in a game because the pitcher "didn't look right when he was warming up" or "said his arm was tired." These statements could be true, but they are unverifiable, making the principal's job of evaluation more difficult, even after the fact, when you might assume all relevant information was visible to both sides. It's a thorny problem without a clear solution, even in a highly public arena like that of professional sports, so that managing it down to an acceptable level may be all you can hope to do if you're the principal in your situation.

# 11

## Throwing Good Money After Bad

### The Sunk Cost Fallacy and Why Teams Don't "Eat" Money

I don't mean to pick on Albert Pujols. He's been a great player, one of the greatest right-handed hitters in the history of the game, and is an icon in St. Louis after he starred for the Cardinals for a decade, playing on two World Series champions and another pennant winner. As thirteenth-round picks go, you can't do any better than the Cardinals did when they took Pujols from a local junior college in 1999.

Pujols's career after he left St. Louis as a free agent, however, is a veritable cornucopia if you want to talk about how bad decisions get made. I covered the mistake the Angels made in the first place when they signed him to an abominably long contract in an earlier chapter, but they have since compounded the mistake by continuing to play Pujols regularly years after he stopped producing enough to earn that playing time.

Pujols's last Pujolsian year was 2010, his penultimate season with the Cardinals, although he was still very good in 2011—14th in the majors in wRC+, an overall measure of offense that also adjusts for ballparks and where 100 represents league average. The Angels signed him after the 2011 season to that ten-year contract, and the party was over immediately. His best offensive season with the Angels, which came in year one of the deal, was worse than his worst season with the Cardinals, that 2011 season. It was all downhill from there: His wRC+ figures, by year from 2012 on, have been 133, 112, 123, 114, 110, 77, 89, and 98.

In years two (112) and five (110), Pujols was bad enough that he was below league-average for a first baseman. From year six onward, he was below "replacement level" according to Fangraphs' metrics, which means that a hypothetical player recalled from triple-A would have performed better than he did. (The offensive standard for a first baseman is higher than it is for most positions, because the position is less demanding defensively and teams often put poor defenders at first base just to get their bats in the lineup.) In short, that says that Pujols shouldn't have been playing at all, because by playing as much as he did, he cost the Angels wins.

Since the Angels signed Pujols, they've only been to the playoffs once, in 2014, which happened to be Pujols's only other year as an Angel where his offensive production was above the median for everyday first basemen. The next year, the Angels missed the playoffs by a single game, finishing at 85–77 while the Houston Astros went 86–76 and took one of the two wild-card playoff spots in the American League, and the Texas Rangers went 88–74 and won the AL West division title.

Pujols's production that year was worth 1.6 Wins Above Replacement, again using Fangraphs' metrics. Out of 20 first base-men across the majors that year who played enough to qualify for the leaderboards (minimum 502 plate appearances), Pujols's WAR ranked 16th. If we drop the threshold to 400 plate appear-ances, Pujols comes in 18th out of 31 qualifiers—better in relative terms but still below the median.

Every American League playoff team had more production from their regular first basemen than the Angels got from Pu-jols, as did three of the five National League playoff teams. (Somehow, the St. Louis Cardinals won 100 games despite replacement-level performance from their first basemen. They had more offensive production from five other positions on the field, including both middle infielders.) The Angels were pay-ing Pujols to be a premium player, but his performance was a detriment to the team when you compare what the Angels got from him to what other teams got from first base, and in 2015, at least, you can point to the difference between his production and the expectations for him as a reason why the Angels missed the playoffs.

At least in 2015, you could justify the Angels putting Pujols in the lineup compared to other options they had in-house, but by 2017, even that had changed, as Pujols's production cratered that year to a career-worst .241/.286/.386. Pujols was a full-time designated hitter that year, and his OBP is the third-worst posted by any designated hitter in this decade, just .003 above the worst mark, Carlos Beltran's .283 OBP in the final season of his career. Pujols's slugging percentage was the fifth-worst of the decade for a DH. It's the worst or second-worst full-season performance by a DH in the 2010s, exacerbated by the fact that Pujols grounded into a league-leading 26 double plays that year. (He's the all-time leader in GIDP, grounded into double plays, well ahead of Cal Ripken Jr. The leaderboard for that stat is great hitters who played a lot, rarely struck out, and didn't run well, but Pujols is well clear of the field already and still playing.)

The Angels didn't come close to the playoffs in 2017, so there is no argument that Pujols cost them a postseason berth, but there is an argument that the decision to play him as much as they did—or at all—cost them in the standings, and would have affected their off-season plans if they were honest with themselves about how little he was likely to produce in that season or subsequent years. Had the Angels gone into 2017 or 2018 with an open mind, and a willingness to bench Pujols some or all of the time— for example, sitting him against most or all right-handed starters, but still using him against left-handers because he would have the platoon advantage there—could have opened them up to acquiring a better replacement or partner for him. Such an incremental improvement, which would have been easy to execute since first basemen or designated hitters who can hit have been plentiful and inexpensive in free agency the last few winters, would have improved the Angels' projections by a few wins, and could then in turn have made additional investments more attractive because their odds of contending for the playoffs were already a bit higher.

Of course, none of that happened. In 2019, Pujols had a marginally better year than he did in the prior two seasons, although this may be a function of the livelier baseball in the 2019 season or just the baseball equivalent of what investors call a "dead cat bounce." Pujols is thirty-nine years old, and any sort of second wind after such an extended period of nonperformance would make him a historical unicorn. Yet the Angels have continued to play him regularly throughout his contract and the decline phase that started quite early for him; the shape of his career, starting his peak at age twenty-three and declining quickly from age thirty-one, looks like a typical hitter's career arc that has been shifted back about three years. Pujols has played enough to qualify for the batting title in all but two of the eight years he's played for the Angels so far; in the other two, he missed due to injuries, not from any decision to play him less often. When his body's been willing, he's been in the lineup.

Pujols's legacy is not in question here; he's a certain Hall of Famer, with no reason for any voter to omit him from their ballots (especially now that we've had our first unanimous Hall of Famer, Mariano Rivera). He'll probably finish his career in the top five all-time in home runs, doubles, and the useless-but-voters-still-like-it runs batted in; and he's already in the top fifteen all-time in total hits, with a chance to get into the top twelve. None of this discussion is about Pujols himself, but about how the Angels have chosen to handle him now that he's nearly forty and a shadow of the superstar he was a decade ago.

So why have the Angels continued to play him despite such an extended sample of mediocre or worse performance? There is an idea within sports that you don't pay a player a starter's salary to sit on the bench, and baseball coverage in the media will often refer to the difficulty of sitting a player who earns a substantial salary, but this is all a function of what economists call the *sunk cost fallacy*. The Angels are paying Pujols regardless of how much he plays: If he gets 600 at bats or zero, the team pays him the same base salary. (Pujols has some bonus incentives in his contract, but he's extremely unlikely to reach any of them now that he's already passed 3,000 career hits to collect that one $3 million bonus.) Therefore, any decision on how much to play Pujols, or whether to play him at all, should be independent of his salary. If you have already paid for something, your choice of whether to use it should be a function of whether you want or need to use it, not a function of the money that is already gone regardless of what you do.

The Angels are hardly the only team to continue to play a player past the point of usefulness, although they probably have the most famous example of the last decade. Miguel Cabrera, another all-time great right-handed hitter who is headed for the Hall of Fame, has been, to put it kindly, burnt toast since the start of 2017, below replacement level when he plays and less durable as well. A brief stretch of productivity to start 2018 was interrupted by injury, and outside of those five weeks he's been "worth" less than zero WAR, meaning the team was actively worse off for playing him. He's earned $28 million, $30 million, and $30 million over those three seasons, with four guaranteed years remaining at a total of $124 million. They might be better off just releasing him, although that's certainly not likely.

Chris Davis of the Orioles probably became the poster boy for sunk costs when he started the 2019 season 0 for his first 33, which, combined with a hitless streak to end the 2018 season, put him at a major-league record 54 at bats without a hit. (He did draw seven walks in that stretch, so it's not the same as making outs in 54 consecutive trips to the plate.) Davis led the American League in home runs in 2013 and 2015, sandwiched around a 2014 season where he slipped to .196/.300/.404—actually still above replacement level, thanks to his 26 homers and a solid walk rate, but hardly the same player he appeared to be the years before or after. The Orioles ignored the 2014 performance, and everyone else in the baseball world saying Davis was too risky for a huge long-term contract, and gave him an eight-year, $184 million contract, even though it wasn't clear if Davis had another bidder for his services at the time.

Davis was fine in year one, worth about 3 WAR in 2016 even though his contact rate was heading down, but by year two he appeared to be finished as a major-league hitter. He was right at replacement level in 2017, and in 2018 had one of the worst seasons in MLB history: he hit .168/.243/.296, producing −2.8 WAR by Baseball-Reference, the 13th-worst figure since 1901 and the second-worst figure this century. Fangraphs had him at −3.2 WAR, which is the worst mark since 2000 by their metrics.

And yet the Orioles . . . just . . . keep . . . playing him. Davis played just about every day in 2016, then 128 games (out of 162) in both 2017 and 2018, and still played regularly in the first half of 2019 before the team finally started to consider superior options at first base, like erstwhile outfielder Trey Mancini, former Oakland bonus baby Renato Nunez, or a fan whose name is pulled out of a hat a half an hour before the first pitch.

The stakes for the Orioles weren't small, either. In 2017, at least, they finished with the same record as the Toronto Blue Jays, with both teams earning wild-card playoff berths. The game was played in Toronto due to a tiebreaker; had the Orioles won one more game over the course of the season, they would have hosted that game. Maybe the outcome would have been the same in Baltimore, but in this universe, the game was held in Toronto, and the Jays won on a walk-off home run by Edwin Encarnacion in the bottom of the eleventh inning. That was the end of the Orioles' run of contention in the 2010s; they fell to fifth place the next year at 75–87, and in 2018 had the worst record in baseball, going 47–115, which cost both manager Buck Showalter and general manager Dan Duquette their jobs.

One of the first columns I ever wrote for ESPN.com, two weeks after I left the Blue Jays to join the Worldwide Leader, covered this exact topic. The Arizona Diamondbacks released pitcher Russ Ortiz on June 13, 2006, even though they still owed him $22 million on the hilarious four-year deal they'd given him eighteen months earlier. The Associated Press newser we ran on our own site said, "The Arizona Diamondbacks decided Tuesday they would rather eat the remaining $22 million of Russ Ortiz's contract than keep him on their roster."[1] That phrasing particularly set me off, because they weren't "eating" anything. That salary was already somewhere in Arizona's GI tract, likely causing indigestion but there nonetheless. Major League Baseball player contracts are guaranteed; there is no way to un-eat that meal. The Diamondbacks did the right thing by cutting Ortiz, who had been a dumpster fire on a train wreck since signing, with a 7.00 ERA in 28 starts over a year and change. They were paying him anyway, so the question was whether they were better off with him on the roster or off it. They made the right choice: they cut him rather than keeping him and continuing to let him pitch for them and give up loads of runs. Ortiz played briefly for four other teams before his career ended, with a 6.38 ERA across all four stops, so even with the benefit of hindsight the calculus hasn't changed. The Diamondbacks were better off giving those innings to their best in-house alternative than giving them to Ortiz. (At the time, the move set what appeared to be a record for the largest remaining dollar amount on a contract when a player was released.)

You'll notice that I haven't named decision-makers for these decisions about playing time. There's a reason for that: while managers or general managers are often presumed to make those macro decisions, such choices could easily come from above them. An owner might say that he's not paying Twerpy McSlapperson $23 million a year to sit on the bench, or that he won't release Joey Bagodonuts because he's paying the guy $19 million this year and he's determined to get something for his money. It's entirely irrational, and can be at odds with the owner's likely goals of winning more games and making more money. However, if you're a manager, and your boss tells you to put Bagodonuts in the lineup every night, you're going to do it.

There's also the clubhouse concern—what might other players think if, say, you bench an icon like Albert Pujols or Miguel Cabrera for performance reasons. Although I tend to think those concerns are overblown, as players are professionals and most will go out every day and perform to the best of their abilities regardless of how such veterans are handled, a manager or general manager may be sufficiently conflict-averse that they choose not to make the cold, rational choice. This probably makes me callous by comparison. I'll accept that, because I'd definitely have benched Pujols or Cabrera some time ago.

The sunk cost fallacy is part of introductory economics. I encountered it in college and again in graduate school, the latter in the required intro to microeconomics course. My professor at the time, Uday Rajan, now the David B. Hermelin Professor of Business Administration at the Ross School of Business at the University of Michigan, explained it with a simple example. In a fit of optimism, perhaps part of a New Year's resolution to get in shape or lose weight, you buy a piece of home exercise equipment—an exercise bike, a treadmill, or, if I were the buyer, an elliptical machine. (I don't own any exercise equipment, for a few reasons, but Professor Rajan's example is absolutely one of them.) When you first buy it, you use it pretty often, as your ardor for exercise has not yet cooled and the novelty of having the new toy—excuse me, machine—hasn't worn off. Over time, however, you're less eager to use the machine, at which point, your brain reminds you: You paid a lot of money for that device. You should use it more!

While exercising more is a good thing, the rationale is all wrong. The amount of money you spent on the machine should have no impact whatsoever on how often you use it. Think about two scenarios: One where you paid $500 for a treadmill, and another where you won the identical treadmill in a lottery and paid nothing. In both scenarios, once the transaction is over and the treadmill is ensconced in your house (probably somewhere that annoys at least one other member of your family), your states are identical: you own a treadmill, outright. The choice to use it is entirely independent of what you paid for it; it's the same machine, and has the same effects on your body and health when you use it, regardless of its cost.

That's not how the human mind works, as I'm sure you've realized. There's a natural compulsion to use the machine more to "justify" what you spent on it. You're probably not justifying it to anyone but yourself, of course, which isn't necessary and involves setting some arbitrary goals to make the purchase seem worthwhile. (Do you have to use it three times a week? More/less? Was it only a good purchase if you use it some minimum number of times in the first year? What if you don't use it for two years and then suddenly decide to use it regularly and as a result you become a healthier person—do we have to amortize back the gains to reflect the time value of lost weight? Yeah, let's not do that.)

If you buy the treadmill and never use it except to hang damp clothes to dry, you may feel that you have wasted the money you spent. That's irrational, at least to a classical economist, but it's a pretty apt description of how people think. Some contemporary economists have argued that considering sunk costs is not irrational, citing "reputation concerns"[2] (for example, "my partner/kids/friends already think I'm an idiot for buying the treadmill, so I'll prove them wrong by using it!") or time and financial constraints ("I don't have the money left over to get a gym membership, so I'll just use this treadmill").[3] I think it's better to think of considering sunk costs as economically irrational, while recognizing there may be intangible or difficult-to-measure considerations to such decisions.

The seminal paper on the sunk cost fallacy was written by Hal Arkes and Catherine Blumer of Ohio University and published in

1985, simply titled "The Psychology of Sunk Cost." The authors believe that this behavior is largely explained by the human desire not to appear wasteful, and run through a series of psychological experiments that shows the fallacy affecting decision-making, like whether to buy a new, superior printing press just a week after you've invested in a custom press at great cost; whether to continue research into a new product that is 90 percent complete but has already been scooped by a competitor; and whether to eat a $5 TV dinner or an identical $3 one after you've cooked both but learned that your guest can't make it. (About a quarter of respondents said they'd eat the $5 one and discard the $3 one, even though *they're the same meal*.)[4]

The sunk cost fallacy can have deadly consequences. It's been used to justify the United States' continued involvement in multiple overseas conflicts, including the Iraq War, which began in 2003 and didn't end until the United States withdrew all combat troops in 2011. President George W. Bush, who was the commander in chief who made the decision to invade Iraq in March 2003, said in July 2006 that the United States would continue its involvement in that country because "I'm not going to allow the sacrifice of 2,527 troops who have died in Iraq to be in vain by pulling out before the job is done."[5]

That's a perfect distillation of the sunk-cost fallacy: The cost already paid in human lives could not possibly justify putting more human lives at risk—if anything, it should have been a deterring argument against continuing the fight. According to the Department of Defense's statistics, another 1,905 Americans would be killed in "Operation Iraqi Freedom" between Bush's statement and August 31, 2010, along with thousands more wounded and many thousands of Iraqi deaths. In March 2008, two economists estimated that the total costs of the Iraq War to the United States would top $3 trillion, a number that would have been lower had the United States withdrawn its troops sooner.[6]

This particular instance of the sunk cost fallacy has its own name, *escalation of commitment*, what I think most of us know as "throwing good money after bad." Eventually, you have to learn to walk away from an investment that will never give you the return you sought, and that investing further—such as holding on to a stock that's well below the price you paid for it, or increasing your bets at the craps table when you're losing—means you've let your emotions take over for your rational side.

Recent research has found that the sunk cost fallacy may even extend to costs that were sunk by someone else. Christopher Olivola, a marketing professor at the Tepper School of Business at Carnegie Mellon University, published the results of multiple experiments involving online surveys (with large sample sizes) that explored the *interpersonal sunk cost effect*.[7] For example, Olivola tweaked a well-known experiment by Richard Thaler where respondents were asked what they would do if they had an expensive ticket to a basketball game but the weather that night was bad and made traveling to the game dangerous. In Thaler's study, respondents were more likely to try to drive to the game if they'd paid more for the ticket. Olivola switched it up by saying the respondent had gotten the ticket from a friend, and then made the key variable whether the friend had paid $200 for the ticket or gotten it for free. Respondents were still much more likely to drive to the game if their friend had paid the $200 than if the ticket had been free. In other words, they were responding to the sunk cost fallacy when the cost wasn't theirs in the first place. Across multiple experiments—finishing a cake when you're already full, continuing to watch a bad movie, choosing between two conflicting trips—Olivola found the same effect:

people consistently acted in accordance with the sunk cost fallacy even when the cost was incurred by someone else.

I'll stop picking on Pujols for now, because there's another example of misunderstanding the sunk cost fallacy in recent baseball history that led to a cascade of bad decisions and helped sink (pun intended) a general manager who wasn't even part of the first mistake.

When Jim Thome reached free agency at age thirty-two after the 2002 season, he was still at the peak of his offensive powers. He had just led the American League in walks and slugging percentage and finished second in the league with 52 homers, after finishing second in homers the year before with 49. He was still a full-time first baseman, although never a particularly good one and likely to need to move to the designated hitter spot at some point in the next few seasons. The Phillies had just finished 80–81 and were 15 games out of a playoff spot in 2002, so they decided to make a big investment in Thome, signing him to a six-year deal worth a guaranteed $84 million that ran through his age-thirty-seven season, past the point where most hitters have begun to decline.

The first year went pretty well; Thome hit . . . and was worth 4.7 WAR, off his pace from his last few seasons with Cleveland but still very productive. He slipped in 2004 to 3.3 WAR, and that's where our story gets interesting, as the Phillies had a somewhat surprising prospect tearing through the minors. Their fifth-round draft pick from 2001 was a husky first baseman from Missouri State University (then known as Southwest Missouri State) named Ryan Howard, and he did two things exceptionally well for a hitter: strike out and hit very long home runs.

To be entirely fair to the Phillies, I don't think anyone saw Ryan

Howard coming—which is amusing, since he's listed at 6'4", 250 pounds, and doesn't move all that fast, so I don't think he's the sort to sneak up on people. The Phils didn't seem to believe that much in his bat; in his first full year in the minors, they left him in low-A at age twenty-two for the whole season, where he hit .280/.367/.460 with 19 homers for the Lakewood BlueClaws, tying for third in the league in home runs behind Walter Young (who, also aged twenty-two, was so big he made Ryan Howard look like Jose Altuve) and phenom Andy Marte.[8] Howard was too old to be left there all season, and as a college product should have at least finished the year at high-A.

In the next season, the Phillies promoted him to high-A Clearwater . . . and again left him there all year, even though he hit fairly well, .304/.374/.514, leading the Florida State League with 23 homers and finishing fourth with 32 doubles. In 2004, they promoted him to double-A Reading, which has long been one of the best parks for home run hitters in the Eastern League, and Howard went off, hitting 37 homers in 102 games for the Reading Phillies, then hitting 9 more in 29 games for triple-A Scranton Wilkes-Barre, and 2 more in a September call-up to the majors for 48 homers on the season in 150 games. Had Howard stayed in double-A, he would certainly have smashed the Eastern League's all-time home run record of 41, which still stands through the 2019 season.

I have omitted one salient point on Howard, however: with those home runs came a lot of strikeouts. Howard finished second in the Sally League in strikeouts in 2002 (behind Julian Benavidez, who never played above double-A), then led the Florida State League in strikeouts in 2003, then finished third in the Eastern League in strikeouts despite leaving that league on July 30 with over a month left in the season. You have to go all the way down to 18th on the Eastern League's strikeout rankings to find the next player who spent any significant time in the majors.

Howard struck out at a rate that, at that time, appeared to be a contraindicator for a player's hit tool. Howard never struck out at a rate below 25 percent, and in both double-A and triple-A he struck out in more than 29 percent of his plate appearances. When Howard struck out in 29.8 percent of the time in double-A, no other player who played even half a season there had a strikeout rate over 25.1 percent. With the benefit of hindsight, we can see that he was an outlier; the players around him on every leaderboard either were unsuccessful in the majors or never sniffed the big leagues at all. At the time, however, I think everyone looked askance at Howard's stat line, figuring it was more likely he wouldn't hit in the majors than that he was the world's biggest unicorn.

The Phillies were helped in their skepticism, however, by the large investment they'd made in their rapidly declining first baseman. Thome's first season as a Phillie was the best season he would have for the remainder of his career, and he'd already shown some slippage at the plate in 2004, his age-thirty-three season. Howard was unproven, and obviously risky, but the Phillies didn't have to pay to acquire him—the cost was playing time, and a roster spot.

They chose to stick with Thome. Howard started 2005 in the minors, while Thome limped to a .203/.347/.304 line in April before his first trip to the disabled list that season. Howard came up for the two-plus weeks while Thome was out, but only started sparingly—the Phillies preferred to slide elite second baseman Chase Utley over to first rather than give Howard regular starts—and returned to triple-A when Thome returned from his injury. Thome only stayed on the active roster for six more weeks, going back on the DL on July 1 and never returning. Howard came up a second time, went 2-for-4 in his first game back, hit .296/.365/.585

with 21 homers the rest of the season, and won the NL Rookie of the Year award. That winter, the Phillies traded Thome to the White Sox to give Howard the full-time first base job; Howard led the NL in homers and RBI the next season, winning the NL MVP award in the process.[9]

There were a lot of factors involved in the decision to play Thome on opening day of 2005, and the subsequent decision to restore him to the starting lineup and demote Howard in late May, beyond just the sunk cost fallacy, but it's clear from contemporary media coverage that Thome's status and contract were important variables. *Sports Illustrated*'s Albert Chen wrote on August 1 of that summer, before Thome had the surgery that ended his season, that if Thome returned from his second DL stint, the Phillies were "expected to keep Howard with the team so they'll have his big bat on their thin bench."[10] That still indicates a preference for the veteran and his contract over Howard, who had just had a very strong July as the starter in Thome's absence, hitting .289/.371/.522 with a 28 percent strikeout rate and reaching base in 21 of his 24 games. Even if the team had more faith in Thome based on past history, the veteran hadn't been productive at all in 2005 and was still dealing with a significant injury. The preference for the established player would have worked against them here, but they were spared the decision by the seriousness of Thome's injury.

Avoiding the sunk cost fallacy in decision-making requires an active accounting of the projected costs and benefits of the decision going forward, omitting costs already expended (and, if applicable, benefits already incurred). It's easier to see if a decision entails throwing good money after bad if you model the potential gains or losses, eliminating those past expenditures from consideration.

Some of the best advice I've seen on avoiding the sunk cost fallacy came from an unexpected source. I'm an avid board gamer and have reviewed games for Paste magazine and other sites for several years now. One of the leading publishers of high-end, critically lauded strategy games is Stonemaier Games, headed by Jamey Stegmaier, who designed games such as Scythe and Charterstone and published the award-winning game Wingspan. Jamey writes often on the Stonemaier site blog, and explained a situation where he fell into the sunk-cost trap by sticking with a vendor he'd used for a long time when the right move was to make a change. He offered a three-step path to getting around the trap:

1. Admit that you have a specific sunk cost issue.
2. Consistently and repeatedly ask yourself if you're happy with the status quo for one week.
3. Act accordingly to the results of your self-survey.[11]

The first step is probably the hardest one, but you can't solve a problem if you don't admit you have it: look for the sunk-cost effect whenever you're making a decision—or deferring making a decision, as Jamey did. Then you can move forward with a rational analysis of alternatives that dispenses with the emotional weight of money, time, or effort already spent—even if someone else spent it—to consider whether you should change providers, end a project, or drive to that basketball game.

# 12

## The Happy Fun Ball

### Optimism Bias and the Problem of Seeing What We Want to See

Do not taunt Happy Fun Ball.[1]

The physical characteristics of the baseball used in MLB began to change after the All-Star break in 2015, leading to a gradual surge in home runs that accelerated in 2019. The Yankees had set the single-season record for home runs by a team in 2018 with 267; *four* teams exceeded that total in 2019, with the Twins and Yankees both crossing the 300 mark. Thirteen teams have accumulated 250 or more homers in one season and seven of those teams did it in 2019.

The problem wasn't limited to the majors. The majors and all affiliated minor leagues had been using different baseballs for several years, but in 2019, the two triple-A leagues switched to using the major-league baseball. As a result, there were more home runs hit in triple-A by the All-Star break in 2019 than there were in triple-A in all of 2018.

Major League Baseball spent most of the first half of the year doing what they did the previous year—denying anything was amiss. They had convened a group of scientists in the spring of 2018 to tell them that everything was fine, but by September 2019, Commissioner Rob Manfred was at least moved to tell *Forbes* writer Maury Brown that "we need to see if we can make some changes that gives us a more predictable, consistent performance from the baseball."[2] That's a tepid response, given how dramatic the effect has been on the field—and remember, for every hitter who's glad he hit an extra home run, there's a pitcher annoyed about it—but it's a start.

The tectonic shift in home run rates around the game poses a quandary for major-league personnel as well. Analysts asked to craft player projections have to grapple with 2019 stats that look nothing like what came before it, and the probability that the baseball itself, and thus league averages and replacement-level baselines, will move in an unknown direction in 2020. If MLB didn't know the baseball was going to be different in 2019, can we assume they will correctly forecast the effects of further changes to the ball? There's hard evidence that the baseballs used in the 2019 postseason differed from those used in the regular season, so which version will the league use in 2020? Scouts must also try to recalibrate their own thinking—what if "average" power doesn't mean what it's meant for the last twenty years? If you predicted that Pete Alonso would hit 37 homers as a rookie, which would itself have been an outstanding total, were you wrong because he hit 53 with the Happy Fun Ball?

This is a trap currently in the making as I write this chapter: Everyone is going into this off-season uncertain of how to evaluate 2019 performances and how to project performances going forward. The default assumption, that all players were equally affected by the altered baseball, is the simplest solution, but doesn't appear to be well supported by the evidence. Individual adjustments for players, however, feels tantamount to throwing darts at a wall and hoping you hit the board. The trap in all this is that the information gap will allow decision-makers to choose what data to believe—a problem known as *optimism bias*, which is just what it sounds like. I want to believe Joey Bagodonuts's spike to 23 home runs in 2019 is real and sustainable, even though he'd never hit more than 6 home runs in any season before. Optimism bias says that people underestimate the probability of negative events and overestimate the probability of positive ones—which likely serves a protective purpose, as otherwise we might never get out of bed in the morning, let alone get on Interstate 95 to drive to work. Unfortunately, bad things do happen, even to good people, and preparing for negative outcomes is part of making good decisions.

The first evidence that the baseball was different in 2019 showed up early, as players were hitting the ball out of the park more often, and often hitting it farther, from the start of the year. MLB saw 1,144 home runs hit through April 30, a record for the season's opening month . . . or for any month, with 25 more homers than MLB saw hit in August 2017. On a per-game basis, it was the fourth-most-homerific month in MLB history.[3,4] May was more of the same, with 1,135 homers in 414 games for a new all-time record of 2.74 homers per game.

The records kept falling; June's rate was higher than May's, and July's higher than June's. Everything peaked in August, with a record 1,228 homers and 2.95 homers per game, both all-time highs. Even a dip in September produced a rate of 2.72 homers per game that was higher than any single month's rate prior to 2019. Meanwhile, Texas's Nomar Mazara tied the all-time Statcast record for home run distance at 505 feet, and the number of home runs projected to have traveled 450 feet or more went up from 82 in 2018 to 183 in 2019, an increase of 123 percent in one year.

What happened? According to Dr. Meredith Wills, an astrophysicist who has discussed the changes to the baseball in multiple columns for the Athletic, the physical characteristics of the baseball have changed at least twice since 2015. The first change, from mid-2015 through the end of 2015, saw an increase in the thickness of the laces on the baseball—Wills is also an avid knitter, and took several baseballs apart to measure the lace thickness—which produced a rounder baseball, reduced the balls' drag coefficient, and may have led to a rise in blister injuries for pitchers.[5]

In 2019, however, the seams' thickness wasn't the issue, but the seams' height was, as they were lower by as much as half. The 2019 baseballs' leather was also much smoother, with Wills finding a reduction in static friction by more than a quarter from the 2018 baseballs. And the 2019 baseballs were slightly rounder. The net result was a significant drop in the drag coefficient of the 2019 baseballs, leading well-struck hits to travel farther, and thus giving us the massive home run surge of 2019 that completely shifted what a typical home run total would look like for an average regular. Here are the number of players who hit at least 20, 25, 30, or 40 home runs in each of the last two seasons, making it stark just how much the thresholds moved in one year:

| Home runs | 2018 | 2019 | % increase |
|---|---|---|---|
| 20 | 100 | 129 | 29% |
| 25 | 48 | 80 | 167% |
| 30 | 27 | 58 | 115% |
| 40 | 3 | 10 | 233% |

Pete Alonso hit 53 homers in 2019, setting the all-time record for a rookie position player, but by WAR he had the third-lowest total value (including defense and position) ever for a player who hit 50 home runs, in large part because, in a world where everyone's hitting more homers, home runs themselves are worth less than they used to be.

Optimism biases are a class of smaller, related cognitive errors that all resolve to us thinking what we want to think. Maybe we pick the forecast that we like the most; maybe we overrate our accuracy in predictions/projections; maybe we overrate our other skills. There's overconfidence bias, where we assume we are better at making predictions and don't accurately estimate the likelihood or range of errors; and the planning fallacy, where decision-makers assume projects will be done sooner than they actually will and/or for a lower cost.

Researchers Neil Weinstein and William Klein opened their 1996 paper called "Unrealistic Optimism: Present and Future" with the blunt yet undeniable statement, "People tend to believe they are better than others."[6] They go on to detail our innate habit of underestimating the likelihood of negative events occurring to us, including how subjects would change their self-reporting of behaviors if it was pointed out to them that such behaviors put them in higher-risk categories.

Awareness of optimism bias goes back at least to 1925, but early research concluded that it was a defense mechanism against anxiety over the uncertainty of future events, not a cognitive error. Kahneman and Tversky later coined the term *planning fallacy* to cover the specific instance of forecasts or plans that "are unrealistically close to best-case scenarios [and] could be improved by consulting the statistics of similar cases."[7]

In general, projecting future performance of professional athletes is a function of determining all of the relevant inputs, such as past performance and age, and using models built on years of prior data to project forward one or more seasons. Such systems will likely miss on significant outliers, players whose performance deviates substantially due to physical or mechanical changes, injuries, or just plain luck, but the goal of a projection system is to project for all players with appropriate error bars, referring to how much variation around the mean projections there should be for each player. If the ground beneath the projections shifts, however, the opportunity for optimism bias becomes wider, because the nature of the baseball itself going forward is uncertain and, in all likelihood, unpredictable.

The rising tide of homers lifted all players, but that doesn't mean it lifted all players equally, nor does it mean that the tide will remain high going forward. If you're trying to project how players will perform going forward—a key component in determining whether to trade or acquire certain players, or how much to pay players you already employ—then what exactly do you do with players like these?[8]

The chart shows the rate at which these players hit balls into play as Barrels, which MLB.com defines as "comparable hit types (in terms of exit velocity and launch angle) [that] have led to a minimum .500 batting average and 1.500 slugging percentage since Statcast was implemented Major League wide in 2015."[9] A Barrel must have an exit velocity of at least 98 mph, and the launch angle range starts at 26–30 degrees and widens as the exit velocity increases.

The Twins have four players here, including Nelson Cruz, who posted the highest slugging percentage of his career at age 38—a late peak worthy of Barry Bonds (who set career slugging highs at 36, 37, and again at 39). The Rays have two players on here whom they acquired from other clubs in 2018. Perhaps those teams are teaching something that helps hitters improve their launch angles

| Name | Team | Barrels/Batted Ball Event | | Increase |
|------|------|------|------|------|
| | | 2018 | 2019 | |
| Mitch Garver | MIN | 5.6% | 15.5% | 9.9% |
| Miguel Sano | MIN | 11.8% | 21.2% | 9.4% |
| Austin Slater | SFG | 2.3% | 10.1% | 7.8% |
| Byron Buxton | MIN | 1.6% | 8.3% | 6.7% |
| Howie Kendrick | WAS | 4.8% | 11.4% | 6.6% |
| Jorge Soler | KCR | 10.3% | 16.9% | 6.6% |
| Rougned Odor | TEX | 7.1% | 13.6% | 6.5% |
| David Freese | LAD | 9.0% | 15.3% | 6.3% |
| Chance Sisco | BAL | 4.3% | 10.4% | 6.1% |
| Austin Meadows | TBR | 6.4% | 12.5% | 6.1% |
| Nelson Cruz | MIN | 13.8% | 19.9% | 6.1% |
| Yandy Diaz | TBR | 4.4% | 10.4% | 6.0% |
| Josh Bell | PIT | 7.0% | 12.7% | 5.7% |
| Jordan Luplow | CLE | 6.8% | 12.1% | 5.3% |
| Roberto Perez | CLE | 5.9% | 11.0% | 5.1% |
| Chris Iannetta | COL | 9.3% | 14.3% | 5.0% |
| JaCoby Jones | DET | 5.9% | 10.7% | 4.8% |
| Eugenio Suarez | CIN | 9.7% | 14.0% | 4.3% |
| Ketel Marte | ARI | 5.0% | 9.3% | 4.3% |
| Marcus Semien | OAK | 4.5% | 8.5% | 4.0% |

(Meadows's went up by 3 full degrees) or otherwise make harder contact—or perhaps it was just the baseball.

Yandy Diaz had one career home run in 299 PA before 2018, then hit 14 homers in half a season before getting hurt in 2019. His average launch angle barely increased and remained in the bottom 10 percent of all MLB hitters, including pitchers. Eugenio Suarez set a career high with 34 homers in 2018, after setting a career high with 26 homers in 2017, and then jumped all the way to 49 homers in 2019, more than doubling his Barrels-batted ball event over two years. His average launch angle did increase to a career high, but his average exit velocity actually went down 2 mph in 2019.

Jorge Soler had his first truly injury-free season in 2019, and more than doubled his career home run total, becoming very much the player the Cubs thought he'd be when they signed him and that I thought he'd become when I first scouted him in the Arizona Rookie League in 2012. But was this a matter of Soler getting healthy, or that the Happy Fun Ball let him post a career-best average exit velocity of 92.6 mph, hitting one of every two balls he put into play at 95 mph or better, so he could hit 48 homers (a Royals franchise record) and 33 doubles? Soler can opt out of his $4 million salary for 2020 this winter and go to salary arbitration—which will have already happened by the time you see this. If you're the Royals, how do you decide how much Soler is likely to be worth next year, knowing that a different baseball in 2020 might have a major impact on his production?

I see players all over this list whose 2019 spikes in Barrel rates or just in home runs look like possible flukes. Some might have come from swing changes. Some could be a matter of getting healthy at the right time. Disentangling the Happy Fun Ball from physical factors that might make these Barrel rate increases sustainable, or from pure random variation, is a major challenge for MLB analysts heading into 2020. Simply buying into Jorge Soler's or Austin Meadows's sudden fulfillment of their long-awaited potential without considering how "real" it is going forward would be the aforementioned optimism bias: believing that, yes, your player's breakout is going to last, without considering that some percentage of these players' power spikes are going to disappear the moment MLB discontinues use of the Happy Fun Ball.

In a similar vein, a scouting director asked me in July, after noting that massive increase in the home run totals in triple-A, "how am I supposed to scout these guys?" Even the International

League, which generally has lower offensive stats than the Pacific Coast League because of the latter's many ballparks in the Rocky Mountains, saw 29 hitters reach at least 20 homers in 2019, with three hitters topping 30 bombs. In 2018, just five hitters reached 20 homers and the league leader hit 23. If you've been scouting triple-A hitters for several years, your internal calibration of what average or good power looks like for that level of baseball is suddenly way off. And what do you do if you scout levels below triple-A, where leagues were still using a different baseball with higher drag coefficients? How accurate might your predicted home run totals be for a player you evaluate in A-ball when he'll be hitting an entirely different baseball in the majors? There's no bias here, just a greater level of uncertainty than we've encountered in baseball since the so-called "rabbit ball" year of 1987, when home runs spiked across the majors—Wade Boggs hit 24 homers that year, and never hit more than 11 in any other year in his career—and MLB also denied that anything was different about the baseball. Scouts' jobs are hard enough without telling them to scout players using one baseball and predict how good they'll be with another baseball.

The 2019 postseason just added to the confusion; MLB denied that they'd done anything to alter the baseballs for the playoffs, saying in a statement that "balls that are used in the postseason are pulled from the same batches as balls used in the regular season. Regular season and postseason balls are manufactured with the same materials and under the same processes." That didn't line up with the physical results of balls hit into play in the postseason, which point to different physical characteristics in the baseball itself. It's as if teams have to prepare three sets of projections for next season: one with the Happy Fun Ball, one with the "de-juiced" playoff ball, and perhaps one in between the two.

# 13

## Good Decisions™

### Baseball Executives Talk About Their Thought Processes Behind Smart Trades and Signings

So far in this book, I've described numerous bad decisions or mistakes that people at all levels of the game of baseball have made because they fell prey to various cognitive biases or illusions—ones that we all endure and for which we must learn to compensate so we can make better decisions going forward. The history of baseball has plenty of good decisions as well, including ones that looked questionable or outright wrong to outsiders at the time but that worked out in the end. I spoke to numerous front office executives, past and present, to solicit ideas for decisions that succeeded against initial expectations, and several were kind enough to speak to me about their own experiences in that line. Here are just a few of the better stories I heard about actual

Good Decisions™ from various general managers and why they made those choices even when the outside view was that their choices were wrong.

When Alex Anthopoulos was first named the general manager of the Toronto Blue Jays in October 2009, one of his first orders of business was to trade Roy Halladay, one of the greatest players to ever wear the Blue Jays' uniform and the team's most popular player at the time, because he was going to become a free agent the following off-season. It was not a situation for the faint of heart, but Anthopoulos pulled off what appeared to be a good trade in terms of value received, dealing Halladay two months later to the Phillies for three prospects who were all former first-round picks.[1] Two of those prospects didn't work out; the third, Travis d'Arnaud, never quite worked out, either, but the Jays used him in a later trade for pitcher R. A. Dickey.

After Anthopoulos's first full season as general manager, he faced a new dilemma around another player heading into his walk year. Jose Bautista had been drafted by the Pittsburgh Pirates, bounced through three other organizations,[2] returned to the Pirates, and then headed to Toronto in a minor trade in August 2008 while Bautista was back in triple-A. The Blue Jays called Bautista up to the majors to finish 2008, but he hit .214/.237/.411 in 21 games and wasn't even a lock to make the club to start the next season.

After a strong April in 2009, he regressed to his usual level of hints of production, with some good on-base skills, but low batting averages. Through August 25, he was hitting .227/.352/.318 with just 3 homers in 258 plate appearances—a very good on-base percentage with nothing else to go with it.

I didn't pick August 25 out of thin air; the next day, as the story goes, he had a conversation with Vernon Wells that led him to change his approach at the plate, particularly his timing. From that date forward, he hit .248/.345/.560 and hit 10 HR, all of which came in September. It was unlike anything he'd ever done before, but it was a small sample and came against expanded rosters in September, a time period baseball executives have long known to distrust: never base evaluations off spring training or September.

In 2010, however, Bautista hit like that all season, going from someone who didn't hit enough to play regularly to a legitimate star and MVP candidate at age twenty-nine, later than most players hit their peak. Bautista hit .260/.378/.617 that year, led the majors with 54 homers—still the fourth-highest mark since Barry Bonds set the all-time record in 2001 with 73 homers—and generated 7 WAR, good for eighth best in the American League. Bautista came into that season at exactly 0 WAR (per Baseball-Reference), so he'd been a replacement-level player through his age-twenty-eight season, and then became a top ten player in the league, making his first All-Star team and coming in fourth place in American League MVP balloting.

After that season, the Blue Jays still controlled Bautista's rights for one more year. They could go to salary arbitration with him, or negotiate a one-year deal beforehand, and he'd then leave as a free agent after the season. They didn't want to let him leave for nothing, so they faced two options: sign him to a long-term deal or trade him. While Anthopoulos explored his trade market, he ultimately chose to sign Bautista to a five-year extension.

The industry reaction to the contract, in general, was disbelief. It looked like they'd made an expensive five-year bet on a player who'd had just one good year and was already thirty years old. I panned the deal, and so did many others in the media and inside MLB front offices. We were wrong; the deal worked out spectacularly, and if anything it was a bargain considering how good

Bautista became. This is how Anthopoulos, with the help of his front office, decided that buying into Bautista's most recent season wasn't just recency bias, but a real change in the player—and he made that decision with data.

"We didn't celebrate it after" the deal was signed, Anthopoulos says now. "By no means did we celebrate it, or think it would work as well as it did, for all parties. We felt like we were dragged to that number.

"If you look at the timing of that deal, it was the off-season of 2010–11," which featured a number of big-name sluggers as free agents, including third baseman Adrian Beltre, outfielder Adam Dunn, and DH Victor Martinez. Their eventual contracts would affect Bautista and the Jays in two separate ways: Bautista, as a player with five full years of service, could compare himself to those free agents in a salary arbitration hearing that February; and he would likely ask for comparable or higher salaries to theirs when he did become a free agent.

Beltre was the best of the group—he's going to end up in the Hall of Fame, and he had just come off a tremendous season with Boston—and, in Anthopoulos's words, "he played out the market," waiting until late January and signing a five-year deal with Texas that guaranteed him $80 million, or $16 million per year. The month before, Dunn had signed a four-year, $56 million deal with the Chicago White Sox, while Martinez signed a four-year, $50 million deal with Detroit. Dan Uggla was Bautista's peer by service time, one year away from free agency, and signed a five-year, $62 million deal with Atlanta after the team acquired him in trade. (Beltre's deal worked out well for his new club, but Dunn's and Uggla's were disasters, while Martinez played well in three years and missed one season due to injury.)

Those salaries—$16 million for Beltre, $14 million for Dunn, $12.5 million for Martinez, $12.4 million for Uggla—all defined the potential market for Bautista as a free agent. He'd be unlikely to sign an extension for anything less than Uggla's deal, and while Beltre was undoubtedly the better player, he also signed his new deal off one all-star season that looked like it could be an outlier. Bautista had every reason to shoot for $15 million a year or more.

"We knew we had an organizational decision to make on him. He was walking into the last year of the deal. It changed the direction of the franchise," recalls Anthopoulos. "We went north of Uggla, above Dunn and Martinez, and just under Beltre as a free agent."

The timing of Bautista's year added another dimension to the decision. Anthopoulos recalled, "2010 was my first year, and we were just into a rebuild. All of a sudden, Bautista has a huge 2010 with one year of control left. He was twenty-nine at the time going into age-thirty season. What are we doing with him? Keep him, trade him, rebuild around him?"

The decision to keep him came down to weighing the risk that the one year (plus a month, if we're being precise) was a fluke against the potential that it was real, which would argue for re-signing him to retain that newfound value. While the Jays weren't going to spend recklessly, they chose to try to keep him.

"We bought into the performance. We thought the swing changes were real. We had exit velocities even back then, and they were fantastic—they were a big part of the decision-making. He had good on-base skills. And he took care of himself."

Anthopoulos and his front office, whom he credited repeatedly for their input into this decision, identified multiple factors, some backed with hard data, that supported the belief that Bautista's breakout year wasn't a fluke, and thus that giving him an expensive new contract was a rational choice rather than a function of recency bias.

First, Bautista had changed key parts of his swing and mechanical approach the previous August. The Blue Jays' coaching staff, including manager Cito Gaston, hitting coach Gene Tenace, and first base coach Dwayne Murphy, had been working with Bautista all season to improve his timing at the plate after noticing that he was consistently late, especially against good velocity. "He was late, with a big leg lift, so he would oftentimes foul balls off to the right side," recalls Anthopoulos. "Before the middle of August [2009], his numbers weren't good—he didn't have any power, and was just fouling everything off to the right side. He couldn't click," even though Gaston set up pregame drills where he'd have whoever was throwing batting practice throw harder than normal to Bautista. Gaston would stand behind the cage and "he would tell Bautista 'Now!'" to try to get the player to start his hands (and thus his swing) sooner.

Bautista was still having trouble making the adjustment and, according to Anthopoulos, was voicing his frustration over his swing in the clubhouse before a game that August when Vernon Wells, who had a neighboring locker, offered some simple advice. "Vernon said, 'Look, just go embarrass yourself, as early as you think you're being. If you're that frustrated, just totally overexaggerate the whole thing,'" recalls Anthopoulos. That night, August 26, Bautista doubled off the wall—his first extra-base hit that entire month—and he stayed with the new approach, trying to get the bat head to the ball earlier so he would have a chance to pull it rather than letting the ball travel and hitting to the opposite field all the time. The change stuck through that huge 2010 season.

Second, the Blue Jays had hard data in the form of exit velocity, which is widespread now thanks to MLB's installation of Statcast equipment in all major-league parks and individual teams' investment in similar technology at most minor-league stadiums. Exit velocity is just what it sounds like—the speed of a ball as it leaves the hitter's bat. The Blue Jays could see that his exit velocities were "fantastic," according to Anthopoulos, and it served as tangible evidence that Bautista's swing changes were yielding different results on batted balls.

Third, the Jays considered other position players who had somewhat similar skill sets to Bautista and looked at how those players aged into their mid-thirties—especially hitters who, like Bautista, were patient and drew a lot of walks even in their twenties. Anthopoulos specifically cited Bobby Abreu, who remained an above-average hitter through his age-thirty-six season in 2010, and who had finished in the top ten in his leagues in walks in nine out of the last twelve years. Abreu never had Bautista's raw power, but did hit a ton of doubles, with 41 at age thirty-six that previous year. The group looked at all historical comparables, asking "how many 29–30 year olds have that type of season and are able to sustain it for an extended period of the time," Anthopoulos said, and the answer, while not definitive, pushed them further toward a deal.

And finally, the Blue Jays felt that Bautista's own character, often referred to as "makeup" in baseball jargon, made him a better bet than most players with his profile. Anthopoulos specifically cites Bautista's work ethic, including how he worked to keep himself in the best possible shape, as one mitigating factor against the risk that might normally come with signing a player into his thirties, as well as Bautista's intelligence and competitiveness. "He was very smart, very competitive, very driven, had a fierce belief in himself," he says. "After he signed the deal, I saw him in the clubhouse. He said, 'Are you worried? Do you see this body?'"

One additional factor unrelated to Bautista himself was the situation the Jays were in. Anthopoulos had just begun a rebuilding effort, having traded a franchise icon in Halladay, and now potentially faced another, similar decision with Bautista. He explored the trade market but found only tepid interest, surmising that the industry was "skeptical" because Bautista had only performed like this for one year. "The only club that showed strong interest at the time was Detroit," he says. "Dave Dombrowski was the general manager at the time. He was aggressive and quick, and said, 'we're in, we have interest,' and he made some good players available." In the end, however, the Jays chose to keep Bautista and try to re-sign him because, if his 2010 season was his new normal, acquiring another player like him would be difficult. "We had a do-over with a player that's hard to acquire. You don't know that you're going to get another chance to get a Halladay-type or Delgado-type player," referring to two of the best players in Jays history, neither of whom ever played in a playoff game for Toronto.

The Jays had another problem heading into that winter—Vernon Wells's contract, which was due to pay the outfielder about $68 million over the next three seasons, the tail end of a seven-year extension the Jays had given him (under previous management) in 2006. The team's limited budget under the ownership of the Rogers Corporation would make it difficult to pay Bautista what he'd demand on an extension, pay Wells what he was owed, and still assemble a competitive team around them. In the first three years after signing the new deal, Wells's production had fallen off dramatically, averaging just 1.4 WAR over those seasons, but he'd had a better year in 2010 at age thirty-one, with 44 doubles, 31 homers, and a 4.0 WAR total for the year—nearly equaling what he did the prior three seasons. That was enough for the Angels to come calling and agree to take on most of Wells's contract in exchange for Juan Rivera and Mike Napoli, whom the Jays almost immediately traded for reliever Frank Francisco. (That second deal didn't work out so well for the Jays.) Anthopoulos cleared about $21 million from his 2011 payroll in one fell swoop, and thus doing a deal with Bautista became much more feasible, especially since the player had started out the talks by asking for a deal in the vicinity of $100 million.

Bautista's side had filed a request in arbitration for $10 million, while the Jays had filed at $8 million. The Jays were hoping to do a three-or four-year deal, while Bautista's side wanted a longer contract, which led the two sides to converge on five years, covering his last year of arbitration (which would be about $9 million, given where the two sides filed) plus four years of free agency at a price that, in theory, would be close enough to the market to satisfy Bautista while providing the Jays a slight discount for guaranteeing this money. It helped that the free-agent market that winter had also settled on four- to five-year deals as the standard for players of Bautista's caliber, and put upper and lower bounds on the average annual salary (often called AAV, for average annual value). The Jays were determined not to match Beltre's $16 million AAV, while Bautista was unlikely to take anything below Martinez and Uggla's.

The two sides still hadn't agreed on a deal when they reached the arbitration hearing room; the Jays had decided that once the hearing began, they would end negotiations on a long-term contract. It nearly broke down over what turned out to be a trivial difference in the dollar figures—"We almost walked away from the deal over $1 million," Anthopoulos recalls—but the Jays agreed to add an option year with a $1 million buyout that brought the total value to $65 million over five years.

The immediate reaction was unkind to Anthopoulos and the Jays, as everyone, myself included, feared they'd fallen into the recency bias trap and overrated the outlier year because it had just happened, rather than considering Bautista's age and larger body of work. Anthopoulos remembers having doubts even a few days after the deal, and hearing criticism from rival agents who called to express their shock and from members of the media. Bautista homered on opening day, homered again two days later, hit .366/.532/.780 in April, and ended up having the best year of his career. He led the American League in homers, walks, and slugging percentage, was second in on-base percentage, and was second in the league in WAR with 8.3. He produced almost 28 WAR over the four years, then 1.1 more in the option year (which the Jays exercised), and had one of the most epic bat-flips in MLB history after homering against Texas in the 2015 AL Division Series.

Anthopoulos and his front office recognized the possibility that they were falling prey to recency bias, and instead looked for additional data to inform their decision, most of which ended up corroborating the superficial data on Bautista's one big season and led the GM to agree to sign the player. "A few of the guys [in the front office] would not have done it, or were uncomfortable with it," Anthopoulos remembers. "We ultimately chose to do this, but I said, 'I don't want you to think that because we did choose to do it that your opinions didn't matter. Don't stop giving me your opinion just because I didn't go with you this one time. Someone has to break the tie.' I didn't want the people who were uneasy with it to think that, oh, they went the other way, I'm not in good standing. As a GM you need both sides of the argument."

Dave Dombrowski, longtime GM for the Florida Marlins, Detroit Tigers, and most recently the Boston Red Sox, faced a similar quandary when he took over the Tigers during their moribund 119-loss season in 2003, the worst record ever for any team that wasn't in its first year of existence. (The New York Mets lost

120 games in 1962, but they were an expansion team, and the expansion drafts at the time barely gave the new franchises any shot at acquiring major-league talent.) Dombrowski set about remaking the club in the 2004 season, signing Ivan "Pudge" Rodriguez, now in the Hall of Fame, as a free agent after the 2003 season, when Pudge was on the World Series–winning Marlins. The club also drafted second in the June 2004 draft and took Justin Verlander, now at 70 WAR and still going strong as I write this. The top prospect in their system going into that season, outfielder Curtis Granderson, hit .303/.407/.515 for double-A Erie and made his major-league debut that September. You could see glimmers of hope on the horizon, but going from 119 losses to playoff contention is usually a slow process, and Dombrowski and Tigers owner Mike Ilitch wanted to accelerate it.

Dombrowski decided to go after a surprising target in free agency in the off-season following the 2004 campaign: White Sox outfielder Magglio Ordoñez, who was thirty-one years old and not far removed from a serious knee injury that required two surgeries. The safe betting was that he was past his offensive prime and more likely to miss time as he got older.

One major reason he chose to target another expensive, veteran hitter, even one whose age might have deterred them from chasing him, was that Dombrowski, with Ilitch's support, was trying to accelerate their rebuild and avoid a long stretch of losing seasons. "We were not very good. We were trying to build talent back in the organization. In addition to the big-league level, there wasn't a great deal of premium talent at the minor-league level," says Dombrowski. *Baseball America*'s list of the Tigers' top ten prospects going into 2005 would support that statement: The list had Granderson, the just-drafted Verlander, and hard-throwing Joel Zumaya, but their number two prospect, Kyle Sleeth, missed all of 2005 with injury and never recovered, while only one of the remaining six names on the list (Ryan Raburn) had more than a cup of coffee in the majors. They had two future All-Stars, but very little depth behind those guys.

Dombrowski and his front office felt that Ordoñez's specific skill set as a hitter would age better than most hitters do, given his contact rates and propensity for hitting for average. "I understand the aging curve, but also when you have premium hitters, they age a little bit differently. We thought he was that type of hitter, a premium hitter who made contact but had power, not a huge power hitter but a big doubles hitter who hit with power; we found when we looked at those types of guys, it was a comfortable age period." The Tigers' brass felt that, given historical comps for this hitting profile, the years the contract would cover would be relatively safe for Ordoñez, where he'd decline some but not as abruptly as most hitters do.

Ordoñez's injury also presented an opportunity to the Tigers, where they could get him on a one-year trial basis, and if the injury recurred or just kept him off the field, they could walk away. "There was definitely risk involved. With the research we did—he went overseas to get treatment—his representative Scott Boras gave us the info that we asked for and our doctors looked at it. The contract was written that if he didn't come out of year one healthy we could void it. We did the same thing with Pudge the year before. We were in a spot where there was risk but it was a one-year risk on a good player. If he came out of the first year healthy, it meant the surgery worked and we would have been fine." The contract didn't cover performance risk per se, but if Ordoñez wasn't healthy enough to play regularly in year one the Tigers had an escape clause.

Dombrowski's longtime strategy with free agents and substantial trades, which he's shown everywhere he's been a general manager, is to target stars, and try to fill the remainder of the roster with internal options or other less expensive players. He'd later trade prospects to the Marlins to acquire Miguel Cabrera and Dontrelle Willis, then pulled off a trade with Tampa Bay where he dealt just one prospect and some fringe major-league talent to acquire David Price. As GM of the Red Sox, he signed Price as a free agent, then traded two of the team's top prospects for Chris Sale, moves that helped Boston win the World Series in 2018. Of that strategy, he says, "I do think you have to realize when you're signing guys like Pudge and Magglio, there is a greater risk that this doesn't last for quite as long. I'd rather take that gamble on premium talent compared to signing another average guy."

On the morning of July 31, 2004, the Boston Red Sox had a record of 56–45, 7.5 games behind the AL East–leading Yankees and a half game behind the Oakland A's for the lone wildcard playoff spot. It's not where the Sox, who had come within five outs of a pennant the year before, wanted to be that late in the season, so GM Theo Epstein, still just thirty years old at the time, decided to make a trade that would alter the future of the franchise.

The deal, which stunned Boston fans and, I think, much of the baseball world, involved four teams, but the crux was that it sent Red Sox star shortstop Nomar Garciaparra and prospect Matt Murton to the Chicago Cubs in exchange for Twins first baseman Doug Mientkiewicz and Expos (RIP) shortstop Orlando Cabrera. Garciaparra had only played 38 games in the first four months of 2004 due to a nagging injury to one of his Achilles tendons (I blame Thetis), but he had been worth nearly 13 WAR in total over the previous two seasons, leading Boston in both of those years. He'd led the American League in batting average in 1999 and 2000, missed most of 2001 due to injury, but returned at about

90 percent of his prior level of production, and was still only thirty years old, young enough to think he could stay productive for a while. And he was a huge fan favorite.

Garciaparra was an impending free agent, which likely increased Epstein's willingness to explore a trade, but there was a bigger, evidence-based logic behind the decision. Nomar was widely regarded as a superstar because of his offensive production and because of the way people saw him play defense—he had a strong arm and would make defensive plays described as spectacular.

The Red Sox' front office believed that was illusory. The evidence they had, which was more detailed and comprehensive than the anecdotal looks that outsiders like fans or media members had, said that Nomar's defense was quite poor. Epstein explained the trade to reporters the next day by referring to the Red Sox' overall defense as a "fatal flaw," saying, "we've made our club more functional. We weren't going to win a World Series with our defense."[3]

I spoke at length to someone who was a member of Boston's front office at the time of the trade, who said specifically that the fatal flaw was their infield defense—and Garciaparra, who wasn't as good as people believed when he was healthy, was actively hurting the club on the field while he was hobbled by his Achilles' injury. His lateral range was extremely limited and his throwing had suffered as well. As a result, the team's internal defensive metrics, advanced for the time but quite crude compared to today's analytical tools, showed Nomar was the worst defensive shortstop in the majors that year by a substantial margin, "worse than everyone by a couple standard deviations," according to the former executive. With Kevin Millar, a well below-average defender at first, also on the infield, the trade allowed Boston to upgrade two spots in one move, turning a major liability into a strength by adding plus defenders at shortstop and first base.

The trade also sent away one of Boston's top prospects just a year after he was a first-round draft pick, when his perceived value in the industry was still quite high. Murton was the 32nd overall pick in the 2003 draft, had begun the 2004 season with high-A Sarasota, and had hit .301/.372/.452 before the trade, a very solid performance for his first full year in pro ball, with a promising on-base percentage and the hope of future power. It turned out that the 13 homers Murton hit in 2004, including those he hit after the trade, would be a career high; he never hit more than that until he left the United States to play in Japan, where he became something of a star, setting the NPB[4] record for hits in a single season in 2010, leading the Central League in batting average in 2014, and playing six seasons as a regular for the Hanshin Tigers. The Red Sox believed that Murton's swing path didn't put the ball in the air enough—a precursor to the current emphasis on optimizing a hitter's launch angle—for him to get to the power a corner outfielder needs to have. They were right, and the industry was late to adjust.

As it turns out, none of the teams in the transaction other than the Red Sox fared very well. The Cubs ended up with Murton and two months of Garciaparra. The Twins got one minor-league pitcher, Justin Jones, who never got out of double-A. The Expos, who would move to Washington for the next season, got three players, all of whom were worth less than replacement level for the team. It was a controversial move at the time, one Red Sox fans seemed to hate when it was made, but I'm pretty sure everyone supported the trade three months later after the team won its first World Series in eighty-six years.

The Red Sox made a number of good, data-driven decisions under Epstein, especially in the first few years of his tenure, while the majority of major-league front offices continued to operate under an older playbook that eschewed any modern thinking in favor of the old-school modus operandi. The 2004 season not only ended that franchise's World Series drought, but brought in a new player who'd be instrumental to their next championship as well.

Dustin Pedroia won the 2007 American League Rookie of the Year and the 2008 AL Most Valuable Player awards in his first two full seasons in the majors. He made four All-Star teams, played for two World Series–winning teams, and, as of this writing, has amassed more than 50 career WAR thanks to a .299/.365/.439 career line and often terrific defense at second base.

Yet when the Red Sox selected him with their first pick in the 2004 draft, taking him in the second round with the 65th overall selection, much of the industry laughed. Pedroia was a great college performer for Arizona State, but he checked very few of the boxes that traditional scouts used to evaluate players. He was a shortstop for the Sun Devils, but lacked the range or the arm to stay at that position in pro ball. He was a well-below-average runner. He didn't appear to have much home run power. And, perhaps worst of all, he just didn't look like a big leaguer: he's about 5'6", and wasn't in great physical shape.

"He was chubby for a 5'6" kid," remembers Jason McLeod, the Red Sox scouting director in 2004, who chose Pedroia with the first ever draft pick he had as the man in charge of the amateur drafts for Boston. (McLeod's run as director would also include the selections of Jacoby Ellsbury, Jed Lowrie, Clay Buchholz, Justin Masterson, Josh Reddick, and Anthony Rizzo.) "I remember going to watch Pedroia at Arizona State. At that time, ASU was wearing the baggy uniforms and the players used to wear their pants knee high. For a guy who's 5'6" and not cut up, the unis did not look good on him," he said with a laugh.

The Red Sox were fully aware of the questions around Pedroia, many of which revolved around his grades in the five scouting tools: hitting, hitting for power, running, fielding, and throwing. Pedroia was clearly below average in the last four, and as an undersized middle infielder, his slow foot speed was like a cardinal sin to pro scouts. The reason Pedroia ended up with Boston was how strongly they believed in his first tool, his ability to hit, and the two ways they supported that belief.

"Looking at our follow reports, and evaluations of the player, we did not think he was ultra-toolsy other than very high grades on the bat," McLeod says. "We even underestimated his super, super-elite hand eye and contact, and I know at that time we were looking at it. We probably didn't realize just how impressive it was at the time that he'd had more extra-base hits than strikeouts." Pedroia managed that feat in his last two seasons at ASU, with an XBH to K ratio above 3 in his sophomore year.

Pedroia's performance history was the second reason why the Red Sox felt like they could discard the conventional wisdom and take Pedroia with their first pick. In three seasons for Arizona State—admittedly, a good environment for hitters—Pedroia hit .386/.466/.544, with 91 extra-base hits, 108 walks, and just 47 strikeouts. College statistics are subject to lots of noise, including some extreme hitting environments and inconsistent competition (the pitching you face on a Tuesday isn't as good as what you'll typically face on a Friday), but Pedroia had three strong years of production, and nothing in his underlying data indicated that it might not be "real" or sustainable. He'd also played on the U.S. collegiate national team for two summers, using a wood bat rather than the aluminum bats college players used at the time, and was still a very tough hitter to strike out, fanning in under 10 percent of his PA. (Also, the U.S. national team coaches had him sacrifice bunting constantly. I thought people went to college to get smarter.)

McLeod also credits the work his staff did on understanding

Pedroia's makeup, calling the player the "fiercest competitor" that he's ever been around in twenty years in the industry. He offers one anecdote from after Pedroia reached the majors as an example of his single-minded focus on winning: "We're in Texas in late August, and I'm on the trip with the team, sitting in the dugout making calls around six-thirtyish. Dustin comes out [of the club-house] and he's the only player in there. He's walking up and down the dugout, checking his batting gloves, getting ready for the game by himself. The PA guy starts doing the pregame announcements and the first thing he says is, 'Welcome to the Ballpark in Arling-ton, home of your Texas Rangers!' Dustin gets on the top step and shouts to the crowd, 'Home of the team that's gonna get their fuckin' asses kicked tonight!' And he did it with a snarl on his face. I'm like, damn, bro, it's a Monday night in August!"

When it came to that year's draft, the Red Sox lined up their top thirty players, even though they didn't pick until No. 65, and Pedroia was on it. "He was the easy guy to say, 'who looks like that in the big leagues,'" says McLeod, recalling one of the most common objections to Pedroia as a prospect—the lack of compa-rable players in the majors at the time. Even today, in 2019, there is only one MLB regular with a listed height of 5'6" or below, the speedy Astros second baseman Jose Altuve. "We felt great about the bat and great about his makeup. We felt that as a second base-man he was going to gobble up everything that was hit to him. We thought he'd get the bat to the ball and to be able to move the ball around the field, so he'd hit for average."

As the Red Sox' first pick approached, Pedroia was still avail-able, as was catcher Kurt Suzuki, ranked just behind Pedroia on Boston's draft board. Suzuki was a true catcher, projected to stay at the position—and he did, still catching in the majors in 2019. There's safety in a catcher who can handle the position defen-sively, as the offensive bar he has to clear to be a major leaguer is quite low. Theo Epstein, Boston's GM at the time, asked the team's draft room, which included McLeod, his predecessor David Chadd, and the team's top scouts, how certain they were that they wanted the diminutive ASU infielder over a surefire catcher. "Give Theo credit," McLeod says now. "He kept at it over those next two to three picks [before Boston's selection]. He made sure that that was our conviction in the player, saying, 'You're telling me we're going to take him and move him to second base, so he's really going to have to fucking hit.'" (Oakland took Suzuki two picks after Boston took Pedroia.)

The story doesn't quite end there. Pedroia zoomed through the minor leagues, and continued to make a lot of contact and rarely strike out; he had more extra-base hits than strikeouts at every stop in the minors except for his first stint for triple-A Pawtucket, although he remedied that when he returned to the PawSox the next year. But when Pedroia reached the majors in September 2006, he looked overmatched, and his soft body, described to me at the time by one scout as "dumpy," didn't fit on a field full of athletes.

"We heard a lot of the mocking of that, people calling him an Oompa Loompa or a midget," says McLeod. I remember sitting in Fenway with the scouts for one of those games in 2006, and when Pedroia hit a weak single to right field, one of the scouts near me said, "A grown man hit that ball," with enough acid in his voice to dissolve the seats beneath us. It wasn't until May 2007 that Pedroia finally started to hit, having spent the previous off-season getting himself into major-league shape, and once he started he didn't stop for a decade.

One thing that everyone—and I am definitely included in this group—missed on Pedroia was his exceptional hand-eye coordination, which is why he was able to foul off many pitches he couldn't hit hard into play. "He'd spoil a lot of those sliders off the dish and then the pitcher would come back with 95 up and in and he'd turn it around and rifle it off the wall. The way he turned around pitches was ridiculous," says McLeod. Improved data sources have made it easier for teams to track and analyze that kind of data, but the first step is recognizing that this is information worth looking at in the first place, and the Red Sox identified Pedroia's exceptional hitting skills better than anyone else at the time.

How good was the Pedroia pick? Through the end of the 2019 season, only one other player from the 2004 draft class, number two overall pick Justin Verlander, has had a more productive MLB career than Pedroia, with Verlander at 71 WAR and likely going to the Hall of Fame someday. Pedroia's career WAR total—and as I write this, there's a good chance he's done as a major leaguer due to injuries—is higher than those of the top player from the second round in 2003 and the top player from the second round in 2005 combined. McLeod, Chadd, area scout Dan Madsen, and Boston's fledgling analytics department of the time made what the industry saw as a risky call, but felt they had the data and the subjective evaluations to justify it.

After the 2011 season, the Cardinals faced a difficult decision with Albert Pujols, who had become one of the best and most beloved players in the franchise's long history, and who was heading to free agency after finishing a seven-year, $100 million–plus contract he'd signed before his fourth season in the majors. The deal turned out to be a screaming bargain for the team, as Pujols was worth 66 WAR just in those seven seasons, winning three MVP awards, finishing second in two other seasons, and capping it off by hitting three homers in the 2011 World Series, the Cardinals' second championship over the course of the deal. But Pujols was about to turn thirty-two that winter, and the market was willing to pay him past his age-forty season.

The Cardinals' GM at the time, John Mozeliak, says it was a difficult decision for myriad reasons, including Pujols's importance to the team and the community over his eleven years with St. Louis. "We don't look at something like this in a vacuum. That negotiation was one that we did in part want to try to find a way to re-sign him, but we also recognized where we were in the marketplace relative to our competitors on what we should be spending or not spending in that arena. Ultimately we had to come to a point where if we couldn't get it done, it wasn't for a lack of effort, it was just that the market moved. As you can imagine, whenever you're negotiating these types of players that have that type of legacy to your community and your team, all of that gets factored in; in the end you have to have the discipline, to be able to move on, if you have to."

One of the factors they did include was their internal projections on Pujols's production going forward, a model developed and overseen under Sig Mejdal, then a senior analyst in their baseball operations department and now the assistant general manager of the Baltimore Orioles. "We couldn't make the math come close to working," given the length and size of the deal in question, recalls Mejdal, who also worked for the Houston Astros and was instrumental in the team's rise from worst to first between 2012 and 2017. Mozeliak adds that "you can run that model out with some confidence, to those out years, based on the aging curve, but I will say that any time you're talking about contracts in length over six years, your confidence when someone's entering free agency at thirty-two is not what it might be when you're thinking about a player at twenty-two."

The market didn't see it that way; the Angels, who ultimately did sign Pujols, were willing to go to ten years, as were at least two other teams, including the Marlins (who, according to published reports at the time, wouldn't include a no-trade clause). The Angels landed Pujols with the highest total pretax offer, $254 million, and didn't try to defer money as the Cardinals did. At the time, the Cardinals were disappointed to lose Pujols, according to Mozeliak, saying that the "push/pull" of the decision included the hard-to-quantify value of a player like Pujols, who was such a fan favorite and active in the community, which doesn't add wins to the team but has some financial value to the franchise as a whole.

In the end, however, the market moved to a point where the Cardinals couldn't justify the required investment, based on the projections that their internal model had for Pujols's production going forward. He was entering his age-thirty-two season, and had shown some signs he might be declining even in 2011, his worst offensive performance by any measure in any of his eleven seasons to that point. It turns out that even the Cardinals' model and offer (about $220 million, but with much of it deferred) were optimistic: as I've detailed, the Pujols contract has been disastrous for the Angels, as he's been worth only 13.7 WAR in the first eight years of the deal and has taken up playing time they might have better spent on other, less famous players. The Cardinals, meanwhile, filled the void with many internal options in the years after Pujols left, with Matt Carpenter, Matt Adams, and Jose Martinez among the players to man first base in the interim, and Paul Goldschmidt, the first regular from outside of their system to play first base regularly since 2011 when the team traded for him before the 2019 season. None of his replacements were as productive as Pujols was in his last year for the Cardinals, but the team put the money they might have spent on him into other players on the roster, reaching the playoffs for the next four years after he left, including one more National League pennant in 2013. The emotion-driven choice would have been to keep Pujols at any cost, but they made their decision on rational grounds, and it worked out even better than they had reason to expect.

# Conclusion

For someone who just wrote a book about how humans can make better decisions, I've made a lot of bad decisions myself. I'm also human—I have DNA evidence to prove this—and fall prey to all of the traps I've mentioned in this book and more. I'm as prone to emotional bias and wishful thinking as anyone. I always try to think and expect the best of other people, which is neither rational nor realistic. I can fall into a Panglossian belief that all is for the best or live by Micawber's expectation that something will turn up.

That might be okay for your philosophy of life, or at least something you can write in some rococo font and post to Pinterest, but it's no way to run your business or even manage your own financial plan. Making better decisions anywhere in life is a function of asking the right questions, every time. Critical analysis is not natural to humans; imagine how long our species would have lasted had early man decided to stop to calculate different scenarios to better evaluate the risks of various strategies while being chased by a wooly mammoth at the start of the Holocene period. Fortunately, you are unlikely to be chased by an enormous mammal at any point in your life, and you will often have the benefit of time when making large or significant decisions. Identifying the questions you must ask and the data or evidence you will need is the first step in decision-making, and you can do that more effectively once you're aware of the pitfalls posed by the cognitive biases and illusions I've cited in this book.

Baseball, and sportsball in general, is perfect fodder for this kind of thinking because it's awash in data—if anything, Major League Baseball teams right now have too much data, and run the risk of "ransacking" it, to borrow Gary Smith's phrase, to find spurious correlations—because when your data set is that large, there will be statistically significant relationships that don't pass the common-sense sniff test. It could mean certain teams will chase illusory advantages within games or in the draft or elsewhere, because their R&D folks find correlations in these massive data sets that don't hold up when tested against new data. But that also means there's little excuse for general managers in 2020 to let the kind of cognitive errors I described in this book determine major decisions—and the same could be said of other executives, writers, and even fans who want to understand more about what they're seeing on and off the field.

I hope that *The Inside Game* has at least explained these concepts clearly enough, with fun examples, that you'll be able to spot these own cognitive biases when they crop up in your life, at home or at work. Companies have made multimillion-dollar mistakes by ignoring the sunk cost fallacy or using only the most recent data to drive large decisions; individuals can do the same, like pouring money into renovating a house that will never return that investment when sold, or basing your long-term budget on an outlier year when your income was temporarily higher. You can't avoid the thoughts themselves; this isn't like training yourself to do mental math or improving your mindfulness to cope with anxiety. You're fighting uphill against thousands of years of evolution, and evolution usually wins. Instead, the solution is to change your process so that these biases can't unduly affect your decision-making, gathering more data or adding steps to your process so that you stop yourself (or your team or your company) before the errant decision becomes permanent.

# Resources

If you'd like to read more about cognitive psychology, biases, and illusions, I have a number of books I can recommend and that I credit with sparking my interest in this subject and/or helping me write this book. The list starts with *Thinking, Fast and Slow* by Daniel Kahneman, which is both fascinating to read and consistently supported by research evidence, although, as I said in the introduction, the prose is dense and I have many friends who started it but couldn't finish it. It's modular enough that you could read parts that you find particularly relevant to your life or work, however. Kahneman won the Nobel Prize for the work that he summarizes in his book, and he and his late colleague Amos Tversky led the creation of this entire field of economics, helping overthrow the tyranny of traditional economic thinking that man is a rational actor who will always act in his or her own best interests.

Richard Thaler, who worked with Kahneman and Amos Tversky for years, has two books in this genre, *Nudge* and *Misbehaving,* the latter of which delves more into cognitive psychology and name-checks Kahneman and Tversky on what seems like every other page. Dan Ariely's *Predictably Irrational* also mines similar territory, and both Ariely and Thaler write more for the mass audience than Kahneman does, bringing more levity to what remains at heart an academic subject.

Gary Smith's *Standard Deviations* describes many ways in which writers, corporate leaders, politicians, and even scientists play games with statistics to mislead readers, including a baseball example or two along the way. It was also invaluable to me in thinking about topics and examples for this book, and it's a great read for anyone who wants to be a more informed consumer of news in an era where the trustworthiness of news outlets and writers is constantly under attack.

*The Invisible Gorilla,* by Christopher Chabris and Daniel Simons, focuses on a half-dozen cognitive illusions that I didn't cover in this book but that are both well backed by evidence and also extremely entertaining in the authors' descriptions. The title refers to a famous experiment on inattention bias, where we can miss even extraordinary things that happen right in front of us because our attention is focused elsewhere.

*Think Twice,* by Michael J. Mauboussin, covers cognitive biases and illusions in a very concise, breezy book that's under two hundred pages, explaining what they are and a little about how they work without a lot of underlying examples. It's great if you don't care as much about the evidence used to support our acceptance that these cognitive errors actually exist and that our decision-making isn't that rational after all. I especially like this title: we all think once as an automatic process, but learning to think about a question or conundrum a second time gives our brains the time and room to consider other options, or to ask whether you're falling prey to any of the biases I described in this book.

*The Hidden Brain,* by Shankar Vedantam. The NPR podcast of the same name is also one of my favorite weekly listens, occasionally delving into cognitive biases and illusions; one of his many guests over the years was Kahneman himself, and I've discovered many other books and research papers that helped me prepare this book through Vedantam's podcast.

*Everybody Lies,* by Seth Stephens-Davidowitz, which uses large data sets like Google search queries to show, for example, that searches for racist jokes or racist comments about the Obamas predicted areas where Donald Trump would beat projections in

the 2016 vote totals; or to show that people lie about "embarrass-
ing" topics like pornography or medical questions but will reveal
the truth in their online search requests.

*Whistling Vivaldi,* by Claude Steele. Stereotype threat is a real
issue in baseball, and I imagine in other sports; I've spoken many
times about my anecdotal experiences with hearing different ad-
jectives used to describe players of different races or national or-
igins, or the differing baseline expectations for players' physical
tools based on skin color. For example, there's an ingrained belief in baseball that black players will be—or should be—faster
runners, or just better athletes overall. That starting belief puts
black players at a disadvantage when they're being scouted, and,
according to the research cited in *Whistling Vivaldi,* may cause
black players to underperform when they know they're under evaluation. Stereotype threat is a major issue in American education
as well, given gaps in performance like the gender gap on math
tests (tell girls they're worse at math than boys and, guess what,
they'll do worse on tests!). It's not a cognitive bias or illusion, and
felt like too big a topic to squeeze into one chapter in this book,
but it is the kind of subtle prejudice that has replaced the overt
racism and sexism that held back people of color or women in
previous generations.

*The Drunkard's Walk,* by Leonard Mlodinow. Mlodinow, a
physicist who cowrote *The Grand Design* with Stephen Hawking,
offers a clear-eyed look at how much random chance exists in our
world and the extent to which it determines things as disparate as
our career paths and what albums or movies become bestsellers.
Its relevance to this book comes from the widespread innumer-
acy that leads people to see patterns in randomness, to pretend
that the typical variations of repeated events are meaningful, even
though they're easily understood with a bit of statistics and normal accident theory.

# Acknowledgments

*The Inside Game* originally stems from a recommendation Sig Mejdal, now assistant GM of the Baltimore Orioles, gave me back in 2014, suggesting that I read Daniel Kahneman's *Thinking, Fast and Slow*, a book he recommended to all new hires with the Astros, his employer at the time. The book had just started to make its way around major-league front offices, so it helped me better understand my own thinking while also giving me a whole set of new tools with which I could evaluate front offices' decisions, whether in trades, the draft, free agents, or tactics within games. If anyone can take credit for this book's existence, it's Sig.

My agent, Eric Lupfer, helped me turn this from a two-sentence idea that I wasn't sure would work in book form into an actual proposal that we could send to William Morrow, the publishers of my first book, *Smart Baseball*, to see if they'd be interested in working with me again. Not only did they say yes, I got to work with the same editor, Matt Harper, who helped shepherd *Smart Baseball* through its construction and editing to turn it into a viable book, and has done even more work here in helping me turn this into a coherent work.

I'm very grateful to the various executives who spoke to me for the chapter on actual decisions from MLB history, sharing details of their thought processes that I don't think had been made public before. Their time and openness gave this book the tie to the real world I was hoping to provide. I'd also like to thank Ehsan Bokhari, Dan Szymborski, and Harry Pavlidis for providing their insight on building statistical projection models for players.

I'd like to thank all of the readers who purchased (or borrowed) *Smart Baseball*, especially those who talked about the book online and shared their recommendations, as well as all of the independent bookstores and venues who hosted me for readings and signings over the past three years. Those events have been my favorite part of this entire process, and I can't wait to do it again and meet even more of you around the country.

Finally, I am so grateful for the support of my daughter, Kendall, and my girlfriend, Meredith, who both provided positive encouragement throughout the eight months it took me to write this book, and who understood when I disappeared into the computer for just about all of September in my most furious bout of writing. I can't imagine getting through all of this without your love and support.

# Notes

## Introduction

1. NobelPrize.org.
2. Hat tip to Dan Ariely, whose *Predictably Irrational* is indeed on my list of recommended books in this field.
3. J. Shanteau, "Cognitive Heuristics and Biases in Behavioral Auditing: Review, Comments and Observations," *Accounting, Organizations and Society* 14, nos. 1–2 (1989): 165–77, doi:10.1016/0361–3682(89)90040–8.

## Chapter 1

1. Ben Walker, "With Each Pitch at Series, Call Gets Louder for Robot Umps," Associated Press, October 29, 2019.
2. Amos Tversky and Daniel Kahneman, "Judgment Under Uncertainty," *Science*, New Series, vol. 185, no. 4157 (1974): 1124–31.
3. Ibid.
4. The correct answer is 40,320. Apropos of nothing, my back-of-the-envelope calculation would be this: 5 x 4 is 20, and 3 x 2 x 1 is 6, so that's 120. Multiply by 6 and you get 720; that times 7 is about 5,000; and that times 8 is about 40,000. I think that's much easier than trying to start the descending order with 56 and then multiplying that by 6 and so on.
5. Also edited by Matt Harper, editor of this book and *Smart Baseball*.
6. Tobias Moskowitz and L. Jon Wertheim, *Scorecasting* (New York: Three Rivers Press, 2012), pp. 14–17.
7. John Walsh, "The Compassionate Umpire," *Hardball Times*, April 7, 2010.
8. Dave Allen, "Does the Umpire Know the Count?" BaseballAnalysts.com, April 6, 2009.
9. Etan A. Green and David P. Daniels, "Bayesian Instinct," August 19, 2008. Available at SSRN.
10. Specifically, Bayes's theorem lets you calculate the odds of event B given condition A if you know three other things: The odds of condition A being true on its own, the odds of event B happening, and the odds of condition A being given that event B has occurred. The formula is then $P(B|A) = P(A|B)*P(A)/P(B)$, where $P(x)$ refers to the probability of x. I learned this in college, and again in grad school, and still have to look

it up to make sure I have it right. Nobody, let alone MLB umpires, is actually doing this calculation in their heads in real time.

11. Teams may receive such additional picks as compensation for losing free agents or for failing to sign the previous year's pick. In this case, I included those picks when they were within rounds, between rounds 1 and 2 (calling those first-round picks), and between rounds 2 and 3 (calling those second-round picks). My categorization follows that of the industry.

## Chapter 2

1. 1901 to the present, position players only.
2. John Drebinger, "Yankee Ace Tops Williams in Poll," *New York Times*, November 12, 1941, p. 37.
3. Ben Bradlee Jr., *The Kid: The Immortal Life of Ted Williams* (Boston: Little, Brown, 2013).
4. "Most Valuable Player Award Voted Di Maggio," *Philadelphia Inquirer*, November 12, 1941, pp. 37–40.
5. George Kirksey, "Joe DiMaggio Edges Ted for Most Valuable Award," *Boston Daily Globe*, November 12, 1941, p. 22.
6. Amos Tversky and Dan Kahneman, "Availability: A Heuristic for Judging Frequency and Probability," *Cognitive Psychology* 5, no. 2 (September 1973): 207–32.
7. Michael Wilson, "Killed by a Stranger: A Rarity, but a Rising Fear," *New York Times*, August 18, 2016, Section A, p. 19.
8. David Finkelhor, "Five Myths about Missing Children," *Washington Post*, May 10, 2013.
9. Jonathan Allen, "Kidnapped Children Make Headlines, but Abduction Is Rare in U.S.," Reuters, January 11, 2019.
10. Finkelhor, "Five Myths about Missing Children."
11. Fred Mitchell, "Green Recalls Blank Check," *Chicago Tribune*, January 7, 2010.
12. Baseball-Reference.com.
13. MLB's home runs per game went from 0.91 in 1986 to 1.06 in 1987 down to 0.76 in 1988. Data from Baseball-Reference.com.
14. Michael Martinez, "Dawson Named NL MVP," *New York Times*, November 19, 1987, pp. 47–48.
15. Fred Mitchell, "MVP! MVP! Dream Comes True for Cubs' Dawson," *Chicago Tribune*, November 19, 1987, section 4, p. 1.
16. Chip Buck, "Mysterious Case of the '87 Award Season," ESPN.com, March 1, 2011.
17. Herbert A. Simon, *Models of My Life* (Cambridge, MA: MIT Press, 1996), p. 234.

18. Robert K. Merton, "The Matthew Effect in Science," *Science*, January 5, 1968, pp. 56–63. If Merton's name is familiar to you, it might be because his son, Robert C. Merton, is a Nobel Prize–winning economist.

19. "Palmeiro Supported Stevens for Award," Associated Press, November 10, 1999.

20. Smith, Gary, *Standard Deviations: Flawed Assumptions, Tortured Data, and Other Ways to Lie With Statistics* (New York: Harry N. Abrams, 2014), p. 42.

## Chapter 3

1. Joe Sheehan, "The Daily Prospectus: Game Four," BaseballProspectus .com, November 1, 2001.

2. No, it doesn't.

3. "It is unclear what the World Series–winning skipper's motive was. In any event, he's better off keeping these 'get off my lawn' takes to himself." Austin Pert, "VIDEO: Diamondbacks Announcer Makes Strangely Offensive Comment About Fernando Tatis Jr.," 12up.com, April 12, 2019.

4. Nassim Nicholas Taleb, "Learning to Expect the Unexpected," *New York Times*, April 8, 2004, Section A, p. 29.

5. J. Baron and J. C. Hershey, "Outcome Bias in Decision Evaluation," *Journal of Personality and Social Psychology* 54, no. 4 (1988): 569–79.

6. Joseph Sheehan et al., *Baseball Prospectus 1997*, Ravenlock Media LLC.

7. Major League Baseball does not test players on teams' 40-man rosters, who have major-league contracts, for marijuana, but tests all minor leaguers for the drug and issues suspensions as they would for other, "harder" drugs. With the changing legal status of marijuana across the United States, I expect the policy to change in the next collective bargaining agreement.

8. N. J.Roese and K. D. Vohs, "Hindsight Bias," *Perspectives on Psychological Science* 7, no. 5 (2012): 411–26, doi:10.1177/1745691612454303.

9. It's a quantum physics reference. Just work with me here.

## Chapter 4

1. Jim Bowden, "Bowden: An Early Ranking of the Top 20 Free Agents Who Will Be Available This Offseason," The Athletic, August 14, 2019.

2. Marc Gonzalez, "Javier Baez to Undergo an MRI on His Ailing Left Thumb," *Chicago Tribune*, September 6, 2019.

3. Ken Gurnick, "Bellinger Gets Protection with Lineup Tweak," MLB .com, May 9, 2019.

4. Chris Nelsen, "Miguel Cabrera Scoffs at Power Outage: 'You Know Who's Hitting Behind Me?'" *Detroit Free Press*, May 4, 2019.

5.  David Laurila, "Player's View: Does Lineup Protection Exist?" Fangraphs.com, May 5, 2015.

6.  Lynn Worthy, "Royals' Ned Yost Talks Danny Duffy Progress, Lineup Changes," *Kansas City Star*, August 20, 2019.

7.  Lynn Hasher, David Goldstein, and Thomas Toppino, "Frequency and the Conference of Referential Validity," *Journal of Verbal Learning and Verbal Behavior* 16, no. 1 (1977): 107–12.

8.  Lisa K. Fazio, Nadia M. Brashier, B. Keith Payne, and Elizabeth J. Marsh, "Knowledge Does Not Protect Against Illusory Truth," *Journal of Experimental Psychology: General* 144, no. 5 (2015): 993–1002.

9.  Ibid. The original study is by Rolf Reber and Norbert Schwarz, "Effects of Perceptual Fluency on Judgments of Truth," *Consciousness and Cognition* 8, no. 3 (September 1999): 338–42. They found that making statements easier for subjects to read made the subjects more likely to rate them as true.

10. Smith, *Standard Deviations*.

11. See Peter Hotez's wonderful, informative book *Vaccines Did Not Cause Rachel's Autism* (Baltimore: Johns Hopkins University Press, 2018) for more about the history of this pernicious myth and the media's role in propagating it.

12. J. L. Mellerson, C. B. Maxwell, C. L. Knighton, J. L. Kriss, R. Seither, and C. L. Black, "Vaccination Coverage for Selected Vaccines and Exemption Rates Among Children in Kindergarten—United States, 2017–18 School Year." *MMWR Morbidity and Mortality Weekly Report* 67 (2018): 1115–22. Based on 94.3 percent vaccination rate and Department of Education enrollment estimates.

13. S. Pluviano, C. Watt, and S. Della Sala, "Misinformation Lingers in Memory: Failure of Three Pro-Vaccination Strategies," *PLoS ONE* 12, no. 7 (2017): e0181640.

14. Corey Seidman, "Here's the Proof That Bryce Harper Has Been MLB's Most Clutch Hitter in 2019," NBC Sports Philadelphia, August 16, 2019.

15. Patrick Brennan, "Revisiting Whether Clutch Is a Skill," Beyondtheboxscore.com, August 22, 2019.

16. Susan Slusser, "Ex-A's manager Tony La Russa Explains Harold Baines' Hall of Fame Election," *San Francisco Chronicle*, December 10, 2018.

17. "Former Twins, Red Sox Slugger David Ortiz Shot, Says His Father," *Minneapolis Star-Tribune*, June 10, 2019.

18. La Velle Neal, "Twins Reach Deal with Jack-of-all-trades Marwin Gonzalez," *Minneapolis Star-Tribune*, February 23, 2019.

19. Gordon Wittenmyer, "Swing and a Myth: Kris Bryant Is a Lot Better at Clutch Hitting than You Probably Think," *Chicago Sun-Times*, August 17, 2019. In the same piece, Wittenmyer writes that Joe Maddon, the Cubs' manager, believes "against data" that there is such a thing as a clutch hitter.

20. Tom Tango, Mitchel Lichtman, and Andrew Dolphin, *The Book: Playing the Percentages in Baseball* (n.p.: Potomac Books, 2008), pp. 97–115.

21. See David H. Rapp and Jason L. G. Braasch, *Processing Inaccurate Information* (Cambridge, MA: MIT Press, 2014), pp. 3ff.

22. Pluviano et al., "Misinformation Lingers in Memory."

23. Dave D'Onofrio, "13 Moments When David Ortiz Defined Clutch," *Boston Globe*, November 8, 2016.

24. Foxsports.com, October 4, 2016.

25. Chris Smith, "David Ortiz's Postseason Greatness: Top 10 Moments of Ortiz's Red Sox Playoff Career," MassLive.com, September 2016.

26. Frank McBride, "In U.S., Percentage Saying Vaccines Are Vital Dips Slightly," Gallup.com, March 6, 2015.

27. "Americans' Views on Vaccines and Infectious Disease Outbreaks," May 2018, Research!America.

28. Patrick Phinck et al., "Institutional Trust and Misinformation in the Response to the 2018–19 Ebola Outbreak in North Kivu, DR Congo: A Population-Based Survey," *Lancet*, March 27, 2019.

29. H. Miton and H. Mercier, "Cognitive Obstacles to Pro-Vaccination Beliefs," *Trends in Cognitive Sciences* 19, no. 11 (2015): 633–36.

30. Daniel Drezner, "What Alex Cora Can Teach America's Leaders," *Washington Post*, October 30, 2018.

31. Miton and Mercier, "Cognitive Obstacles."

32. JoNel Aleccia, "Measles Outbreak Sends Vaccine Demand Soaring, Even Among the Hesitant," NBCNews.com, February 7, 2019.

## Chapter 5

1. Just to be clear, this is not a thing. Exceptions do not prove rules. If they did, they would no longer be exceptions.

2. Throughout this discussion, when I refer to "college" players, I mean those drafted from four-year schools. Many major-league players came through two-year colleges, but they rarely go in the first round; there were 16 first-rounders taken from junior colleges from 1985 through 2015.

3. It also includes three players who didn't sign, another risk with high school players who may choose college over pro ball, and Doug Million, who died of an asthma attack during fall instructional league in Arizona in 1997. He was only twenty-one.

4. Philip E. Tetlock, *Expert Political Judgment: How Good Is It? How Can We Know?* (Princeton, NJ: Princeton University Press, 2017), pp. xix–xx.

5. A. Tversky and D. Kahneman, "Evidential impact of base rates," in D. Kahneman, P. Slovic, and A. Tversky, eds., *Judgment under Uncertainty: Heuristics and Biases* (Cambridge: Cambridge University Press, 1982), pp. 153–60.

6.  D. Kahneman and A. Tversky, "On the Psychology of Prediction," *Psychological Review* 80, no. 4 (1973): 237–51.
7.  Tom Verducci, "From Trackman to Edgertronic to Rapsodo, the Tech Boom Is Fundamentally Altering Baseball," *Sports Illustrated*, March 25, 2019.
8.  FIP looks like Earned Run Average (ERA), but is an estimate based on the pitcher's rates of strikeouts, walks, and home runs allowed, thus removing any potential bias from good/bad defense behind the pitcher, unusual luck on balls hit into play, or the results of pitchers before or after the one in question. It does a better job of predicting subsequent performance than ERA itself does.

**Chapter 6**

1.  Per Baseball-Reference. Fangraphs has him with about four wins less, because their calculation assumes that Kershaw's ability to limit hits on balls in play was random chance and not a skill. The difference isn't really meaningful here; Dodgers scouting director Logan White made one of the best picks in history by taking Kershaw, regardless of how you calculate it.
2.  Also called survival bias, which I just think sounds strange, as, yes, I am biased in favor of my survival.
3.  Jordan Ellenberg, *How Not to Be Wrong: The Power of Mathematical Thinking* (New York: Penguin Books, 2005), pp. 8–9.
4.  Smith, *Standard Deviations*, various pages.
5.  John P. A. Ioannidis, "Why Most Published Research Findings Are False," *PLoS Medicine* vol. 2, no. 8 (2005): e124, doi:10.1371/journal.pmed.0020124.02.
6.  Regina Nuzzo, "Scientific Method: Statistical Errors," *Nature*, February 12, 2014.
7.  Stephanie M. Lee, "Sliced & Diced: Here's How Cornell Scientist Brian Wansink Turned Shoddy Data into Viral Studies About How We Eat," *BuzzFeed News*, February 25, 2018.
8.  K. J. Dell'Antonia, "Varied Snacks Nudge Kids toward Healthier Eating," *New York Times*, December 18, 2012. As of this writing, the research paper has not been retracted.
9.  S. Lyman, G. S. Fleisig, J. R. Andrews, and E. D. Osinski, "Effect of Pitch Type, Pitch Count, and Pitching Mechanics on Risk of Elbow and Shoulder Pain in Youth Baseball Pitchers," *American Journal of Sports Medicine* 30, no. 4 (2002): 463–68, https://doi.org/10.1177/03635465020300040201.
10. I'm not even going to get started on the absurdly high pitch counts in the Japanese high school tournament held in Koshien, where it is common to see teenagers throw 200+ pitches in a single day.

11. Matt Kelly, "The Story Behind Nolan Ryan's 235-Pitch Start," MLB.com, June 14, 2019.

12. Testuya Matsuura, Iwame Toshiyuki, and Koichi Sairyo, "Exceeding Pitch Count Recommendations in Youth Baseball Increases The [*sic*] Elbow Injuries." *Orthopaedic Journal of Sports Medicine*.

## Chapter 7

1. Bill Shaikin and Mike DiGiovanna, "Pharmacy Raid Linked to Athletes," *Los Angeles Times*, February 28, 2007.

2. For one example, see J. R. Anderson and M. Matessa, "A Production System Theory of Serial Memory," *Psychological Review* 104, no. 4 (1997): 728–48, doi:10.1037/0033-295x.104.4.728.

3. Richard Hébert, "Code Overload: Doing a Number on Memory," Association for Psychological Science, September 26, 2001.

4. V. Arnold, P. A. Collier, S. A. Leech, and S. G. Sutton, "The Effect of Experience and Complexity on Order and Recency Bias in Decision Making by Professional Accountants," *Accounting and Finance* 40, no. 2 (2000): 109–34.

5. Dan also gets some amusing notes from fans who think he's somehow rigging the forecasts, or coming up with them by hand, rather than generating them by algorithm. The best story he has of such emails, however, was the reader who was angry that Dan was citing ZiPS forecasts without properly crediting their creator—who, of course, is Dan himself.

6. Meaning that 60 percent of the time he hit a ball in play that month, he reached base safely. LaHair had 70 plate appearances in April, drawing 10 walks, striking out 25 times, and hitting 5 home runs, so he had 30 balls he hit into play, and 18 of those became hits. League average BABIP is usually a shade over .300, with clear variations among hitters by skill level, but the hitter whose true talent level is even at a .400 BABIP hasn't been born yet. Since baseball integrated in 1947, the highest full-season BABIP by a qualifying hitter is .408 by Rod Carew in 1977.

7. Apropos of nothing, the day I revised this chapter, I had a conversation around poinsettias, and said to someone that they were "highly poisonous." Questioning my own belief in this, I googled "poinsettias poisonous" only to find out that my belief was inaccurate: Eating parts of the poinsettia can make a child or a pet sick, but they're not toxic, and certainly not dangerous enough to worry about having one in your house. I fell for the illusory truth effect before I found evidence to the contrary.

8. James Wagner, "Research Supports the Notion of the 'Hot Hand'; Baseball Players Always Believed in It," *Washington Post*, July 16, 2014.

The research paper Wagner cites, however, doesn't actually support the notion of the hot hand, due to methodological problems and a failure to account for confounding variables like playing environment.

9. Mark Saxon, "Q&A with John Mozeliak: Is the Cards' Success Proof They Didn't Need to Add Pitching at the Trade Deadline?" The Athletic, September 12, 2019.
10. Justin Toscano, "Todd Frazier, Zack Wheeler and Justin Wilson Key Victory for Mets over the Diamondbacks," NorthJersey.com, September 10, 2019.
11. Thomas Gilovich, Robert Vallone, and Amos Tversky, "The Hot Hand in Basketball: On the Misperception of Random Sequences," *Cognitive Psychology* 17 (1985): 295–314.
12. Russell Carleton, "Baseball Therapy: Going Streaking." BaseballProspectus.com, March 8, 2010. I also very strongly recommend Russell's book *The Shift: The Next Evolution in Baseball Thinking*, published in 2018 by Triumph Books.
13. German Lopez, "John Oliver Exposes How the Media Turns Scientific Studies into 'Morning Show Gossip,'" Vox.com, May 9, 2016.
14. Brett S. Green and Jeffrey Zwiebel, "The Hot-Hand Fallacy: Cognitive Mistakes or Equilibrium Adjustments? Evidence from Major League Baseball (revised)," *Management Science*, November 2018, pp. 4967–5460.
15. See http://tangotiger.com/index.php/site/comments/streaks-in-baseball#6, by the commenter Kincaid.
16. See http://blog.philbirnbaum.com/2015/12/a-new-hot-hand-study-finds-plausible.html. Birnbaum points out the flaws in the original study's methodology, including the discarding of relevant data.
17. Smith, *Standard Deviations,* p. 199.
18. Joshua Miller and Adam Sanjurjo, "Surprised by the Hot Hand Fallacy? A Truth in the Law of Small Numbers," *Econometrica* 86, no. 6 (November 2018): 2019–47.
19. Ibid.
20. Ben Cohen, "The 'Hot Hand' Debate Gets Flipped on Its Head," *Wall Street Journal*, September 30, 2015.
21. George Johnson, "Gamblers, Scientists and the Mysterious Hot Hand," *New York Times*, October 17, 2015.
22. Jesse Singal, "How Researchers Discovered the Basketball 'Hot Hand,'" TheCut.com, August 14, 2016. Singal himself has come under fire for his reliance on questionable science in his writing about transgender kids.
23. Tom Haberstroh, "He's Heating Up, He's on Fire! Klay Thompson and the Truth about the Hot Hand," ESPN.com, June 12, 2017.
24. Joshua Miller and Adam Sanjurjo, "Momentum Isn't Magic—Vindicating the Hot Hand with the Mathematics of Streaks," *Scientific American*,

March 28, 2018. Reprinted from *The Conversation*.

25. Tamar Haspel, "In the Fight Against Obesity, the Real Enemy Is Oversimplification," Undark.org, October 13, 2016.

26. The second quote was transcribed and tweeted by Mike Wilner of The Fan 590 in Toronto, January 23, 2018.

27. Ben Markham, "Diaz's Hot Start Not as Unsustainable as You Might Think," VivaElBirdos.com, April 19, 2016.

28. Tyler Kepner, "Astros Begin Again, Starting with Youth and Hope," *New York Times*, August 12, 2012.

## Chapter 8

1. https://twitter.com/TurnerSportsPR/status/1049805952164085760.

2. "Status Quo Bias in Decision Making," *Journal of Risk and Uncertainty* 1 (1988): 7–59.

3. Peter Gammons, "The Hub Hails Its Hobbling Hero," *Sports Illustrated*, November 10, 1986. https://www.si.com/vault/1986/11/10/114340 /the-hub-hails-its-hobbling-hero-even-though-bill-buckner-let-game-6 -slip-through-his-injured-legs-the-fans-in-boston-showed-last-week-how -much-they-admired-his-courageous-play-in-the-world-series.

4. Tyler Kepner, "For McNamara, a Final Out That Wasn't Meant to Be," *New York Times*, November 7, 2011, https://www.nytimes.com/2011/11/08 /sports/baseball/former-red-sox-manager-john-mcnamara-recalls-final -out-that-wasnt-to-be.html. McNamara's recollections of many parts of that game do not match those of some of his players.

5. Daniel Kahneman, Jack Knetch, and Richard Thaler, "The Endowment Effect, Loss Aversion, and Status Quo Bias," *Journal of Economic Perspectives* 5, no. 1 (Winter 1991): 193–206.

6. In this book, I'll stick to the convention of referring to trades as teams trading players, when in fact, teams are trading contractual rights to those players, for a limited, defined duration. Such rights extend either to the end of the player's current contract or, for players who have less than six years of major-league service time and no long-term deal, until they exceed that threshold and become free agents. Teams aren't actually trading people, which sounds rather distasteful if you stop to think about it. They're just trading those rights.

7. To qualify to lead the league in ERA, a pitcher must throw at least one inning for each game his team plays in that season. Most teams will play 162 games in a full season, so pitchers on those teams would have to throw at least 162.0 innings to qualify.

8. Michael Strahilevitz and George Loewenstein, "The Effect of Ownership History on the Valuation of Objects," *Journal of Consumer Research*, December 1998.

9.  Campbell Pryor & Amy Perfors & Piers D. L. Howe, 2018. "Reversing
    the endowment effect," *Judgment and Decision Making,* Society for
    Judgment and Decision Making, vol. 13(3), pages 275-286, May.

## Chapter 9

1.  Sizemore missed 2012 and 2013 and made a comeback in 2014–15, but
    was below replacement level between his much-reduced offensive ability
    and his lack of mobility in the outfield.
2.  David Rowell and Luke B. Connelly, "A History of the Term 'Moral
    Hazard,'" *Journal of Risk and Insurance* 79, no. 4 (December 2012):
    1051–75.
3.  Robin Pearson, "Moral Hazard and the Assessment of Insurance Risk
    in Eighteenth- and Early-Nineteenth-Century Britain," *Business History
    Review* 76, no. 1 (2002): 1–35.
4.  In this discussion I am referring to his age based on his official date of
    birth of January 16, 1980.
5.  "Wood Has No Regrets about His 13-Inning Outing in 2009," *Houston
    Chronicle,* June 9, 2011.
6.  A player becomes draft-eligible in the year when he finishes high
    school, or finishes either year at a two-year college, or finishes his
    third year of eligibility at a four-year college, or if he turns twenty-one
    within forty-five days of the end of the draft regardless of his year in
    college.
7.  William Poole, "Moral Hazard: The Long-Lasting Legacy of Bailouts,"
    *Financial Analysts Journal* 65, no. 6 (2009): 17–23.

## Chapter 10

1.  Jon Tayler, "Ozzie Albies's Contract Extension Is Insultingly Low," *Sports
    Illustrated,* April 11, 2019.
2.  Michael Baumann, "Ozzie Albies's New Deal Could Be the Worst an
    MLB Player Has Ever Signed," TheRinger.com, April 11, 2019.
3.  Jeff Passan, "Passan: Baseball Is Obsessed with Value—and It's
    Changing Contracts Forever," ESPN.com, April 12, 2019.
4.  Ibid.
5.  Like most published authors, I have used the services of a literary agent
    to help build my book proposals and negotiate the book contracts.
6.  Joel G. Maxcy, Rodney D. Fort, and Anthony C. Krautmann, "The
    Effectiveness of Incentive Mechanisms in Major League Baseball,"
    *Journal of Sports Economics* 3 (2002): 246.
7.  Ibid.
8.  Ibid.
9.  Ibid.

10. *Baseball Between the Numbers* (New York: Basic Books, 2006), pp. 199–207.

11. For example, the FDIC insures individual depositors' accounts with commercial banks—checking or savings accounts—against losses, but not brokerage accounts at investment banks.

12. Frederick Mishkin, "Over the Cliff: From the Subprime to the Global Financial Crisis," *Journal of Economic Perspectives* 25, no. 1 (Winter 2011): 53.

13. Michael Jensen and William Meckling, "Theory of the Firm: Managerial Behavior, Agency Costs and Ownership Structure," *Journal of Financial Economics* 3 (1976): 305–60.

14. S. J. Grossman and O. D. Hart, "An Analysis of the Principal-Agent Problem," *Econometrica* 51, no. 1 (January 1983): 7–45.

15. William P. Rogerson, "The First-Order Approach to Principal-Agent Problems," *Econometrica* 53, no. 6 (November 1985): 1357–67.

16. Major League Baseball Official Rules, Rule 21(d): Gambling. Retrieved from MLB.com.

17. Ryan Rodenberg, "Pete Rose's Reckless Gamble," *Atlantic*, August 22, 2014. Few players in MLB history have provided so much fodder for content over as long a period as Rose has.

18. Murray Chass, "Truth Is Revealed in Bets Rose Didn't Make," *New York Times*, March 16, 2007.

19. My "favorite" example of this is Red Sox reliever Kerry Lacy, who was an adequate middle reliever at the very end of Boston's pitching staff in 1997, working short stints of up to 36 pitches in an outing. On June 1, 1997, the Red Sox played an extra-inning game against the Yankees. Lacy entered that game with a 2.30 ERA over 15 not terribly impressive innings, in the eleventh inning, and was left in to throw 81 pitches, more than double his career high. Lacy, who had only made 10 starts in his minor league career, visibly tired as the game went into the fifteenth inning, giving up a homer, double, and single before leaving the game. After June 1, he gave up 25 runs in 25 innings, went on the disabled list at the end of August, and then missed all of 1998, after which Boston released him. He never pitched in the majors again.

20. Jessica E. Lessin and Joann S. Lublin, "Apple Required Executives to Hold Triple Their Salary in Stock," *Wall Street Journal*, February 28, 2013.

## Chapter 11

1. "Diamondbacks Designate Right-hander Ortiz," Associated Press, June 14, 2006.

2. Randolph McAfee, Hugo Mialon, and Sue Mialon, "Do Sunk Costs Matter?" *Economic Inquiry* 48 (2010): 323–36.

3. Ibid.

4. Hal R. Arkes and Catherine Blumer, "The Psychology of Sunk Cost," *Organizational Behavior and Human Decision Processes* 35, no. 1 (February 1985): 124–40.

5. Barry Schwartz, "The 'Sunk-Cost Fallacy,'" *Los Angeles Times*, September 17, 2006.

6. Daniel Trotta, "Iraq War Hits U.S. Economy: Nobel Winner," Reuters, March 2, 2008.

7. Christopher Y. Olivola, "The Interpersonal Sunk-Cost Effect," *Psychological Science* 29, no. 7 (2018): 1072–83.

8. In an unfortunate coincidence, both Young and Marte died in their mid-thirties, Young of an apparent heart attack, Marte in a car accident in his home country, the Dominican Republic.

9. Howard wasn't even the most valuable player on the right side of the Phillies' infield in 2006, let alone in the National League. Chase Utley was worth more than a full win more than Howard, since Utley was an outstanding defender at second base while Howard, even in his prime years, was a below-average defender at first base.

10. Albert Chen, "First Priority," *Sports Illustrated*, August 1, 2005.

11. Jamey Stegmaier, "Overcoming the Sunk Cost Fallacy (KS Lesson #268)," Stonemaiergames.com, July 11, 2019.

**Chapter 12**

1. "Happy Fun Ball" is the name of a fake advertisement that ran on *Saturday Night Live* on February 16, 1991; this line is a direct quote from the sketch.

2. Maury Brown, "Manfred: 'We Need to Make a Change to the Baseball,'" *Forbes*, September 25, 2019.

3. MLB has been starting its season earlier the last few seasons, so April totals include the last few days of March, which means that the rate here is more telling than the total, with 437 total games in March/April 2019.

4. Noah Frank, "Home Run Happy? MLB's Record-Breaking April Sign of Times," WTOP, May 1, 2019.

5. Meredith Wills, "Yes, the Baseball Is Different—Again. An Astrophysicist Examines This Year's Baseballs and Breaks Down the Changes," TheAthletic.com, June 25, 2019.

6. N. D. Weinstein and W. M. Klein, "Unrealistic Optimism: Present and Future," *Journal of Social and Clinical Psychology* 15, no. 1 (1996): 1–8, doi:10.1521/jscp.1996.15.1.1.

7. Kahneman. *Thinking, Fast and Slow*. p. 250.

8. Source: Daren Willman's BaseballSavant at baseballsavant.mlb.com. This isn't a complete leaderboard; I've deleted some players due to low playing time, known injuries, etc.
9. MLB.com Statcast Glossary.

## Chapter 13

1. I'm including Brett Wallace, whom the Jays acquired in a trade involving one of the three prospects they got from the Phillies, Michael Taylor, the same day.
2. Not counting the Mets, who had him on paper for a few minutes on July 30, 2004, and immediately traded him again.
3. Bob Hohler, "Sox Trade Nomar to Cubs at Deadline," *Boston Globe*, August 1, 2004.
4. Nippon Professional Baseball, the Japanese equivalent to MLB.

# Index

# About the Author

KEITH LAW has written about baseball since June 2006, spending thirteen years at ESPN before joining The Athletic at the start of 2020. His first book, *Smart Baseball: The Story Behind the Old Stats That Are Ruining the Game, the New Ones That Are Running It, and the Right Way to Think About Baseball,* was first published in April 2017 by William Morrow. He also covers board games for multiple sites, including Paste Magazine, Ars Technica, and Vulture; and writes about other topics, including music, movies, and food, on his own long-running blog *The Dish.* He lives in Delaware with his daughter.